SPICE

SPICE

THE 16TH-CENTURY CONTEST THAT SHAPED THE MODERN WORLD

ROGER CROWLEY

YALE UNIVERSITY PRESS
NEW HAVEN AND LONDON

For information about this and other Yale University Press publications, please contact:
U.S. Office: sales.press@yale.edu   yalebooks.com
Europe Office: sales@yaleup.co.uk   yalebooks.co.uk

Set in Adobe Caslon Pro by IDSUK (DataConnection) Ltd
Printed in Great Britain by TJ Books Ltd, Padstow, Cornwall

Library of Congress Control Number: 2024930692

ISBN 978-0-300-26747-1

A catalogue record for this book is available from the British Library.

10 9 8 7 6 5 4 3 2 1

To Jan with love

The scent of the clove is said to be the most fragrant in the world. I experienced this coming from Cochin to Goa, with the wind from the shore and at night it was calm when we were a league from the land. The scent was so strong and so delicious that I thought there must be forests of flowers. On enquiry I found that we were near a ship coming from Maluco with cloves.

— Garcia de Orta, sixteenth-century Portuguese botanist

Although we call them the 'Old World' and the 'New World', that's because we only came across the latter recently, and not because there are two worlds; there is but one.

— Inca Garcilaso de la Vega, 1609

CONTENTS

CONTENTS

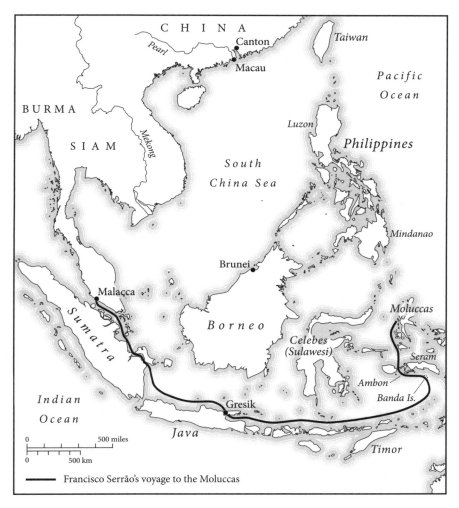

Map 1. The Malay Archipelago, the coast of China and the voyage of
Francisco Serrão.

Map 2. *Magellan's voyage and the circumnavigation of the world, 1519–22.*

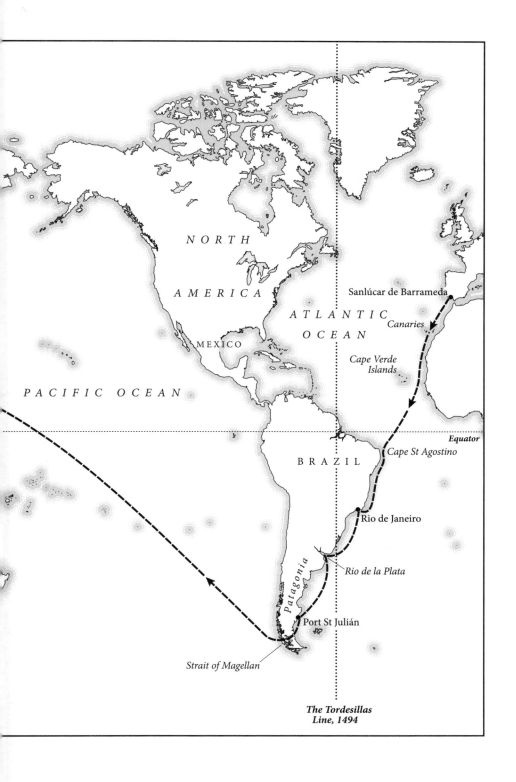

NORTH

AMERICA

ATLANTIC
OCEAN

MEXICO

Sanlúcar de Barrameda

Canaries

*Cape Verde
Islands*

PACIFIC OCEAN

Equator

BRAZIL

Cape St Agostino

Rio de Janeiro

Patagonia

Rio de la Plata

Port St Julián

Strait of Magellan

**The Tordesillas
Line, 1494**

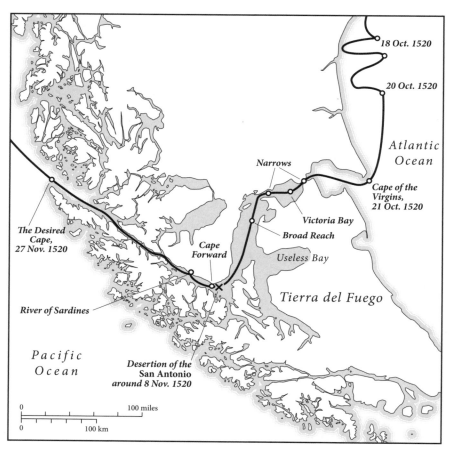

18 Oct. 1520

20 Oct. 1520

Atlantic
Ocean

Narrows

Cape of the
Virgins,
21 Oct. 1520

Victoria Bay

Broad Reach

The Desired
Cape,
27 Nov. 1520

Cape
Forward

Useless Bay

Tierra del Fuego

River of Sardines

Pacific
Ocean

Desertion of the
San Antonio
around 8 Nov. 1520

0   100 miles

0   100 km

Map 3. The transit of the Strait of Magellan.

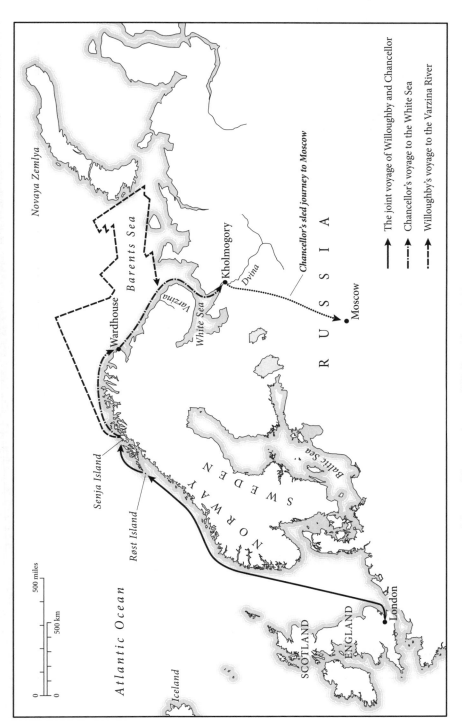

Map 4. The expedition of Willoughby and Chancellor, 1553.

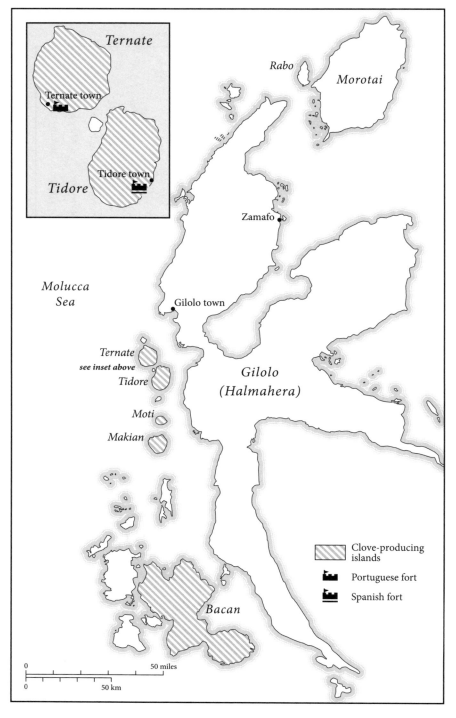

Ternate

Ternate town

Tidore town

Tidore

Rabo

Morotai

Molucca
Sea

Zamafo

Gilolo town

Ternate
see inset above

Tidore

Gilolo
(Halmahera)

Moti

Makian

Bacan

	Clove-producing islands
	Portuguese fort
	Spanish fort

0   50 miles

0   50 km

Map 5. The Moluccas (Maluku).

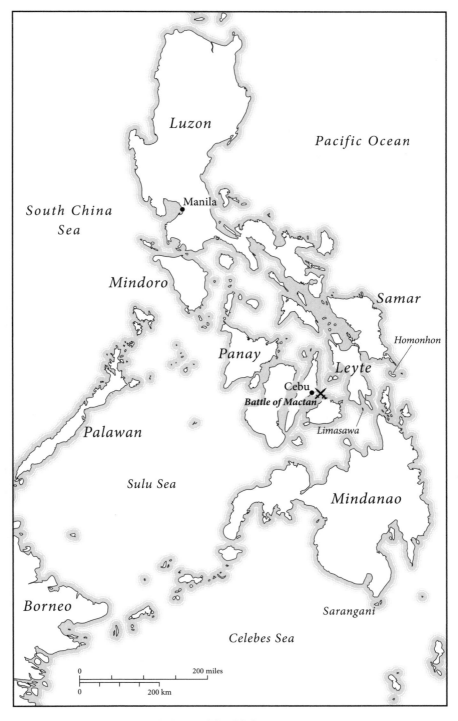

Luzon

Pacific Ocean

South China
Sea

Manila

Mindoro

Samar

Panay

Homonhon

Leyte

Cebu

Battle of Mactan

Palawan

Limasawa

Sulu Sea

Mindanao

Borneo

Sarangani

Celebes Sea

0   200 miles

0   200 km

Map 6. The Philippines.

COLLISIONS

Seen from space the Malay Archipelago is a splatter of islands. It's as if a giant had dropped an enormous porcelain plate from a great height and stood back to admire the effect. Tipped south-east of Malaya, the dynamic barriers of Sumatra and Java trail thousands of disintegrating fragments across a 4,000-mile arc that spans a quarter of the earth's circumference. Some of these islands are shaped like spiders, others neat circular blobs topped by symmetrical volcanoes as in a child's drawing. At the centre, the blunt chunk of Borneo and the 7,000 pieces that comprise the Philippines. To the east, New Guinea acts as an end-stop before the vast Pacific void. And at the heart of the chain, too small to be significant on any world map, another thousand tiny islands that make up a group known to history as the Moluccas – Maluku. This is the deepest tropics, a place through which the equatorial line runs like an arrow, dividing day and night into exactly equal halves.

The whole archipelago is the epicentre of one of the most geologically active regions on earth. Here four tectonic plates collide, grinding against each other, forcing up new volcanic islands, driving Australia north and pushing up the mountains of New Guinea in restless and unceasing agitation. The 450 volcanoes that comprise the western end of the Ring of Fire – an immense horseshoe-shaped belt that rims the Pacific Ocean – are some of the most destructive on earth. The world has heard their echo; the Krakatoa explosion of 1882 produced the loudest recorded noise in history, and in our own time the submarine quake of 2004 launched a tsunami 100 feet high, ripping across the Indian Ocean at 500 miles an hour to hammer fourteen countries. The peoples on this fault line live with permanent terrestrial instability. They feel the planet tremble, landmasses continuously remade. The nineteenth-century naturalist Alfred Russel Wallace noted that 'on many of the islands the years of the great earthquakes form the chronological epochs of the native inhabitants, by the aid of which the ages of their children are remembered, and the dates of many important events are determined',[1] and how the island of Makian in the Moluccas:

> was rent open in 1646 by violent eruption which left a huge chasm on one side, extending into the heart of the mountain. It was, when I last visited it in 1860, clothed with vegetation to the summit, and contained twelve populous Malay villages. On the 29th of December, 1862 . . . it again suddenly burst forth, blowing up and completely altering the appearance of the mountain, destroying the greater part of the inhabitants, and sending forth such volumes of ashes as to darken the air at Ternate, forty miles off, and to almost entirely destroy the growing crops on that and the surrounding islands.[2]

These collisions are not only geological. It is here that two sets of species – those derived from Australasia and those from Asia – meet across a frontier now known as the Wallace Line. In the rich volcanic soil of the island chain, the monsoon rains and tropical temperatures, abundant species of plants, insects and animals have evolved in unique and diverse ways. Life here is so teeming that a Dutch zoologist in the nineteenth century counted as many fish species off the shores of one island as in all the rivers and seas of Europe, and the tropical forest is so luxuriant that the last Japanese soldier to surrender after the Second World War could remain undetected on the pocket-sized island of Morotai for thirty years.

The archipelago has been a laboratory of evolution. It was its astonishing diversity of species that propelled the Moluccas into history. Five microscopic volcanic islands – Ternate, Tidore, Moti, Makian and Bacan – were the only places on the planet where clove trees grew. Four hundred miles south another handful of islands – the Bandas – were the unique source of nutmeg. The fruits of these plants gave the Moluccas the title of the Spice Islands and would bring them, in time, to the attention of the world.

The lure of spices reaches far into antiquity: 4,000-year-old clove buds have been excavated from cities on the banks of the Euphrates, sculpted reliefs of spice fleets recorded in the Valley of the Kings. Chinese emperors in the Han dynasty required courtiers to sweeten their breath with cloves and the Romans held spices to be olfactory portals to the divine – to scent sacrificial offerings and to waft the souls of the dead up from funeral pyres. Spices have been valued as antiseptics, analgesics and aphrodisiacs, to cheer up food and drink, as intimations of paradise. They have been instrumental in the development of long-distance trade routes by land and sea, the growth of cities and the spread of religions by the merchants who carried them. Lightweight and durable, they were the first truly global commodity; the mark-up as they passed through many hands has been so astonishing – as much as 1,000 per cent by the time they reached Europe – that they could be worth more than their weight in gold; at times they have been a currency in their own right.

In the Middle Ages, Europeans resented that the spice trade was largely in the hands of Muslim merchants and that their bullion was draining away in payment. The secrets of the source of cloves and nutmeg were unknown. It was the rumours of lone travellers that whetted the appetite. Marco Polo thought that cloves came from

China – he must have seen whole clove branches there imported from the Moluccas – and nutmeg from Java. The Franciscan missionary Odoric of Pordenone, who passed through Java in the early fourteenth century, understood that they came from somewhere further east, without being able to identify the exact spot. The Italian traveller Ludovico di Varthema claimed to have visited both the Bandas and the Moluccas around 1505 and described the cultivation of both cloves and nutmeg. His account was quickly in printed circulation.

This swirl of speculation and desire was the driver of European exploration. Columbus had set out westward for the 'Indies' – China, Japan and the Spice Islands – to track the riches of the Orient back to their source and cut out the Islamic middlemen. The annotations in his Latin copy of Polo's travels, which still exists, indicate his interests: spices, gold and gems. Instead, he hit the American barrier. Vasco da Gama sailed east to India: by 1511 the Portuguese had reached Malacca on the Malay Peninsula, almost within sighting distance of Sumatra.

What followed is the subject of this book. The Moluccas were destined to become the epicentre of a sixteenth-century great game that literally shaped the world – first a vicious struggle between Portugal and Spain that had ricocheting consequences, later a global contest. It would launch scores of expeditions via Malaya, the Strait of Magellan, the coast of Mexico and the Arctic circle. It despatched fleets from Seville and Lisbon and London that involved conquistadors from Castile, Portuguese and Basque pilots, Flemish cartographers, English seamen, German and Italian bankers. It created violent clashes with the Ottoman empire and brought Europeans into contact with the ancient kingdoms of China and Japan.

The years 1511–71 saw Europe, hungry, competitive and aggressive, shift decisively from the margins to the centre and briefly transform Spain into a world power. In these six critical decades Europeans demonstrated that the world was spherical, started to fill in the blank of the Pacific Ocean, created the first global cities, and linked up the oceans. Their maritime empires would dominate the seas of the planet for nearly half a millennium. The epic voyages and the collisions of peoples and cultures produced extraordinary stories of endurance, courage and suffering, alongside appalling acts of cruelty and genocide against indigenous peoples. They ushered in a new age of information through the development of printing and built the networks for a global trading system. Its mechanism would be the worldwide flow of silver as a universal medium of exchange; its springboard the lure of spices. All this would feed into the political, commercial, cultural and ecological make-up of the modern world.

In 1511 three Portuguese ships set sail from Malacca to track cloves and nutmeg back to their source. They were poised to reap enormous rewards.

PART I
LANDFALLS:
THE RACE TO THE EAST
1511- 22

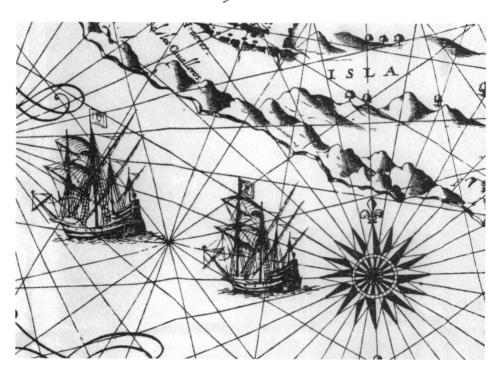

One

The Heaven of Francisco Serrão
1511-19

1 April 1512, from Cochin on the west coast of India. A letter from Afonso de Albuquerque, the Portuguese governor-general in India, to the king, Manuel I. Included with the letter, the copied fragment of a large map:

> It seems to me, Sir, that this was the best thing I have ever seen, and your Highness will be very pleased to see it ... I send this piece to Your Highness, which Francisco Rodrigues traced from the other, in which Your Highness can truly see where the Chinese and Gores [Ryukyu islanders] come from, and the course your ships must take to the Clove Islands, and where the gold mines lie, and the islands of Java and Banda, of nutmeg and spices, and the land of the king of Siam, and also the end of the navigation of the Chinese, the direction it takes, and how they do not navigate farther.[1]

The larger version to which he alluded had been lost in a shipwreck that had nearly cost Albuquerque his life, but what remained was of immense value. Complete with 'rhumb lines and direct routes followed by the ships',[2] it was a blueprint for sailing to the Spice

Islands, the final objective of European exploration after centuries of speculation, and it offered the dizzying prospect of making direct contact with China, rendered fabulous in the European imagination by Marco Polo.

Eight months earlier the Portuguese had captured the strategic city of Malacca near the tip of the Malay Peninsula that linked the trades of the farthest Orient to those of India and the Middle East. It was the conduit by which spices passed through the hands of many middlemen to the markets of Europe at vastly inflated prices, and it now provided the Portuguese with the springboard for a final push to purchase cloves and nutmeg at source. They were moving fast. With Malacca secured, Albuquerque immediately sent embassies to Burma, Thailand and Sumatra announcing the Portuguese presence and offering trade and goodwill. What the letter back to King Manuel had not said was that an expedition to the Spice Islands was already at sea with Francisco Rodrigues, 'a young man . . . with very good knowledge and able to make maps',[3] as pilot. Among those who had participated in the taking of Malacca were two young men of the minor Portuguese nobility, Francisco Serrão and Fernão de Magalhães, the man who would become Magellan.

Three ships set sail from Malacca, probably in November 1511, 'to go to Molucca for cloves and Banda for nutmeg'[4] under the command of António de Abreu: the *Santa Catarina*, the *Sabaia* captained by Francisco Serrão, and a light caravel piloted by Rodrigues. It was manned by 120 Portuguese with 60 enslaved men to work the pumps. The commanders were battle hardened from the fight at Malacca. Abreu was recovering from a musket shot in the face that had smashed his teeth and destroyed part of his tongue, but this expedition was framed as a peaceful trading venture. It also carried two Malays familiar with the sailing route. Albuquerque was aware that word of the Portuguese capture of Malacca would have rippled through the communities of the Malay Archipelago and threatened to disrupt their trade. He despatched a junk to pave the way, captained by a Persian master called Ismael, 'so that when António de Abreu reached these ports . . . seeing that our name was feared among those people, we wouldn't be badly received'.[5] Rounding the tip of Malaya, the Portuguese were turning the corner into a new sea and a new world: the Malay Archipelago, with its thousands of islands, multiple languages, tiny fragmented kingdoms and unknown sailing conditions. In the process they were morphing from conquerors into traders, now on the periphery of the Portuguese empire.

The ships sailed along the north coast of Java, steering by the line of volcanoes rising above green terraced rice fields. Putting in to resupply at the port of Gresik, Serrão acquired a Javanese wife, a 'monsoon bride', in the custom of seasonal traders along the coast. As they threaded their way through a chain of reefs, the *Sabaia* was wrecked and had to be abandoned. The two remaining ships set their course north. Rodrigues was astonished by the isolated volcanic island of Gunung Api, rising out of the sea – 'from its highest point streams of fire run down continuously to the sea, which is a wonderful thing to behold'.[6] He mapped this new world as they went and sketched the coastlines that they passed.

The voyage, however, was mistimed to reach the clove-bearing islands of the Moluccas. Instead, contrary winds forced them to turn east then south in search of nutmeg in another island group, the Bandas, ten tiny spots in the sea, wrapped around the sunken caldera of a vanished volcano. The new arrivals anchored in the bay of Lontar, the largest of the islands, 'shaped like a billhook',[7] according to the Portuguese historian Barros. Rising above them was a live volcano spewing sulphur from its mouth. The slopes of the islands were brilliantly green with the nutmeg trees they had come to find, sheltered by other species. To the Portuguese it was everything they could have imagined: 'it seemed like a garden in which Nature with that particular fruit had created something of delight'. The flowers of the nutmeg 'had a complex fragrance, unlike anything that we have. After the flowers, the nutmeg, green in colour . . . and as they begin

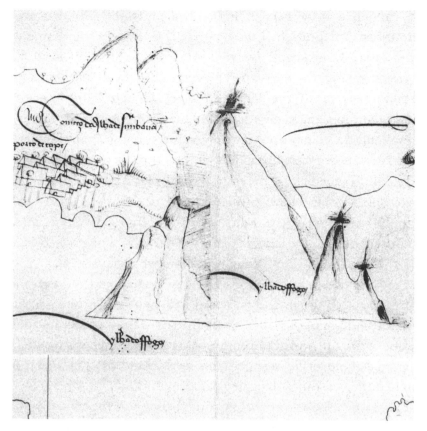

1. The line of volcanoes along the coast of Java sketched by Francisco Rodrigues. In the centre the volcanic island of Gunung Api belching fire.

to ripen, a multitude of parrots and various other birds come . . . it's quite another spectacle to see the sheer variety of species, songs and colours that Nature has given them.'[8] The birds played an intricate role in the richly woven fabric of the islands' ecology, disseminating the nutmeg seeds. The curious Portuguese also closely described the people and social structure of the islands.

If the Portuguese saw, they were also seen. According to one account, the inhabitants of these islands were overawed by the arrival of Abreu's fleet and the size of their ships. The new arrivals were quick to exploit the potential, both practical and psychological, of their stout sailing vessels. Rui Brito de Patalim, the captain of the fort of Malacca, reported that 'for the Moluccas, Banda, Timor and Java, we need large ships, even though the inhabitants are frightened of them'. He suggested sending out one or two *naos* (large sailing ships) of 500 tons, 'because apart from asserting our authority, they can take great abundance of spices which could not be done in smaller ships. Moreover, the route is already known and easily navigable.'[9]

The Bandanese had wide trading networks with the surrounding islands. They received cloves from the Moluccas and also made voyages to Java, and occasionally Malacca. They greeted the newcomers as just one more trading party. They were particularly welcome because the Portuguese themselves had ruptured their commercial system and they needed business. Guided by the advice of Malaccan merchants, the Portuguese had come with suitable trading items: cloth, rice and Chinese porcelain. Javanese gongs – musical instruments – were extremely popular and could be traded for large quantities of spices: 'With these and with basins of metal and tin they make themselves music.'[10]

Here they loaded up with nutmeg and mace (the more delicately flavoured outer coating of the nutmeg), as well as imported cloves, and purchased a Bandanese junk to replace the *Sabaia*. Neither of their surviving ships was in good shape, nor was the junk. These craft, though suitable for inter-island voyages, were not particularly seaworthy and were equipped only with wooden anchors, but nutmeg was a bulky cargo and they needed the hold space. It was Francisco Serrão who commanded this ship as they set out on the return journey across the Banda Sea. In mid-sea the junk started to ship water. They were wrecked on the reef of a barren island with nothing but turtles for company. There was no other food source and no fresh water. Their plight, however, had not gone unnoticed. The Lucopina islands were evidently a known graveyard for ships crossing the Banda Sea, and provided pickings for sea scavengers. A war canoe appeared on the horizon to see what could be salvaged. Advised by their Muslim pilots, the Portuguese hid in ambush, took the sea robbers by surprise and commandeered their vessel. The tables were turned and the would-be pirates, themselves now potential castaways, were forced to row their own canoe to the settlement of Hitu, on the nearby island of Ambon.

The small band of Portuguese, eight or nine in all, stepped ashore in their steel armour, bearing muskets. They made an immediate impression. Hitu was involved in a contest with the people of Luhu, on the neighbouring island of Seram. The pattern of inter-island warfare consisted of canoe attacks in which they 'make sudden raids from one island to another, making war, and taking captive or slaying one another'.[11] It was a style of fighting with which the Portuguese incomers were soon to be deeply familiar, along with the complexity of local politics. Serrão's small band, co-opted by Hitu, had a decisive impact on the contest. News of the incomers and their feats of arms spread fast across the archipelago. It soon reached the clove-bearing islands of the Moluccas, 300 miles north, and was of immediate interest to their rulers.

The two tiny islands of Ternate and Tidore are dominated by symmetrical volcanoes rising sheer out of the sea, their slopes fringed by forest-clad slopes. Separated by just a few hundred yards of water, at that moment they were locked in combat. Both had been casually Islamicised by Muslim merchants, and their sultans were fierce rivals, each leading a confederacy of other islands and settlements. The pattern of warfare was already familiar to Serrão and his colleagues from their participation on Ambon. These attacks were carried out in large, fast war canoes called *kora-koras* or *joangas*, carrying up to a hundred rowers. Ternate had the largest fleet of these vessels, and it was one of their kora-koras that reached Serrão at Hitu with an invitation to come to the island.

The Portuguese adventurers were welcomed warmly by the sultan, Bayan Sirullah: 'he received them in his country and did them great

2. Ternate and its volcano in an eighteenth-century Dutch print.

honour'.[12] He claimed to have had a prescient dream about the arrival of men in iron who would extend his rule. They quickly established themselves – a mercenary strike force that gave Ternate the upper hand against Tidore. In the process, Serrão became the indispensable adviser and confidant of the sultan. When, in 1514, Bayan Sirullah wrote a letter to the king of Portugal offering vassalage, it was not only because Portugal's control of the spice-trading hub of Malacca was critical to Ternate's clove exports. He also saw the Portuguese as the means for decisive control of the adjacent island kingdoms. Serrão was the man to accomplish this. The Portuguese saw the relationship rather differently. In September 1515 Albuquerque was writing to the king with 'news of Serrão who was alive and in power of the clove islands and governed the king and all the land',[13] implicitly on behalf of his royal master.

Malacca was the most eastern hub of Portuguese power. Its limited human resources were spread thinly across a chain of forts and bases stretching from Africa to the Persian Gulf and the west coasts of India, a vast arena. The Moluccas were two monsoons and 9,000 miles away from royal power, and Serrão, it seems, was increasingly shedding his allegiance to a far-distant king in Lisbon. In the years after his arrival in 1512 Portuguese trading vessels reached the island, loaded up with cloves, and sailed away again. Serrão stayed, ignoring any injunction to return home. Semi-independent of Portugal, he was meddling in the internal politics of the islands. He was living the life many a Portuguese adventurer dreamed of, driven not by the desire to serve the royal edict but simply to get rich and live in the imagined luxury of the Orient, a rajah in an exotic world. Albuquerque's letter suggests that he was at least tolerated.

Serrão remains a shadowy figure, of whom little is known, but his name runs as a thin seam through the chronicles of the age and he was destined to occupy a small, perhaps pivotal role in what was about to happen. His voice is muffled. Like many of the records of the Portuguese, his letters were probably lost in the Lisbon earth-quake of 1755, and only exist as echoes in contemporary chronicles. But it is known that Serrão was writing letters, despatched with the scent of cloves, in departing Portuguese ships, to the king, and to his friend, Fernão de Magalhães.

The Portuguese were inquisitive gatherers of information on the Spice Islands. Of the Bandas, they noted their unique political organisation: 'they have no king, they are ruled by the elders'; the appearance of the people; their diet, which depended on sago: 'made from the pith of a tree and baked very hard . . . and it is used for money'; along with population numbers, the geography of the islands and landing arrangements; above all, their trading networks and the details of costs and spice production. They were curious to discover and describe the cultivation and harvesting of nutmeg and mace: 'trees like unto bay trees, whereof the fruit is the nut; over it spreads

3. The nutmeg and its outer coating of mace.

the mace like a flower, and above that again another thick rind. One quintal of mace is worth here as much as seven of nutmeg.'[14] 'The mace is a fruit like peaches or apricots, and when it is ripe it opens and the outer pulp falls, and that in the inside turns red, and this is the mace on the nutmeg, and they gather them and put them to dry. The fruit is ripe all through the year; it is gathered every month.'[15]

Clove production in the Moluccas came in for similar scrutiny:

17

The woods of these islands are full of certain trees like unto bay trees and their leaves are like those of arbutus; whereupon grow the cloves in clusters like orange or woodbine flowers. It grows very green and then turns white, but when it is ripe it is of a fine red colour. Then the natives gather it by hand and spread it out to dry in the sun, when it turns black; and if there is no sun they dry it in smoke-houses. When it is dry, they sprinkle it with a little salt water that it may not become mouldy and may preserve its full virtues. And of this they gather so great a quantity in these five islands that it cannot be conveyed out of the country . . . if it is not gathered for three years the trees run wild, and that which they yield thereafter is worthless.[16]

These accounts collected by factors and merchants were effectively commercial handbooks, providing a continuous stream of feedback to Portugal's national project on all aspects of geography, ecology, trade, power structures and anthropology. Europeans were garnering information about the world and none of it was quite innocent.

In 1519 King Manuel commissioned an exotic book of maps, now known as the Miller Atlas. It is both an extraordinary and beautiful work of art and a celebration of the nation's discoveries. In it, the Moluccas are picked out in gold and pinned to the sea by a Portuguese flag, like a rare butterfly in a collector's cabinet. This was an assertion of ownership, to the reality of which the peoples of the islands were yet to awake. On the book's world map, the Moluccas are ringed by a semi-circular set of shoals, suggesting that the islands were inaccessible. The islands themselves are reasonably accurately positioned but the shoals do not exist, and the clove-bearing Moluccas are further protected by a labyrinthine maze of imaginary islands through which navigation looks to be immensely difficult. Even more startling is that the Pacific, first sighted by the Spanish four years earlier and now widely known, does not exist. The book's world map is anachronistic – a throwback to the worldview of the ancient geographer

4. The clustered fruit of the clove tree.

Ptolemy. It shows the Atlantic to be enclosed by an encircling landmass with no possible exit to the east. The Miller Atlas was not an
objective description of what the Portuguese knew, more a geopolit-
ical tool aimed at buttressing Portugal's hegemony of the spice trade
and deterring inquisitive rivals – specifically Spain – from making an
attempt on the Moluccas by breaking into the Pacific around, or
through, the Americas.

The same year the Spanish were planning to do just that with
the active Portuguese involvement of Fernão de Magalhães and the
knowledge of Francisco Serrão. King Manuel was certainly aware
of this.

Two

Maps and Speculations
1513-19

The Spanish had been playing catch-up in the race to the Indies. Doubts about Columbus's claims of being close to Japan were creeping in; so far his exploits had produced little of value. The continuous advances of the Portuguese were causing envy and concern the other side of the frontier. Portugal and the Crown of Castile – the latter now consolidating other kingdoms of the Iberian Peninsula into a unified Spain – were tied together by marriage and proximity into a relationship that might be described as passive-aggressive: bitter rivals whose monarchs addressed each other as dear friends. Across this frontier there was an interpenetration of maritime skills and knowledge. Alongside Iberians, both depended on outsiders. These included Venetians, Genoese and Frenchmen, but generally the flow of expertise was one way: from the Portuguese, the front runners in exploration, to Castile's information hub at Seville.

Areas of exploration for both parties were bound by the Treaty of Tordesillas. In 1494, in the wake of fierce clashes in the Atlantic Ocean, Castile and Portugal had agreed to allocate discrete areas of exploration via an imaginary line running through the Atlantic from pole to pole. Its position was calculated from the Cape Verde islands to a point 270 leagues west. This was intended to define exploration and territorial claims in regard to the Atlantic, but as the Portuguese pushed east to the Spice Islands, the full implications became apparent. The demarcation line must run right round the world, like a knife dividing an orange exactly in half. The critical issue was who 'owned' the highly desirable sources of nutmeg and cloves in the other hemisphere. Whatever their disagreements, between them the Iberian pioneers peremptorily claimed monopoly rights on the discovery of the whole planet, as a privatised political space. 'Show me Adam's will,' was the derisive comment of Francis I, king of France, Spain's bitter rival. Crucial to the question of where the antemeridian might cut through the Malay Archipelago was the issue of the size of the orange. Columbus had believed that the world was smaller than in fact it was. A smaller world suited Castilian ambitions. It allowed them to claim large reaches of territory in the East which the Portuguese had already abrogated. The Portuguese had trav-elled further than their rivals and had a more realistic assessment, though neither had yet grasped the vastness of the Pacific.

The Tordesillas Line proved to be a curse laid on the pretensions of the Iberian pioneers. Given the inability to accurately measure longitude – that is the east–west position of anywhere relative to the Cape Verde islands – defining exactly how and where it allocated rights of appropriation in the deep tropics was an impossibility. Obsessive as the hunt for an elusive subatomic particle, the issue of the line of demarcation was destined to run through the sixteenth century, spawning a torrent of documents, claims and counterclaims, diplomatic stand-offs and wars. It seemed that only possession could decide the issue, a nicety lost on indigenous peoples.

In the light of Tordesillas, for the Spanish the only way to compete for the spice trade was to sail west, and this required a channel through the barrier of the Americas – or rounding a final cape, symmetrical to the Cape of Good Hope that had carried the Portuguese east to India – into a sea that lay beyond. The idea that there might be a connecting strait was the subject of intense interest. The first two decades of the sixteenth century saw repeat probes down the coast of South America, some Portuguese, some Spanish, to find a way through – nosing up rivers and inlets, following the coastline as it appeared to taper south-west into colder latitudes. In 1513, when the conquistador Vasco Núñez de Balboa crossed the narrow isthmus of Panama and waded into the surf of a new ocean that he called the *Mar del Sur*, the South Sea, it was taken as an encouragement. It suggested that the continent might be permeable. The same year, a famous map by Martin Waldseemüller, the first to label the continent as America, includes a channel in this region. Ferdinand of Aragon had already instructed Juan Díaz de Solís, a navigator probably of Portuguese origin, to seek such a channel. Solís departed in 1514, after an initial objection from the Portuguese king, to find a westward route to 'the islands of Maluco, which is inside the limits of our demarcation, and you will take posses-sion of it'[1] – an assertion to be endlessly repeated in Spain during the decades that followed. Solís sailed up the River Plate in the hope that this might be the trans-continental channel but was killed in an encounter with the tribal people and eaten. But the hope of a passage remained, as did the Spanish claim.

Europe was rippling with intellectual curiosity about the world unfolding from Lisbon and Seville. German and Spanish bankers were funding voyages, anxious to seek profits. Cartographers scram-bled to assemble new pictures of the world. Speculative maps and globes projected the wish fulfilment of explorers – straits that led into the new sea. A map based on the voyages of the Portuguese pilot, João de Lisboa, in 1514, shows South America tapering to a point. The following year the globe of another cartographer, Johannes Schöner, includes both Waldseemüller's central channel and a strait round the tip of South America, separating the Americas from the labelled but as yet undiscovered Antarctica. Schöner's accompanying commentary claimed that:

The Portuguese, thus, sailed around this region, the Brasilie Regio, and discovered the passage very similar to that of our

Europe (where we reside) and situated laterally between east and west. From one side the land on the other is visible; and the cape of this region about 60 miles away, much as if one were sailing eastward through the Straits of Gibraltar or Seville and Barbary or Morocco in Africa, as our Globe shows toward the Antarctic Pole. Further, the distance is only moderate from this Region of Brazil to Malacca, where St Thomas was crowned with martyrdom.[2]

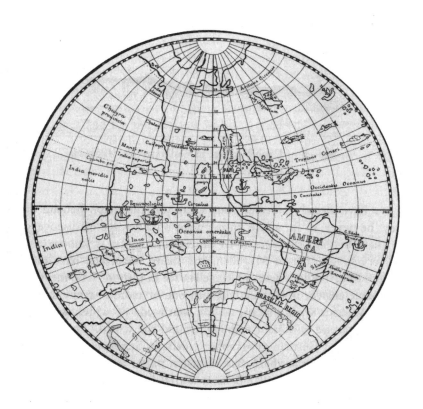

5. *The 1515 globe of Johannes Schöner. North America hardly exists but South America is reasonably shaped and shows a strait into the Pacific. Schöner may have confused the notion of a strait with the River Plate. Brazil is shown beneath it. His globe was probably one of a number of maps that encouraged Magellan to believe that a strait existed.*

Schöner was providing European audiences with the prospect of a comfortable analogy of sailing out of the Mediterranean, and then, by vastly shrinking the world, it would be a short hop across a narrow sea from the Americas to Malacca. Behind this may lie distorted accounts of the probes up the River Plate.

Into this arena of speculation and exploration stepped Francisco Serrão's friend, Fernão de Magalhães. Magalhães, whose origins lay in Portugal's lesser nobility, had the typical upbringing of his age and class, steeped in the late medieval ideals of chivalry with its commitment to great deeds and personal glory. There had been the conventional early attachment as a page to the court of King Manuel in Lisbon, from which all preferment stemmed, then adventures in the vibrant world of Portuguese overseas expansion – an opportunity for chancers, fortune seekers, wild risks and glory. Like Luís de Camões, the epic poet of Portugal's age of discoveries, he had witnessed siege, shipwreck, sea battles, prospects of wealth and sudden reversals of fortune. Magalhães had gone out to India with the annual imperial Portuguese fleet of 1505; participated in the ransacking of the coast of East Africa; fought at the critical sea battle at Diu in 1509; been present at the capture of Malacca in 1511; saved the life of Serrão in an ambush and voyaged with him as far as Sumatra. Subsequently he lost all the wealth that he had accumulated in the East when wrecked in the Maldives, where he seems to have acted with bravery and a cool head. He made it back to Goa almost destitute, so poor that Afonso de Albuquerque gave him a second-hand suit of armour. Finally returning to Portugal he went on campaign against the Moors in Morocco. Somewhere along the way, either in the East or in Morocco, he acquired a leg wound. Thereafter he always walked with a limp. Magalhães had seen the world of the Orient, glimpsed its possibilities and he had the letters from Serrão on the riches of the Spice Islands; he was engrossed in charts and the suggestions of cartographers.

The Morocco adventure in 1513–14 proved his undoing as far as preferment in Portugal was concerned. He was accused of having illegally sold some booty. He managed to clear his name but something in his nature – a streak of stubbornness and prickly pride – riled King Manuel. When he requested the return of a court stipend, this was refused. Obstinately, he asked again, and was pointedly turned down a second time. With his prospects blunted and a burning sense of injustice he looked across the frontier to neighbouring Castile.

It may have been Serrão's letters as well as gleanings from his own travels that ignited his attraction to the Moluccas. His own consideration of maps and globes convinced him that there must be a way of reaching the Spice Islands by sailing west. In which case, given the Tordesillas treaty, the opportunity to profit lay not with Portugal, but with Spain. Shaking the dust of his native country from his feet, and with his opportunities there gone, he crossed the frontier in the autumn of 1517. By 20 October he had arrived in Seville, Castile's centre of exploration and endeavour, where he took an oath of loyalty to the kingdom and rebranded himself as Fernando de Magallanes. He carried with him his CV: Serrão's letters, persuasive maps and charts, and his own self-confidence. This portfolio also included two enslaved people – a man called Enrique de Malacca and a Sumatran woman – to add credibility to his knowledge of the East. What he needed now was connections.

In Seville it was the institution of the Casa de Contratación that controlled all exploration and the business of the Americas, headed by the powerful Juan Rodríguez de Fonseca, Bishop of Burgos. In the city, Magalhães also found a small but influential group of Portuguese emigres. These included Diogo Barbosa, a well-established Portuguese exile, with whom he became so familiar that he had married his daughter within two months; and Juan de Aranda, who had connections with the Casa de Contratación. Magalhães also had a partner in the enterprise that he had come to promote, the somewhat eccentric Rui de Faleiro, a cosmographer and astrologer who claimed to have cracked the problem of determining longitude.

Faleiro, who shared his belief that the Moluccas lay on the Spanish side of the line, followed him to Castile in December.

By chance, Magalhães had arrived at an opportune moment in the affairs of Castile and of all Spain. A month after his arrival, the 18-year-old Charles Duke of Burgundy landed in the country to take up the throne as Charles I of Spain, which he had inherited through dynastic alliances. Almost all his advisers were Flemings from northern Europe, and Charles spoke no Castilian, but his arrival betokened a decisive break point in the affairs of his new kingdom. Castile was reaching out over the world to the Americas and was hungry for more; at the same time, the kingdoms of Spain would coalesce into a coherent bloc under the boy king. Charles was soon installed in Valladolid, the effective capital of Spain, and it was there that Juan de Aranda offered to broker Magellan's pitch. In January 1518 Magellan and Faleiro set off to the capital under the guidance of Aranda.

Aranda was a businessman looking for a cut of the anticipated profits, with whom disagreements on the subject quickly arose – but he did have the contacts. On 17 March he engineered the opportunity for the two men to put their case to a convocation of ministers. It consisted of three of Charles's Flemish advisers and the formidable Juan de Fonseca. Magellan produced the evidence: the letters from Serrão, 'giving him to understand that he had discovered yet another world, larger and richer than that found by Vasco da Gama',[3] a glimpse of this exotic world in the form of Enrique and the Sumatran, and persuasive maps and globes. Faleiro laid out the case for the Spice Islands lying within the Spanish sphere. Together they conjured up a golden mirage, talking up the wealth, the riches that were at Spain's door and her natural right. The critical question was: how might the Moluccas be reached, given that no strait or exit had, as yet, been discovered through the barrier of the Americas? Magellan's self-confidence, based on whatever he knew or had deduced from previous voyages, rested on a globe that he produced.

An eyewitness to this meeting was Bartolomé de las Casas, a Dominican priest. According to las Casas, Magellan, like a magician who refuses to reveal his trick, 'brought with him a well painted globe showing the entire world, and thereon traced the course he proposed to take, save that the strait was purposely left blank so that nobody could anticipate him'.[4] In effect he refused to reveal the secret of his secret, like an entrepreneur pitching a patent product whose contents he could not actually reveal on grounds of commercial sensitivity. It was a stunning display of self-confidence and single-handed bravado. Whatever he knew or guessed or hoped, his plan was based on his wishes, and his will. At any rate, this man, whose Spanish was not good, and whose credentials as a faithful citizen of a new country were questionable, should have been turned down flat.

Las Casas' follow-up question should certainly have proved the knock-out blow to anyone making a pitch to sceptical investors. 'I asked him what route he proposed to take. He replied that he intended to take that of Cape Santa María, which we call Rio de la Plata, and thence to follow the coast along until he found the strait. I said, "what will you do if you find no strait to pass into the other sea?" He replied that if he found none he would follow the course that the Portuguese took [by sailing east].'[5] Given the testy relations between the two kingdoms and the over-concern not to encroach on each other's space, this should have been a non-starter. It was also an implicit admission by Magellan that his secret route round the Americas might not exist at all. Overall, the council of ministers was not in favour: they were doubtful about the existence of a strait and dubious about the integrity of its proponent. Las Casas left a pen portrait of the 37-year-old Magellan standing in front of them. 'This Hernándo de Magallanes must have been a brave man, valiant in thought and for undertaking great things, although his person did not carry much authority, since he was of small stature and did not look like much, so that people thought they could put it over him for want of prudence and courage.'[6] People certainly misjudged him.

Magellan might prove to be imprudent but he was certainly brave. With this went a prickly and secretive nature, stubbornness and a high sense of his own worth and abilities: 'he thought of becoming a great lord'.[7]

Astonishingly, Magellan's proposal was put to the king in a positive light. Perhaps, overlooking the technical question mark as to how to get there, the dazzling wealth of the Moluccas beguiled: they thought it was worth the bet, and ruefully looking at the triumphal claims to the spice trade emanating from Portugal there was the fear of missing out. Charles appears to have overruled any misgivings. With astonishing speed – on 22 March 1518, less than five months after Magellan had announced himself for Castile – he granted royal approval to 'find in the domains that belong to us and ours in that area in the Ocean Sea, within the limits of our demarcation, islands, main lands, rich spices'.[8] The issue around exploration zones was particularly topical and repeatedly re-emphasised: 'You must so conduct this voyage of discovery that you do not encroach upon the demarcation and boundaries of the most serene king of Portugal, my very dear uncle and brother, or otherwise prejudice his interests, except within the limits of our demarcation'[9] – a complex piece of doublespeak given the uncertainties of the Tordesillas Line. Two months later to the day, Charles would be signing a treaty for the marriage of his sister to King Manuel of Portugal. The go-ahead for Magellan did not go down well with the Bishop of Burgos.

In the contract for the voyage, Magellan asked for the inclusion of a curious clause: that if more than six islands were discovered he would be able to retain two for himself. It hints that he might have been aiming to create a fiefdom of his own, as Serrão had done in the Moluccas. It was known that there were five spice-bearing islands in the Moluccas. It was also clear that the Portuguese were well installed there. Might he be aiming not to go to the Moluccas at all?

Back in Seville, he began preparations in earnest. From the start these were bedevilled. He was to be provided with five ships, all of them small – the largest 130 tons – and none of them newly built. Even so, the costs of purchasing, overhauling, provisioning and recruiting were huge. When it came to the crucial issue of funding, Charles decided that the majority of the investment, about 80 per cent, would be met by the crown. It was to be an imperial project. The remainder provided scope for private capital. Magellan and Faleiro were to be appointed joint captains and their expedition was to be designated the *Armada de Molucca*. Later, Magellan and Faleiro were further gratified to be made knights of the Order of Santiago, an honour that conferred authority and status on the Portuguese incomers.

And yet, a thread of distrust runs through Charles's orders. Behind the scenes, in the Casa de Contratación, the powerful Juan de Fonseca was working to undermine Magellan's authority. One of his placemen, Juan de Cartagena, was given the post of inspector-general of the fleet (accountant), a position that put a check on Magellan's overall authority. Unknown to Magellan, Cartagena also had secret orders from the king:

> You will advise us fully and specifically of the manner in which our instructions and mandates are complied with in the said lands; of our justices, of the treatment of natives of said lands . . . [and] how said captains and officers observe our instructions, and other matters of our service.[10]

Cartagena's presence implied concern about the Portuguese. He was there to keep Magellan and Faleiro in check. He had no seafaring background, but his salary was far higher than Magellan's. Cartagena was not a nobody. He was Fonseca's 'nephew', a euphemism for illegitimate son. Fonseca similarly sought to pack other key positions. The ships' captains, with the exception of those commanded by Magellan and Faleiro, were placemen chosen by him. All the conditions were in place for trouble.

The nervousness over the Portuguese contingent was overt. Orders were given to limit their number to twelve. These mainly comprised the experienced pilots. In effect, nearly all the ships' captains were Spanish, while the navigators were Portuguese. The total company of the fleet was to be limited to 235. Magellan did his best to trim the Portuguese contingent to the quota, but it was difficult to recruit sufficient seamen from Castile. In the end the number of Portuguese rose to thirty-seven. The day before departure he was compelled to swear a statement that he had made all reasonable attempts to recruit Spaniards: 'I proclaimed in this city, in squares and markets and busy places and along the river that anyone – sailors, cabin boys, caulkers, carpenters, and other officers – who wished to join the Armada should contact me … None of the villagers born here wanted to join the Armada.'[11] One man who did sign on was Juan Sebastián Elcano, an experienced seaman from the Basque region.

There was one curiosity among the ships' complement. An Italian nobleman and scholar, Antonio de Pigafetta, got himself attached to the expedition as a supernumerary. Pigafetta, widely read, cultured and inquisitive, was there for the ride: 'knowing … by reading many books … the very great and awful things of the ocean, I deliberated, with the favour of the Emperor [Charles] … to experiment and go and see with my own eyes a part of those things',[12] and to write up the expedition. He was to be Magellan's hagiographer. Hardly a

6. *Signature of Juan Sebastián Elcano. Here he signs himself as Del Cano.*

critical word about the commander crosses his many pages. At the same time, he came to produce the fullest and most fascinating account of the voyage – and he was curious. By turns natural historian, ethnologist, disciplined compiler of languages, student of astronomy and climatology – and survivor, Pigafetta was the product and celebrant of the Renaissance spirit of enquiry.

Back in Lisbon, there was fury and disquiet about the proceedings. Numerous Portuguese had crossed the frontier to seek opportunities in Castile, but the possibility that Magellan could do real damage to the national interests led him to be branded a traitor. Attempts were made by the Portuguese ambassador to Spain to woo the two men back with a mixture of promises and threats. The offer to return to Lisbon and have their proposal considered by King Manuel fell on deaf ears. Magellan perceived capture and execution as being the more likely outcome. The outside possibility of being assassinated led Charles to provide them with bodyguards.

Magellan was fighting on many fronts. Despite the royal mandate, anti-Portuguese sentiment was rife, particularly in the Casa de Contratación. In October it erupted in an incident in the Seville dockyard, when Magellan was seen hoisting a flag misinterpreted as being that of the Portuguese crown. There was a riot. A pilot was stabbed. Magellan loudly protested to the king that he recognised Sebastião Alvares, the Portuguese agent in Seville, among the crowd and that he was the instigator.

As late as 18 July 1519, less than a month before departure, Alvares was still trying to subvert Magellan's mission. In a letter to King Manuel, he describes catching the navigator in a rare domestic moment: doing his packing for the voyage. 'I went to Magellan's house, where I found him filling baskets and chest with preserved victuals and other things.'[13] Though a mixture of threats, bribes and emotional appeals failed to turn Magellan, they evidently unsettled him. 'He then bewailed himself greatly, and said he was much concerned about it all, but that he knew nothing which could justify his leaving a king who had shown him such favour.'[14] There were other ways of discomforting the turncoat: the well-informed Alvares warned him to watch his back: 'He, Magellan, thought he was going as admiral, whereas I knew that others were being sent in opposition to him, of whom he would know nothing, except when it would be too late to save his honour. And I told him that he should pay no heed to the honey that the Bishop of Burgos put to his lips.'[15] Alvares had accurately sized up the fractures in the command structure and the malign influence of the bishop. The preserves he had casually mentioned would later prove critical to survival.

Alvares also had detailed knowledge of the expedition's planned route. He wrote back to Manuel: 'the route which is reported they are to take is direct to Cape Frio [by Rio de Janeiro], leaving Brazil on the right ... and thence to sail direct to Maluco, which land of Maluco I have seen laid down on the globe and chart [they are taking]'.[16] To which he added a curse: 'May God the Almighty grant that they make a voyage like that of the Corte Reals, and that your Highness may remain at rest.'[17] The Corte Reals, Portuguese explorers, had vanished without trace in the northern seas.

Alvares was also aware that something was amiss with Rui Faleiro. 'I spoke to Ruy Faleiro twice ... it seems to me that he is like a man affected in his reason, and that this his familiar has taken away whatever wisdom he possessed.'[18] Others also noticed that Faleiro was showing alarming signs of mental instability. The man who was half astronomer and half astrologer was wandering. A week later he was replaced with the vague promise of participating in a second fleet.

The departure of Faleiro opened up for the bishop the chance to tighten his hold over Magellan's supreme command. Faleiro needed to be replaced; the role of co-commander now went to Juan de Cartagena, a position that had Fonseca's fingerprints all over it. He was appointed as 'conjoint person', as Faleiro had been, an ambiguous title that further scrambled the chain of command. Was he still subordinate to Magellan, or was he his equal? Each man undoubtedly put his own interpretation on the position. It was one further ingredient in the recipe for trouble once the fleet was at sea. It certainly implied that Magellan should confer with Cartagena on all matters of importance.

On 8 May 1519, Magellan received final instructions from Charles. These were, as was the case of the time with monarchs attempting to control the uncontrollable, minutely detailed and totally unrealistic given the harsh realities of sea voyages. Cartagena also received a copy of the orders, as inspector-general, from which he might assume that he had a rank equal to that of Magellan. Charles was compounding the fault lines in the structure of the voyage. There was the repeated edict not to impinge on Portuguese territory, though it was clear to anyone thinking about this that, at the very least, the armada would have to sail through Portuguese territorial waters along the coast of Brazil. As for the Moluccas, the question of the line was unresolved.

There is a possibility that Charles himself remained open to doubt as to the intentions of his chosen captain. Repeated and insistent orders that he was 'to proceed straight to the spicery'[19] suggest a suspicion that Magellan might have some other destination in mind. The clause about the six islands was suggestive. Alvares reported back to Manuel the high level of dissent between Magellan and the Casa officials: they could not stomach him. The conditions were being laid down for serious trouble when the going got tough: the rifts between Magellan and Cartagena, between Portuguese and Spanish factions – and whatever wandering fancies existed in the mind of the intransigent Magellan.

Above all, Magellan's orders were insistent that he must share information with the captains and officers of all the ships in the armada; a plan was to be made and set down in writing. The captains were to follow the customary practice of the sea, by personally saluting the flagship every afternoon, and to follow set procedures should they get separated. In other words, the expedition was to be based on close collaboration. In Magellan's mind it was quite clearly otherwise. When asked by Alvares about the chain of command, Magellan answered 'once at sea he would be able to do as he liked'.[20]

By early August 1519 the ships were fully loaded with two years' worth of supplies and ready to sail. Two months earlier, on 28 June, Charles had been elected to the title of Holy Roman Emperor, following a great deal of bribery. Henceforth, with his vast holdings in Europe and the Americas, he believed it to be his destiny to be the world monarch. His personal motto was *Plus Ultra*, 'Further'. Magellan was to be an agent of this mission.

Three

The Molucca Fleet
1519-20

'In the name of God and of good salvation. We departed from Seville on the tenth of August, in the year 1519, to go and discover the Molucca islands.'[1] So begins an anonymous account. There were five ships: Magellan's flagship the *Trinidad*, then the *San Antonio*, which carried the bulk of the stores, the *Concepción*, the *Victoria*, and the smallest, at 75 tons, a scouting vessel, the *Santiago*.

According to Pigafetta, the Armada de Molucca left to a triumphant volley of gunfire, the ships gliding away down the Guadalquivir – the Great River of Muslim Spain – through fertile flatlands and estuarine marshes. The river was not deep enough to carry ships of large tonnage and navigation was tricky. They had to dodge the submerged columns of collapsed stone bridges, on their way to the port town of Sanlúcar de Barrameda. Here they stayed a month, finalising their provisioning. 'Every day we went ashore to hear mass in a village called Nostra Dona de Barrameda, near Sanlúcar. Before the departure, the captain-general wished all the men to confess and would not allow any woman to sail in the fleet for the best of considerations.'[2] The landlubber Pigafetta, whose version of Magellan's leadership was consistently loyal, anticipated seeing the wonders of the world. For him and just seventeen others, Sanlúcar was destined

35

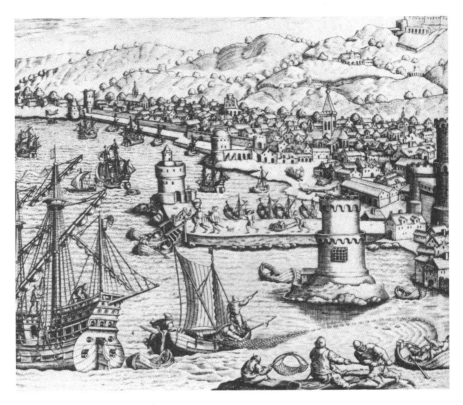

7. The busy port of Sanlúcar de Barrameda.

to be the beginning and the end of an extraordinary cycle of human experience.

On 20 September they departed, heading for Santa Cruz de Tenerife, the largest island in the Canaries, for further replenishment and to obtain pitch for caulking the vessels. At Tenerife, according to the Portuguese chronicler Gaspar Correa, came the first inkling of trouble ahead. A fast caravel brought a message to Magellan from his father-in-law, Diogo Barbosa, to the effect that he should watch his personal safety and beware mutiny from disaffected captains. But he had probably already factored that in.

The fractures in the command structure were soon to show. When they set sail again from Tenerife on 3 October, it was apparent that

Magellan was not pursuing a conventional course across the Atlantic towards Brazil; nor was he following the firm instructions that he had been given to share details of the route with the senior captains and officers: once at sea he would do whatever he liked. It would be standard to swing south-west away from Africa to pick up the trade winds that would carry a ship rapidly across the Atlantic. Magellan did not do so: he kept the fleet running south, parallel to the African coast. The Portuguese had enough knowledge of African exploration to know that following this trajectory was hard work. Cartagena, with his undefined co-responsibility for the voyage, demanded to know the reason. Magellan refused any explanation and ordered him to just follow the flagship. This was not in the brief and it was by no means any attempt to harmonise the fleet. It was perhaps intended to demonstrate Magellan's unchecked authority, but the reasons for taking the route remain unclear. It is possible that a rumour that the Portuguese had sent out an interception fleet may have led him to avoid a conventional crossing, or it may have been a strategy to flush out dissent in the fleet. Tactically it was a disaster. The fleet was hit by ever-changing weather. Pigafetta recalled:

> many days did we sail along the coast of Guinea . . . with contrary winds, calms and rain without wind, until we reached the equi- noctial line having sixty days of continual rain . . . before we reached the line many furious squalls of wind and currents of water struck us head on . . . in order that the ships might not be wrecked, all the sails were struck; and in this manner did we wander hither and yon on the sea, waiting for the tempest to cease . . . when it rained there was no wind. When the sun shone, it was calm.[3]

During one storm, Pigafetta experienced the phenomenon of St Elmo's fire: brilliant electric flashes of blue light crackling at the mast head. For the superstitious sailors this was taken as a holy visitation. The men fell weeping to the deck. 'When that blessed light was about to leave us, so dazzling was the brightness . . . that we all remained blinded and calling for mercy. And truly when we thought that we were dead men, the sea suddenly went calm.'[4]

The arm-wrestle with Cartagena went on. Magellan offered no explanations, made no attempt to share information, showed no inclination to follow Charles's orders. Within the fleet there was a slow-burning guerrilla war between the larger Spanish faction and that of Magellan's Portuguese. A pressure cooker of resentment was building against arbitrary authority. Cartagena resorted to calculated snubs. As part of the ritual that kept the fleet together it was customary for the other ships to salute Magellan's flagship at the end of each day with a formal greeting: 'God keep you, sir Captain-general and master, and good company.'[5] Titles were critical to prickly Renaissance gentlemen, so when Cartagena pointedly started to address Magellan simply as 'Captain', it rankled. Furthermore, it was the quartermaster rather than Cartagena who gave the salute. When rebuked by Magellan, Cartagena replied that he would ask a page to deliver the daily greeting next time. For three days he failed to have it delivered at all.

Just then a new disciplinary crisis emerged. The master of the *Victoria*, a Sicilian called Antonio de Salomón, was caught in an act of sodomy with his cabin boy. The set punishment for such was death but it called for a formal court martial. All the captains of the other ships were ordered to a meeting on the *Trinidad* in the captain's cabin. It was time for a face-to-face between the factions.

Magellan had evidently prepared the next move. When Cartagena again raised the subject of leadership and sailing route, Magellan was ready. He grabbed his rival by the throat and had him secured in the hold. He put his own relative Álvaro de Mesquita in command of the *San Antonio*, the largest ship in the fleet. He threatened to maroon Cartagena on the coast of Brazil, but was dissuaded from doing so. In the end Cartagena was put into the custody of Gaspar de Quesada,

another Castilian, under pledge to keep him secured. He had neutral-
ised his co-commander. Pigafetta recorded none of this. He had
spent his time fishing for sharks and wondering at the bird life of the
deep ocean.

Whatever the reasons for Magellan's change of route – perhaps
the Portuguese fleet that never materialised – it had served one
purpose. By deliberate provocation he had engineered a showdown
and stamped his authority as sole commander on a querulous Spanish
faction. But the cost had been high. It had taken three months to
make a voyage that could have been achieved in six weeks. It had
inflicted unnecessary hardship on the crews, used up valuable
supplies, halved their rations and consumed goodwill. Dissent was
still smouldering as they approached the coast of Brazil, steered by
the Portuguese pilot João Lopes Carvalho, who had spent four years
on this coast. They made landfall at Cape Santo Agostino, north of
their intended destination of Rio de Janeiro. According to the
Tordesillas treaty, they were trespassers, but there were no Portuguese
to object.

After several days they sailed on, arriving at a place they called
Guanabara, the bay of Rio de Janeiro. On this stretch of coast, they
encountered the Tupi people, with whom relations were friendly.
Carvalho had been here before. He re-met a son he had fathered by
a local woman and took him on board. They managed to secure
supplies: according to Pigafetta, 'a plentiful refreshment of fowls,
potatoes, many sweet pine apples, in truth the most delicious fruit
that can be found, the flesh of the *anta* [a tapir], which resembles
beef, sugarcane, and innumerable other things'.[6] The exchanges were
beneficial. The manufactured trade goods the ships carried were
highly desirable: fish hooks, mirrors, scissors and bells. 'For a king of
diamonds ... which is a playing card, they gave me six fowls and
thought that they had even cheated me,' Pigafetta recalled.

From the sailors' viewpoint it was a welcome respite, and a place
where all their fantasies about the innocence of tribal peoples might

be realised. The Europeans were seen as a blessing. There had been a long dry spell. 'When we reached the port,' Pigafetta recounted, 'it happened to rain, whereupon they said that we came from the sky and that we had brought the rain with us.'[7] For Pigafetta these people 'live according to the dictates of nature', and he gathered as much information as he could on their lives, appearance and customs. He wrote objectively of their cannibalism: 'they eat the human flesh of their enemies, not because it is good, but because it is a certain established custom'. He even jotted down a simple list of Tupi words. Like many of the peoples encountered, they had no iron – they constructed their canoes with stone axes – and were hungry for metal objects.

Of particular delight to the rank-and-file sailors were the sexual trades to be made for these: 'The men gave us one or two of their young daughters for one hatchet or one large knife, but they would not give us their wives in exchange for anything at all.'[8] For Pigafetta there was plenty of lubricious copy to appeal to European ideas of the sexuality of indigenous peoples: 'One day a beautiful young woman came to the flagship, where I was, for no other purpose than to seek what chance might offer. While there and waiting ... [she] saw a nail longer than one's finger. Picking it up very delightedly and neatly, she thrust it through the lips of her vagina, and bending down low immediately departed, the captain-general and I having seen that action.' This South Seas idyll had its dark side. On 20 December the death sentence for sodomy was carried out on Antonio de Salomón by strangulation.

The fleet prepared to depart on 27 December, much to the disappointment of both sides. For the pious there were simplistic ideas that these people could easily be converted to Christianity. Mass was said twice on shore, 'during which these people remained on their knees with so great contrition and with clasped hands raised aloft, that it was an exceeding great pleasure'. According to Pigafetta, the Tupi had 'built us a house as they thought that we were going to stay with them for some time'.[9] The sailors had to be prised away. Several

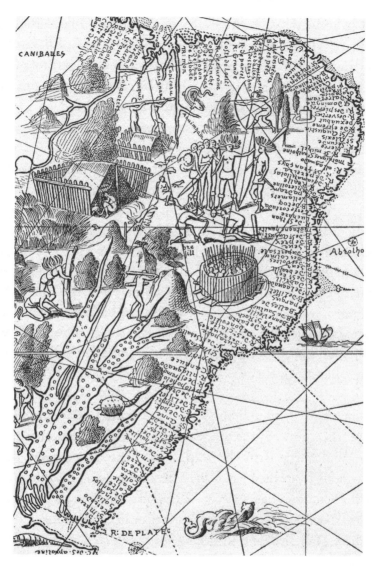

8. *A sixteenth-century map of Brazil, crammed with anthropological
information and hearsay about the lives and culture of the indigenous peoples.
The coast is minutely mapped down to the River Plate. The word 'caniballes'
in the top left-hand corner reflects a European fixation, probably drawn
from the fate of Juan Díaz de Solís and the account of Pigafetta.*

women stowaways were discovered in the ships. Duarte Barbosa, a close ally of Magellan, tried to desert, with the aim of living life in this apparent Eden. He was hauled away and confined to the ship. The Tupi regretfully saw them off in their canoes. It was almost the last comfortable moment of the expedition.

As they headed south, the coast seemed to be tapering promisingly to the west. From then on Magellan began obsessive investigation of bays and inlets in search of the promised strait. The going got harder. They were battling against counter-currents and the weather worsened. A severe storm blew them off course; regrouping, they found themselves in the vast estuary of the River Plate. This was the furthest that the Portuguese had been, and it was a place of ill-omen. It was here that Juan de Solís and his band had been killed and eaten by the native people three years earlier. Undeterred, the smallest ship, the *Santiago*, was sent to reconnoitre for promising signs of a thoroughfare. However, the water was fresh and too shallow to allow the possibility of transit. The local people, despite their reputation as cannibals, fled from them:

> One of them, in stature almost a giant, came to the flagship to assure [the safety of] the others his friends. He had a voice like a bull. While he was in the ship, the others carried away their possessions from the place where they were living into the interior, for fear of us. Seeing that, we landed a hundred men in order to have speech and converse with them, or to capture one of them by force. They fled, and in fleeing they took so large a step that we, although running, could not gain on their steps.[10]

It was the first sighting of the people Europeans were to call Patagonians – giants.

The fleet was hit by increasingly violent storms and deepening cold. Each degree of latitude south sharpened the temperature. Nosing into bays and creeks brought danger. On 13 February the

Victoria struck bottom on a shoal and was close to being wrecked. Magellan was forced to stand further offshore. He continued to search for an opening, retracing parts of his route for fear of having missed something. On 27 February they reached a place they came to call Bahía de los Patos, Duck Bay.

> Coasting along the land, we came to anchor at two islands full of geese and sea wolves [sea lions]. Truly, the great number of those geese cannot be reckoned; in one hour we loaded five ships [with them]. Those geese are black and have all their feathers alike on body and wings. They do not fly, and live on fish. They were so fat that it was not necessary to pluck them but to skin them. Their beak is like that of a crow. Those sea wolves are of various colours, and as large as a calf with a head like that of a calf, ears small and round, and large teeth.[11]

The landing party clubbed some of these; but a sudden squall made return to the ship impossible. The shore party spent a wretched night exposed to the cold and in fear of the wildlife. When a rescue party landed next morning, they found the sailors huddled under the bodies of their dead prey, seeking shelter from the cold, filthy, wretched, stinking, but alive.

The torment at Duck Bay was not over. Making it back to the ships, the fleet was struck by another fierce squall. One by one the *Trinidad*'s cables gave way. Just one still held – the anchor of hope. All the crew could do was to pray and make promises of pilgrimage to the church of Nuestra Señora de la Victoria back in Seville. The cable held; the storm abated. Midnight following, another storm lashed the ships, sheering away forecastles and poops. Again, all that was left were prayers and pledges of pilgrimage. The storm died down; the fire of St Elmo sparked on the mastheads. It raised hopes of God's great mercy but the prospects were deteriorating.

It was time to take shelter to see out the winter weather. Six days later they seemed to have found a suitable bay, with a narrow entrance, but storms pursued them inside this haven. They endured six days of violent weather. The fleet was being tested to the limit. Another landing party was stranded, destined to survive on the frozen shore for a week, eating raw shellfish with their bare hands.

With the deepening cold, the unpredictable storms, the relentless searching with no evidence of a strait, the danger of shipwreck off a hostile coast, the shortening days, fear and exhaustion were now digging deep into the souls of the men. There were doubts about the judgement of their commander, who they believed was not complying with his orders. When asked about the rift with Cartagena during an enquiry on return to Spain, Juan Sebastián Elcano stated that Magellan was tasked with taking decisions jointly but when confronted with this objection said he knew of no such undertaking. 'The other captains asked Magellan to take counsel with his officers, and to tell them the route by which they were going. They also asked him not to make port for the whole winter, and in that way use up all the provisions. And they urged that they should proceed to some region where they could endure the cold.'[12]

Whenever it was this conversation took place, Magellan took no notice. On 31 March he led the fleet into another sheltered bay, which they called St Julian. According to one source, Magellan again probed it to see if this was the magic door. It was not. The imperative was to find a secure refuge. At 49° south, they were cold, lost and surviving on half rations. All the dissatisfactions with the commander now boiled over. They could only see that 'the land stretched uninter-ruptedly to the south, and that no hope remained of its terminating or of the discovery of a strait through it, and that a severe winter was imminent, and that many of them were dead of starvation and hard-ships; and declared that they could no longer bear the rule which he had made about provisions, and begged that he would increase the allowance of provisions, and think about going home'. They added for emphasis that Charles had never intended 'that they should too obstinately attempt what nature itself and other obstacles opposed'.[13]

9. The port of St Julian.

The response was unflinching. 'In reply, Magellan who had already made up his mind either to die or to complete his enterprise, said that his course had been laid down for him by Caesar [Charles] himself, and that he neither could nor would depart from it in any degree, and that he would in consequence sail till he found either the end of the land or some strait (through it).'[14] There was also some taunting of the Spanish for their lack of courage: 'They had done nothing as yet worthy of admiration, or which could serve as an excuse for their return, in as much as the Portuguese crossed the tropic of Capricorn by as much as 12° not only every year, but almost every day, when they were sailing eastwards.'[15] With morale at a low, and Magellan's peremptory style of leadership demanding nothing but blind obedience, the scene was set for confrontation; the taunts of Spanish timidity in the face of the achievements of the Portuguese did not help. The captains' request had been something of an ulti-matum. His response almost invited a showdown.

1 April 1520, Palm Sunday. Magellan invited the ships' captains to dine with him after mass. Sensing a trap, two men – Gaspar de Quesada, and Juan de Cartagena, who was meant to be in his custody – snubbed the mass, and only Álvaro de Mesquita, Magellan's rela-tive, turned up for dinner on the *Trinidad*. He then returned to his ship, the *San Antonio*.

That night Mesquita had a rude awakening. 'While I was in my cabin on the said ship, and everyone was at rest, after the first watch had passed, Gaspar de Quesada, captain of the ship the *Concepción*, and Juan de Cartagena came armed with about thirty men, all armed, and they approached my cabin with drawn swords, and they took me, laid hands on me, their weapons to my chest ... and they put me in the cabin of Geronimo Guerra, scribe of the said ship, and clapped me in irons.'[16]

The ship's master, the Basque Juan de Elorriaga, tried to intervene: 'I require you in the name of God and the King Don Carlos that you go to your ship. This is not the time to be wandering around ships with armed men, and I also require you to release our captain.'[17] He tried to summon the crew to arms. Quesada shouted, 'We cannot be foiled in our work by this fool!'[18] and stabbed him several times with his dagger, leaving him to die. While the ship's chaplain was confessing the apparently expiring man, the crew were disarmed. In fact, Elorriaga's end would prove to be slow and very painful: he lingered for three months.

The mutineers now held the *San Antonio* and the *Concepción*. The *Victoria*, whose captain, Luis de Mendoza, was also deeply opposed to Magellan, joined the mutineers. Only the small scout ship *Santiago*, captained by Juan Serrano, remained loyal to Magellan on the *Trinidad*. Magellan was heavily outnumbered, but the mutineers would have done well if they had assessed their captain's character as shrewdly as Bartolomé de las Casas had back in Valladolid: 'since he was of small stature and did not look like much ... people thought they could put it over him for want of prudence and courage'.[19]

Magellan's response was quick and decisive. He decided first to tackle the *Victoria*, on which there were a large number of foreigners likely to be loyal to him. A boat was despatched with a letter to Mendoza, summoning him to a meeting. Mendoza was not to be fooled so easily but the five men who delivered it carried concealed weapons. As he replied in the negative, daggers were drawn and he was cut down on the deck. Simultaneously a boatload of fifteen more men, captained by Duarte Barbosa, rushed the ship. The suddenness of the coup surprised the crew, who surrendered without a fight. Magellan's standard was hoisted at the mast head, and the ship was moved to the narrow mouth of the bay alongside the *Trinidad*. The *Santiago* was also moved up alongside. The three ships now had the mutineers bottled up. The initiative had swung decisively to Magellan.

Inside the bay the mutineers on the *San Antonio* and the *Concepción* pondered their next move. They were called on to surrender but declined. The only recourse now was to break the pinch-point blockade and make for the open sea, and their best chance was at night. The timing was totally predictable. Magellan readied his men for the engagement. As the *San Antonio* sailed forward she was attacked on both sides, bombarded by the heavy guns of the *Trinidad*, then boarded by a swarm of men. It was very quickly all over. Mesquita was freed; Quesada and the other mutineers were seized and shackled. For the *Concepción* there was now no option; when a boat drew up to demand surrender, Juan de Cartagena complied. The mutiny had been scotched in twenty-four hours.

Magellan's vengeance was swift and ghastly. There was a show of due process but the sentences carried out were intended as both punishment and deterrent. The body of Mendoza was slung from the yard arm head down, then brought ashore, publicly decried as a traitor, and hung, drawn and quartered and spiked on poles. The death of Quesada was grimmer; his complicit servant, Luis del Molino, was given an option: die yourself or execute your master. Faced with the choice, Molino had little option but to wield the sword. The butchered remnants of Quesada joined Mendoza on the stakes. The devices of the inquisition were brought to the interrogation of others. Andrés de San Martín, astronomer to the expedition, was put to the strappado, hung by a rope from his bound hands, stretched by weights on his feet. Somehow he survived. Another man, Hernándo Morales, whose limbs were subsequently described as 'disjointed', did not. Forty more mutineers were condemned to death but their sentences were commuted. The loss of so many men would hamper the expedition's ability to sail the ships, would certainly have cast a deepening pall on the morale of the surviving crew and risked widening a Portuguese–Spanish schism. Each man was brought to Magellan, given a blow on the head, and spent the time in port chained and carrying out hard labour. Among them was Juan Sebastián Elcano. On 27 April, the cabin boy convicted of sodomy with Antonio de Salomón was thrown overboard.

There would be subsequent criticism that Magellan, the man who had said he would do what he liked at sea, had exceeded his authority: 'for these were certain servants of the king, upon whom no one but Caesar [Charles] and his Council could lawfully pronounce a sentence of death'.[20] Perhaps in the light of that, he was careful with Juan de Cartagena, certainly the king's man. His fate was to be different, or more exquisite. He was to be marooned on an island in the bay, along with a priest, Pedro Sánchez de Reina, held complicit in the mutiny. The ever loyal Pigafetta hardly mentions the ghastly contest in St Julian's Bay, preferring to concentrate on the flora and fauna.

The fleet was destined to sit it out at St Julian for a whole winter, repairing the ships and living on constrained supplies, but for Magellan the hunt for the strait still went on. At the end of April, the small *Santiago*, captained by Juan Serrano, was despatched south to investigate. On 3 April it reached a broad river, which Serrano christened the Rio Santa Cruz, and found well stocked with fish and game. Shortly after, disaster struck the ship as it headed further south. Caught in a storm, it was wrecked. The crew survived but were now marooned on the shore in a flat winter wasteland 70 miles from the fleet. With a desperate effort, two men managed to raft across the 3-mile-wide Santa Cruz on planks salvaged from the wrecked vessel and dragged themselves across the frozen tundra through swirling blizzards. When they staggered into St Julian's Bay, eleven days later, the haggard, frozen and starving figures who greeted the fleet were said to be unrecognisable. Magellan sent out an overland rescue party to the shipwrecked crew, who said they had had nothing to eat for thirty-five days.

On 24 August, the whole fleet said goodbye to the torments of St Julian's Bay, taking with them two captive Patagonians as 'ethnographic specimens'. They had been there five months. Now they were to move to the Rio Santa Cruz. Shortly before, the sentence was carried out on Cartagena and the priest. They were given a small quantity of biscuits and two swords and landed on the island. From here they were left to watch the ships dwindle into the distance and vanish, to die in their own time. Those on the departing vessels who could bring themselves to a backward glance would have shuddered. It was an example and a warning, designed to haunt the surviving crew and to impress on them their captain's authority: 'no one from that time dared to disparage the power of the commander'.[21]

On 21 November, the pilot, Francisco Albo, whose log book consists of little more than terse sailing data – course directions and observations of the sun – becomes almost voluble: 'we saw an opening like a bay and it has an entrance, on the right hand a very long spit of sand ... and from the spit of sand to the other side, there may be a matter of five leagues, and within this bay we found a strait.'[22] The ever loyal Pigafetta later claimed that, in the face of doubters and after so many false hopes, Magellan knew this was the strait: 'had it not been for the captain-general, we would not have found that Strait, for we all thought and said that it was closed on all sides'.[23] It was St Ursula's Day, in honour of which the sandy headland would be christened the Cape of the Eleven Thousand Virgins. The ships entered the bay. The water was extraordinarily deep, 'impossible to find a bottom [for anchoring]', Pigafetta recorded.[24] How deep they could not know. The strait was a chasm forged by geological forces, at its shallowest 90 feet deep, in places dropping sheer to 3,500 feet.

Turning into the bay, Magellan sent two ships forward, the *Concepción* and *San Antonio*, to reconnoitre. As they set out, the bay was lashed by a sudden storm so that the *Victoria* and *Trinidad* were forced out to sea. Hit by the ferocity of the weather, it appeared that the scouting ships were sailing into a dead end. In the outer bay there was an anxious wait. Three days passed. The only signs of the reconnoitring party were ominous smoke signals. 'We thought that they had been wrecked,' Pigafetta recalled. 'And so, while in suspense, we saw the two ships with sails full and banners flying to the wind, coming toward us. When they neared in this manner, they suddenly discharged a number of mortars, and burst into cheers.'[25] In the storm they had miraculously found a narrow opening that passed into a second bay, then through a second set of narrows into a broad reach. It was difficult going, battling against wind and current, with tidal surges of 24 feet, but initial indications were good; the impossibility of sounding the bottom was suggestive that this might not be a closed bay, even if it made anchoring tricky.

Magellan's ships had stumbled into a place that seemed like the end of the world. They were probing a shattered labyrinth of tidal estuaries, pinched narrows, broad bays, a complex set of channels that offered multiple choices. Each had to be explored. Above them to their right, jagged snow-capped peaks, glaciers of a piercing blue glittering in the light, tumbling waterfalls. It was a landscape to make humans feel terribly alone, a desolate crevice in the earth's surface.

Despite high summer and only a few hours of night, it was cold; their progress was slowed by the unrelenting wind, their visibility blurred by fog. Cautiously they progressed through the set of narrows then broad reaches, vast bays that had to be scouted one after another, to see if each was a dead end or the promise of an exit.

In the second bay, they sighted signs of habitation on the coast to the south. An armed longboat went to reconnoitre; on the shore was the decaying carcass of a whale. The 'village' turned out to be a native graveyard. They saw no signs of people, except distant fires, which were probably caused by lightning strikes rather than human activity. They called this land Tierra del Fuego.

As they sailed on, they plotted their course and charted everything they saw, creating a route map for ships that might come after, and giving names to features as they went: Victoria Bay, Useless Bay, St Ann's Point. They eliminated the dead ends by a process of patient reconnoitring. The going was continuously tough: the tide rips, the wind, the impossibility of sounding a bottomless sea, the difficulty of tethering the ships, the promising waterways that turned out to be enclosed baffles, the cold and the short rations, the echoing silence of the glacial moraines. The landscape seemed to have been scraped clean of any comforting human presence; for company there were only seals, whales and penguins.

If the crew were on edge, so was Magellan, doubtless concerned not only for the need to discover a way through the strait, but also fearful of further dissent. He was given to mood swings, according to one witness, Ginés de Mafra: 'Now he was happy, now sad.'[26] His authority, his future, his dreams depended on there being a way through the maze. However, the efficiency of the scouting process, investigating and discarding possible divergent openings, paid off. Around 1 November the *Trinidad* and the *Victoria* made a right angle turn round a point they called Cape Froward and nosed their way into a narrow channel. The sequence of events is jumbled in the surviving accounts, but at about this time they seem to have realised from the tides and currents and the consistent salinity of the water that this was in all likelihood a waterway into another sea.

Sometime about now Magellan called on his captains and chief officers, nominally to ask their opinion about whether they should proceed. If this was presented as an open exchange of views, that was not its purpose. After the Saint Julian episode, dissenters were edgy about giving an opinion.

One man, however, did speak up. Estêvão Gomes, a fellow Portuguese, pilot of the *San Antonio*, voiced his opposition to proceeding. Gomes was a realist; he had been instrumental as pilot of the *San Antonio* in scouting the strait and he realised how testing it was. The crew, according to one man, the pilot Vasco Gallego, were 'disgusted with that long and doubtful navigation',[27] the way ahead was uncertain, the ships battered, supplies limited, the voyage already too punishing. The unknown sea ahead he called 'a great gulf'. They had discovered the strait. It would be wiser to head for home with this achievement and return with a better-prepared expedition. Magellan's reply brooked no dissent: 'Even if we have to eat the cowhides that wrap the masts, we had to go [on] and discover what was promised to the Emperor.'[28] If Gomes's argument was rational, Magellan's reply was couched in the heroic language of the role he had cast for himself. Free speech was not what he had in mind. He ordered the death penalty for any who questioned the wisdom of the route or the limited stores. His words about the cowhides would return to haunt them all.

Shortly afterwards, the *San Antonio* vanished. Sent out on another scouting mission, it failed to return. There were strenuous efforts to find it, or spy a wreck, searching right back to the entrance of the strait. Messages, indicated by crosses, were left on two prominent hills. No trace was found. Gomes had engineered a mutiny, overpowered the nominal captain Mesquita in a knife fight, and followed his own counsel. They carried away with them one of the two Patagonians, who died as they crossed the Atlantic. They made it back to Seville where they would face intense questioning and prison.

The loss of the *San Antonio* was serious. It was the largest ship and carried a substantial proportion of their supplies. Proceeding up the new channel, the three surviving vessels – the *Victoria*, *Trinidad* and *Concepción* – dropped anchor at a point they called the River of Sardines. The strait was narrower here, a canyon no more than 2 miles wide in places that hemmed them in. It was potentially dangerous. In the event of a squall there was nowhere to hide, but the vegetation was verdant and the water teemed with fish. The forbidding landscape of the early stages of the transit had given way to lush forest. The ever-optimistic Pigafetta celebrated this new stretch of water: 'one finds the safest of ports every half league in it, water, the finest of wood, fish, sardines and *missiglioni* [mussels], while celery, a sweet herb, grows around the springs. We ate of it for many days as we had nothing else. I believe that there is not a more beautiful or better Strait in the world than this one.'[29] Little did they realise the value of this source of vitamin C.

Four days were spent at the River of Sardines. 'During that period, we sent a well-equipped boat to explore the cape of the other sea.' The men returned within three days, and reported that they had seen the cape and the open sea. 'The captain-general wept for joy and called that cape, Cape Dezeado [the Desired Cape],' according to Pigafetta.[30] It appeared that the way was clear.

Yet Magellan remained anxious – about the morale of the men after the battering in the strait, about supplies, about the loss of the *San Antonio*, about the potential rift between Spanish and Portuguese, about the possibility of a second mutiny. He was isolated, reliant only on himself and taking big risks. Ginés de Mafra had noted the manic-depressive streak in the captain-general earlier, when he was seeking the opening of a strait down the South American coast. While his moods swung violently his determination was unlimited. He was 'preoccupied, at times full of joy, at times downcast. When it seemed to him that *this* was the strait he had promised, he was so joyful that he expressed great delight, then plunged into despondency if for some reason it appeared it wasn't.' Above all, it was the will power: 'In the end he was determined to pursue this undertaking to the bitter end.'[31] It was this that scared the men. Was he a gambler leading them to destruction at the ends of the earth or was he inspired? Could he be trusted? Should he be followed? Alone, on the forlorn tip of South America, there were plentiful reasons to feel very afraid.

The realisation that there was an exit into the South Sea was a crucial breakpoint. Now the question was: should they continue or turn back? Magellan knew which he wanted and was evidently determined to obtain his officers' support, but sensed tacit opposition: 'that to all of you my determination to go on is a serious matter, because the window of opportunity for making this voyage is short'.[32] For a second time he canvassed their opinion, this time by letter, avoiding the unpleasantness of a face-to-face meeting. It was a complex piece of manipulation, designed to command a consensus and provide documentary evidence to cover his back if and when return to Seville led to official enquiries.

Rather than overt threats, Magellan tried a new tack, beginning with a breath-taking lie disguised as reasonableness. 'Because I am a man who never despised the advice and opinions of anyone, rather all my decisions are taken jointly and communicated to everyone, without anyone being offended ... I ask you on behalf of His Majesty and myself ... individually to give me your opinions in writing, the reasons for going on or turning back, without respect for anything that prevents you from telling the truth.'

He went on with a disingenuous attempt to quell their reservations about speaking up by directly addressing the St Julian incident: 'It is because of what happened in the port of St Julian concerning the death of Luiz de Mendoza and Gaspar de Quesada, and the marooning of Juan de Cartagena and the priest Pedro Sánchez de Reina, the rest of you are frightened to speak out and give advice that would be of service to His Majesty and the wellbeing of the fleet.'[33] Far from being a reassurance it was intended as a reminder, a threat and a taunt. The memory of the gibbet at St Julian, the last receding backward glance at the castaways doomed to a slow death – these afterimages were burnt in their minds.

Andrés de San Martín, the chief navigator, was one of those faced with the unwelcome essay writing task. Given that he had been hung up by his arms at St Julian, his reply, on 22 November, was understandably guarded but covertly echoed the queasiness of Gomes the mutineer. He chose his words with care. 'It seems that, for now, Your Lordship should go on, while we have high summer in our hands; and depending on what we find or discover by mid-January 1522, Your Lordship may then have reason to turn back to Spain, because from then on the days will shorten and the weather worsen.' Reading between the lines he was against sailing on but couldn't spell it out: the weather was likely to prove stormy and 'the crew are weak and exhausted and the supplies insufficient to go by the aforementioned route to Maluco, and from there make it back to Spain'. Finally, the let-out from a definitive negative: 'Your Lordship shall do as seems best, and God leads him.'[34]

Having cowed his captains into obedience and gathered valuable written evidence of their support, His Lordship did as He saw fit. The next day, 23 November, the *Victoria*, the *Trinidad* and the *Concepción* began to work their way up the enclosed narrows that led to the ocean. The Strait of Patagonia, as they named it at the time, had tested them to the limit. It had taken thirty-six days to navigate 350 miles. For Magellan it represented a triumph of the will; yet it was already evident from the sheer toil of the voyage that this could never comprise a viable regular sailing route.

'Wednesday, November 28, 1520, we debouched from the strait, engulfing ourselves in the Pacific Sea.'[35] 'Engulfing' might have been a corrected afterthought to Pigafetta's experience, as was 'Pacific'. The small ships felt the hit as the tidal flow of the strait smacked the incoming sea. A carefully choreographed ceremony took place on the ships; flags were flown; the Te Deum sung; celebratory cannon fired. 'Everyone thought himself fortunate to be where none had been before,'[36] recalled Ginés de Mafra. 'We went with great joy.' Magellan wept. Mafra, looking back, saw the strait vanish in the fog, 'leaving it, three leagues out to sea, its entrance could no longer be seen'.[37] As if its jaws had released them, then snapped shut.

Magellan had conceived a small world and a small sea. Like Columbus and optimistic cartographers, he believed it now to be a short hop to the Moluccas. It wasn't. The Pacific Ocean's 60 million square miles comprise the largest body of water on earth. In numbers it is staggering. It occupies almost one hemisphere, covers 30 per cent of the earth's surface, is larger than all the planet's landmasses

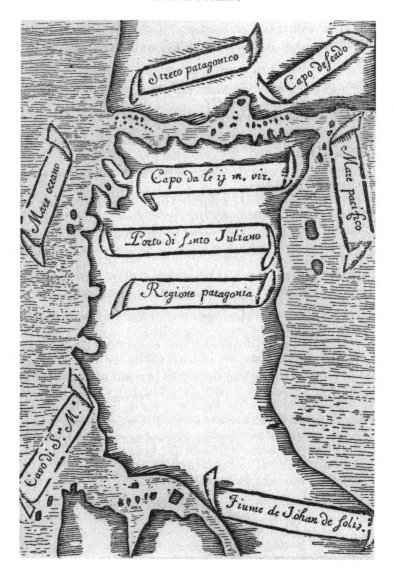

10. *Pigafetta's sketch, orientated to the south, is the first depiction of the Strait of Magellan – here the Strait of Patagonia. He has picked out the River Plate (the River of Juan Solís), the port of St Julian, the Cape of the Eleven Thousand Virgins and the Desired Cape. He is already referring to the new sea as the Pacific Ocean.*

combined. Its submarine chasms plunge down 7 miles and would leave Mount Everest submerged. The distance from the Strait of Magellan to the Moluccas is 9,500 miles. None of this was known to the sailors jubilantly setting forth.

Four

To the Spice Islands
1520-1

Initially the sea was heavy. The current drove them north, running parallel to the continental mass of the Americas. On 17 December, they turned north-west out into the ocean wastes. The following day all sight of land was gone. They would not see it again for three months. At this point they were picked up by the steady trade winds that would carry them serenely forward. For seamen used to all the sudden manoeuvres of Atlantic sailing it was an eerie experience: 'for days on end the mariners had neither to touch nor trim the sails, as if that vast ocean on which they sailed was a canal or a gentle river'.[1] They were travelling so fast it was hard to compute distance. Pigafetta, the landlubber, guessed daily runs of 50, 60 or 70 leagues. The size of the ocean, 'more vast than mind of man can conceive',[2] amazed and confounded. 'We travelled about four thousand leagues during those three months and twenty days through an open stretch in that Pacific Sea. In truth it was very pacific, for during that time we did not suffer any storm.'[3] There was little for the sailors to do. Pigafetta spent his days fishing, stargazing – 'we saw a cross with five extremely bright stars straight toward the west'[4] – and expanding his vocabulary list of the language of the one surviving Patagonian.

It may have been pacific, but it was also dangerous. The eerie serenity of the voyage belied its slow-burning menace. As the days and weeks passed without incident or accident the crew weakened. It became a descent into hell, graphically chronicled by Pigafetta. 'We were three months and twenty days without getting any kind of fresh food. We ate biscuit, which was no longer biscuit, but powder of biscuits swarming with worms, for they had eaten the good. It stank strongly of the urine of rats. We drank yellow water that had been putrid for many days.' They had to hold their noses as they did so. And Magellan's defiant willingness to eat the cowhides of the mast came horribly true:

> We also ate some ox hides that covered the top of the mainyard to prevent the yard from chafing the shrouds, and which had become exceedingly hard because of the sun, rain, and wind. We left them in the sea for four or five days, and then placed them for a few moments on top of the embers, and so ate them; and often we ate sawdust from boards. Rats were sold for one-half ducat apiece, and even then we could not get them. But above all the other misfortunes the following was the worst. The gums of both the lower and upper teeth of some of our men swelled, so that they could not eat under any circumstances and therefore died. Nineteen men died from that sickness, and the giant together with an Indian from the country of Verzin [Brazil]. Twenty-five or thirty men fell sick [during that time], in the arms, legs, or in another place, so that but few remained well. However, I, by the grace of God, suffered no sickness.[5]

It was scurvy that was killing the men. Without vitamin C, one by one the men weakened and died of hunger. And it wasn't God who saved Pigafetta. It was the preserves that Magellan had been packing at his house in Seville, which must have seemed a lifetime back. The ship carried fifty pots of quince jelly, a delicacy exclusively for consumption by the officers. It was probably spoonfuls of this that saved the ship from drifting lifelessly on a sea of death. For Pigafetta it was to be a staggering experience. 'Had not God and his blessed mother given us so good weather we would all have died of hunger in that exceeding vast sea. Of a verity I believe no such voyage will ever be made [again].'[6]

Their first sight of land was a bitter disappointment: a desert atoll, with no anchorages, 'surrounded by reefs that seemed to have been armed by nature to defend itself from the sea'.[7] They named it the Unfortunate Isle, then a second similar atoll, the Island of Sharks. Sometime shortly after, they crossed the equatorial line. Magellan was well aware that the equator ran directly through the Moluccas. It would have been logical at this point to steer due west and run along the line to his destination. He did not. The ships maintained a north-west course that would take them to a destination the Spanish called the Islands of the West – which would become *Las Filipinas*, the Philippines. Had this been his intention all along, when he had written into his contract that he could keep two islands for himself if he discovered more than six?

On 6 March, a shout from the topsail – 'Land! Land!'[8] The sailor aloft had at last spied two islands that looked more promising: green hills, coconut palms, thatched huts – signs of habitation. The crew were shattered but 'with these unexpected words everyone was so overjoyed that those who exhibited few signs of delight were deemed to be mad'.[9] Here was the possibility of food, a chance to reprovision. They came to anchor in the bay of Guam, one of the islands in the Mariana chain. The islanders sailed out to them but the greeting they received was dumbfounding. No sooner had the ships anchored than they swarmed on board and started to steal whatever came to hand. Others cut the rope that attached Magellan's personal skiff and carried it away. The astonished sailors were almost too weak to prevent the pilfering. Things were getting out of hand. Fighting broke out. The incomers were thrown off the ship and artillery was deployed to kill some of the marauders.

Magellan was furious. The following day he led a punitive raiding party ashore, burned the nearest village, killed a number of the inhabitants, seized food supplies and regained the lost boat. The reaction of the wounded and dying was both extraordinary and pitiful:

When we wounded any of those people with our crossbow-shafts, which passed completely through their loins from one side to the other, they, looking at it, pulled on the shaft now on this and now on that side, and then drew it out, with great astonishment, and so died. Others who were wounded in the breast did the same, which moved us to great compassion.[10]

Pigafetta, ever the ethnologist, never lost an opportunity to describe these people; their appearance ('tall as us and well-built'),[11] their clothing and their weapons – just spears tipped with fishbones. He concluded that these people thought, 'according to the signs which they made, that there were no other people in the world but themselves'. Weirdly, between outbreaks of fighting, the local people tried to trade with them. Something was being lost in translation between the Europeans and the Chamorro people.

What particularly astonished Pigafetta were their outrigger canoes – so fast and dextrous that 'it was a marvel'. It was their first sighting of the native craft of the western Pacific and the Malay Archipelago, the *proa*:

Those boats resemble *fucelere* [Venetian oared boats], but are narrower, and some are black, [some] white, and others red. At the side opposite the sail, they have a large piece of wood pointed at the top, with poles laid across it and resting on the water, in order that the boats may sail more safely. The sail is made from palm leaves sewn together and is shaped like a lateen sail. For rudders they use a certain blade resembling a hearth shovel which have a piece of wood at the end. They can change stern and bow

at will [literally: they make the stern, bow, and the bow, stern],
and those boats resemble the dolphins which leap in the water
from wave to wave.[12]

Swarms of these craft pursued them as they left, the women crying
and tearing their hair out for their dead.

There was one horrible footnote to this landfall: 'some of our sick
men begged us if we should kill any man or woman to bring the
entrails to them, as they would recover immediately'.[13] More effective
than cannibalism were the fresh fruit and vegetables they had acquired.
Magellan initially called these the Islands of the Lateen Sails and, as
they left, Las Islas de los Ladrones – the Islands of Thieves. For the
one Englishman on the voyage the fresh provisions came too late.
The master gunner, Andrew of Bristol, died on the day they left, 9
March. They sailed on. Magellan had just three weeks to live.

*11. A characteristic proa, the boats of the Australasian peoples. Proas were of
variable styles and sizes. They were reversible, so that they could be sailed from
either end, and employed outriggers for stability. This one has its sail furled.
The proas of the Chamorro people were extremely fast.*

On 16 March, they spied land again: the green coast and mountainous profile of the island of Samar. It was their first sighting of the archipelago of the Islands of the West. Going by the church calendar, Magellan named it St Lazarus. They had, by accident or design, touched this sprawling maze of thousands of islands at its midpoint – a splatter of fragments wedged between the two largest landmasses to north and south: Luzon and Mindanao. They coasted past Samar's reefs and landed briefly on a small island. When they dropped anchor again the next day at the island of Homonhon it was as if they had entered a new world. After the bleak terror of the strait, the uninhabited atolls and the Islands of Thieves, it seemed a place to relax. A shelter was erected for the sick; they killed a pig they had taken from Guam; there was fresh water. On 18 March a proa approached carrying nine men. Tensing for the encounter, Magellan ordered his men to remain stock still and silent. 'When those men reached the shore', according to Pigafetta, 'their chief went immediately to the captain-general, giving signs of joy because of our arrival.'[14] It was clear they had entered a different world. The visitors were friendly and not given to alarm. The Europeans gave their customary reassurance gifts – bells, caps, mirrors. The natives indicated by sign language that they would return with food.

In the days that followed, the intercourse between the two groups was amicable. The local people were evidently accustomed to visitors. 'These people became very familiar with us. They told us many things, their names and those of some of the islands that could be seen from that place ... we took great pleasure with them, for they were very pleasant and conversable.'[15] Morale was high. 'Our captain went ashore daily to visit the sick, and every morning gave them coconut water from his own hand, which comforted them greatly.' Pigafetta marvelled at the multiple uses of the islanders' staple food – the coconut. He had time to observe closely the appearance of the people – the tattooed chief with his gold earrings and armlets; the men with holes in their ears 'so large that they can pass their arms through them'; the way they oiled their bodies as a protection against the elements. Magellan gave a demonstration of cannon firing, 'whereat they exhibited great fear, and tried to jump out of the ship'.[16] These repeated displays were never entirely innocent. Magellan was flexing a muscle.

On Monday 25 March, in the run-up to Easter, as they prepared to sail on, Pigafetta nearly lost his life: 'I went to the side of the ship to fish, and putting my feet upon a yard ... they slipped, for it was rainy, and consequently I fell into the sea, so that no one saw me.' He was a non-swimmer. Only luck saved him. 'When I was all but under, my left hand happened to catch hold of the clew-garnet of the main-sail ... I held on tightly, and began to cry out so lustily that I was rescued by a small boat ... That same day we shaped our course southwest between four small islands.'[17]

As they moved further into the heart of the Philippine archipelago, encounters became more fruitful. On the 28th they met a boat whose occupants Magellan's servant, Enrique, could converse with in Malay. It was a touchstone moment. For Magellan, who had sailed east into the Malay-speaking world as far as Sumatra, it was evidence of the linkage of worlds, and it spoke of the breadth of contacts that the people of the Philippines had. The language link widened the possibilities for contact. After an initial offer of gifts, floated on a plank across the water to the hesitant locals, they paddled away to inform their king. 'About two hours later we saw two *balanghai* [native sailing boats] coming. They are large boats and are so called [by those people]. They were full of men, and their king was in the larger of them, being seated under an awning of mats.'[18] Via Enrique's interpretation, friendly contact was established. They all came aboard apart from the king, Rajah Kolambu, who stayed on his boat. On departure he offered Magellan a bar of gold as a present; strangely it was refused. He had calculated that not showing overt interest in precious metals would drive down its subsequent price when it came to bargaining.

The next day was Good Friday. For Magellan the religious festival seems to have been supercharged with significance. This time the king did come on board and presents were exchanged. Magellan linked into local alliances by declaring he wished to establish blood brotherhood with Kolambu, ruler of the island of Limasawa.

As well as showing off the rich merchandise the ship carried, Magellan demonstrated European weaponry, first firing 'all the artillery, whereat the natives were greatly frightened. Then the Captain-General had a man armed as a soldier, and placed him in the midst of three armed men with swords and daggers, who struck him on all parts of the body. Thereby was the king rendered almost speechless.' Magellan, warming to his theme, declared that one of his armed men was worth a hundred of the king's men. 'He showed the king cuirasses, swords and bucklers, and had a review made for him.'[19]

If the king was overawed by what he saw, Magellan's calculations of military superiority imbued him with a dangerous sense of invulnerability. As the relationship developed, Pigafetta and another man went ashore, where they feasted with the king and stayed the night. Pigafetta's scrupulous eye for detail preserved for posterity the rituals, the houses, the king's appearance:

He was very grandly decked out and the finest looking man that we saw among those people. His hair was exceedingly black, and hung to his shoulders. He had a covering of silk on his head, and wore two large golden earrings ... he wore a cotton cloth all embroidered with silk, which covered him from the waist to the knees. At his side hung a dagger, the haft of which was somewhat long and all of gold, and its scabbard of carved wood. He had three spots of gold on every tooth, and his teeth appeared as if bound with gold. He was perfumed with storax and benzoin. He was tawny and painted [tattooed] all over.[20]

31 March 1522, Easter Day. Exactly a year since the terrors of St Julian and a world away. An atmosphere of heightened emotion.

Pigafetta attributed his recent escape from death to the intercession of the Virgin. On Limasawa, the onrush of good fortune – the acceleration of religious feeling, the ease with which the native people could be overawed, the emergence into a tropical paradise after the torment of the strait – all this worked on the spirits of the crew, and it seemed to suggest to Magellan that anything was possible. His gambles had paid off. He might have brushed from his mind the possibility that the *San Antonio* could well be en route back to Spain with its own version of the death of Juan de Cartagena, and that there might be a price to pay.

On the Holy Day he seems to have been seized with religious fervour. Pigafetta recorded how:

> When the hour for mass arrived, we landed with about fifty men, without our body armour, but carrying our other arms, and dressed in our best clothes. Before we reached the shore with our boats, six pieces were discharged as a sign of peace ... We landed; the two kings embraced the captain-general, and placed him between them. We went in marching order to the place consecrated, which was not far from the shore. Before commencement of mass, the captain sprinkled the entire bodies of the two kings with musk water.[21]

The kings participated, copying the rituals of the service. Mass was followed by a fencing display, then the parading of a cross. Later the cross was erected on the top of a nearby mountain. While this was explained as a spiritual protection it was also a covert symbol of possession. Magellan had further schemes in mind. He asked the king 'whether he had any enemies, so that he might go with his ships to destroy them and to render them obedient to him'.[22] The king made an evasive answer to the effect that it wasn't convenient just now. Food supplies were somewhat limited on the island; when asking where they might be found, the nearby island of Cebu was suggested. There was a further two-day prevarication over providing pilots, suggestive of some hesitation. When they did set out, the king came with them in his own boat.

At noon on 7 April, they reached the port of Cebu, again rattling a local populace with blasts of gunfire. The king, Humabon, welcomed them cordially but pointed out that it was customary to pay tribute in the port. Magellan was beyond conciliatory gestures. His interpreter relayed an intransigent reply: 'he did not pay tribute to any signior in the world, and that if the king wished peace he would have peace, but if instead, war'.[23] It took a visiting merchant from Siam, who had experience of the Portuguese, to take the king aside and point out that these men were dangerous: 'If they are treated well, they will give good treatment, but if they are treated evil, evil and worse treatment, as they have done to Calicut and Malacca.'[24] Humabon provided the visitors with food, thought about it for a day and waived the tribute.

There followed elaborate rituals of fraternisation: gift giving, feasting, the blood brother ritual, Spanish displays of mock combat. The aim was to both impress and intimidate. There were warnings and enticements: that 'our arms were soft toward our friends and harsh toward our enemies; and as handkerchiefs wipe off the sweat so did our arms overthrow and destroy all our adversaries'.[25] Magellan was upping the stakes: claiming the country for Spain, seeking controllable allies. This was followed by Humabon himself offering tribute to the most powerful king in the world. Pigafetta, meanwhile, was recording detailed descriptions of the islanders' lifestyle, their beliefs and their startling sexual practices. The sailors (and Pigafetta himself) took full advantage of the delights offered by the local women.

By now Magellan seemed to have been seized by religious fervour and a sense of omnipotence beyond the bounds of caution. He personally preached the power of the Christian faith to Humabon and led him towards baptism. The day fixed for this was 14 April.

Magellan staged an elaborate spectacle of set-piece theatre. The ceremony was accompanied by the firing of artillery and the construction of a ceremonial platform hung with banners, on which the king and the captain-general sat on chairs of red velvet; Magellan orchestrated the baptism clad in white. According to Pigafetta hundreds were baptised on the spot. 'Before that week had gone, all the persons of the island, and some from the other islands, were baptised.'[26] The king and his wife were given Christian names – Charles and Joanna – and to the latter was given a wooden image of the infant Christ; more cannon were fired; tears were shed by the grateful queen. Then the iron fist: 'We burned one hamlet which was located in a neighbouring island, because it refused to obey the king or us. We set up the cross there for the people there were heathen.'[27]

Beneath the unctuous piety of the Christian accounts, what the Cebu king and his subjects understood is impossible to know. They failed to destroy their wooden idols and continued to sacrifice to them. In an astonishing extension of Magellan's risk-taking style, he offered to cure a grievously sick man. Magellan baptised him and he recovered. Whatever took place astonished the people. According to Pigafetta, 'the people themselves cried out "Castile! Castile!" and destroyed those shrines'.[28]

Magellan was cruising on a wave of self-belief. In the name of Humabon, he was looking to consolidate personal suzerainty over the neighbouring islands. The intention of establishing his own personal kingdom, perhaps signalled by the strange request in his contract with King Charles to retain islands for himself, now seems manifest. He was oceans away from the royal orders and 'once at sea he would do whatever he liked'. On the small neighbouring island of Mactan, however, where authority was split between two kings, he met with resistance. On 26 April one king, Sula, sent his son with tributary gifts; the other, Lapulapu, could not understand why he should submit to Humabon, and refused. When Sula asked him for a boatload of men to sort Lapulapu out, Magellan rose to the bait and decided to crush this resistance himself.

That day he planned an attack. Humabon offered to provide military support but Magellan's bravado would not countenance it. He thanked Humabon for the offer but suggested he should watch and be instructed, 'to see how the lions of Spain fought'.[29] Wiser heads advised him not to do this. 'He was more courageous than wise,' Ginés de Mafra reflected years after the event. 'A man who carried such weighty business had no need to test his strength . . . and victory would yield little fruit, rather the fleet, which was more important would be set at risk.'[30] 'We begged him repeatedly not to go,' even ever-faithful Pigafetta recalled.[31] Juan Serrano was another who argued against a needless battle. For the first time voices directly challenged his judgement 'and from this he lost a lot of authority'.[32] Magellan would go without local help. Self-confidence was toppling into dangerous risk-taking. He chose to believe that the overawing power of gunpowder and plate armour would indeed be worth a hundred warriors.

Pigafetta described how the attack unfolded. 'At midnight, sixty of us set out armed with corselets and helmets.'[33] They were accompanied by Humabon and his men in twenty or thirty boats. They reached the harbour of Mactan, 5 miles away, three hours before dawn. Magellan directly advertised his intent by sending a message to Lapulapu: submit to Humabon and pay tribute 'otherwise they should wait to see how lances wounded. They replied that if we had lances they had lances of bamboo and stakes hardened with fire.'[34] Lapulapu asked him not to attack until dawn, when he would have more men. Magellan ignored the overt invitation to attack in the dark and fall into carefully dug pit holes.

Dawn broke. The tide was out and the water low. It was impossible to bring the boats close to the shore because of reefs. They were forced to stand off. Forty-nine men jumped into the water and started to wade thigh-deep towards the shore – a distance of half a mile. Another eleven waited offshore, together with Humabon's ships; further out to sea the *Trinidad*, *Concepción* and *Victoria*. Every aspect of this venture was ill conceived. They had sacrificed any element of surprise. The boats were too far out to give any support and the ships further back would be unable to provide effective cannon fire. The timing of the attack, at low water, meant an exhausting beach landing in heavy armour. They had consigned their allies to the role of passive spectators. Magellan was relying on sheer bravado.

Pigafetta, ever loyal, was one of the band who struggled through the surf in the tropical dawn 'more than two crossbow flights' – about a mile. They were massively outnumbered. Awaiting them were Lapulapu's men, 'more than fifteen hundred'. Each of Magellan's men now had to be worth the hundred of their opponents. 'When they saw us, they charged down upon us with exceeding loud cries, two divisions on our flanks and the other on our front.' Magellan correspondingly formed his small band into two divisions, 'and thus we began to fight'.[35] For half an hour the musketeers and the crossbow men fired, to little effect. From a distance the shots hardly penetrated the islanders' wooden shields. Magellan shouted at the men to stop firing, but in the confusion his orders went unheeded. Reloading took time. 'The natives would never stand still, but leaped hither and thither, covering themselves with their shields.' Meanwhile the Spaniards were bombarded with arrows, bamboo spears, pointed stakes, mud and stones. 'We could scarcely defend ourselves.' Magellan decided to fire some of the village huts to terrify and distract. But the only effect was to rouse the defenders to greater fury. Two of the fire party were cut off and killed. The situation was deteriorating. Magellan was hit in the leg by an arrow.

Now there was nothing for it but to contrive an orderly retreat. But according to Pigafetta, some took flight, leaving just a handful with the captain. 'The natives shot only at our legs, for the latter were bare; and so many were the spears and stones that they hurled at us, that we could offer no resistance. The mortars in the boats could not aid us as they were too far away.'[36] They continued to fall back, a crossbow shot from the shore, up to their knees in water, and being relentlessly pursued by their furious opponents, who, 'picking up the same spear four or six times, hurled at us again and again'. They identified Magellan and targeted him, knocking off his helmet twice.

In the shallow sea they made a last stand, holding out for an hour. Accounts of his death are various; Pigafetta pictures his hero in his final moments:

An Indian hurled a bamboo spear into the captain's face, but the latter immediately killed him with a lance ... then, trying to lay a hand on sword, he could draw it out [only] halfway, because he had been wounded in the arm by a bamboo spear. When the natives saw that, they all hurled themselves upon him. One of them wounded him on the leg with a large cutlass ... that caused the captain to fall face downward, when immediately they rushed upon him with iron and bamboo spears, and with their cutlasses, until they killed our mirror, our light, our comfort, and our true guide.[37]

Too late, some of the Cebuans came to their aid.

Pigafetta affords him a martyr's death, describing Magellan checking to see that all the others had made it to the boats before securing his own safety. 'Thereupon, beholding him dead, we wounded retreated as best we could to the boats, which were already pulling off ... had it not been for that unfortunate captain, not a single one of us would have been saved by the boats.'[38]

Requests to retrieve Magellan's body were snubbed by Lapulapu. They offered all the merchandise he wished: 'they would not give him for all the riches in the world, but that they intended to keep him as a memorial'.[39]

Back on the ships it was essential to choose a new commander quickly. It resulted in a joint command – the Portuguese Duarte Barbosa, Magellan's brother-in-law, and the Castilian Juan Serrano – privileged positions both men were to hold for just two days.

The disaster had other consequences. Humabon apparently wept at Magellan's death, but he also recalculated. The Spaniards were not invincible. After the battle on Mactan they could not provide protection against blowback from Lapulapu. The treaty with the intruders was dead. On 1 May he asked the leading men to a feast to receive some jewels he had promised to Magellan.

Some thirty went ashore, approximately a quarter of the whole crew. Pigafetta meanwhile continued to lead a charmed life: he had been wounded in the face by a poisoned arrow and stayed on board. He was startled when he saw two men returning to the ship. 'They told us that they saw the man who had been cured by a miracle take the priest to his house. Consequently, they had left that place, because they suspected some evil. Scarcely had they spoken those words when we heard loud cries and lamentations.'[40] A massacre was taking place. The ships weighed anchor and closed on the shore, firing their mortars into the houses. One man appeared on the beach. He was wounded and his hands were tied. It was Juan Serrano, desperately pleading for rescue; he called out that the others were all dead, except Enrique the interpreter. Serrano had been sent to bargain: his life for some goods. Accounts differ. For Pigafetta, Serrano was cold-bloodedly abandoned by his friend, João Carvalho, who sailed away with Serrano's curses ringing in his ears that God would ask for Carvalho's soul. Others tell a different story. The price for his life was two cannon. Carvalho had these delivered to the shore but had then been asked for more. Serrano understood their game and, with a belief they were hoping to capture the ships, shouted that they should go 'since it were better for him to die than that they all should perish'.[41] They sailed off with his dying shrieks in their ears. The cross that had been planted on a nearby peak was torn down.

The death toll had been heavy. The fleet had lost its new leaders, Barbosa and Serrano, the astrologer Andrés de San Martín, a priest and many more. Some may have been enslaved. One who seems not to have died was Enrique the translator. It was claimed that he was complicit in the massacre in revenge for maltreatment by Barbosa in the wake of Magellan's death. He vanishes from the scene. Magellan had been hungry for personal glory and perhaps a kingdom of his own to equal that of his friend Francisco Serrão. He had blundered into a complex world of tribal loyalties and power structures that he did not understand and had paid the price.

On 2 May 1521 the ships weighed anchor. The ineffective Carvalho was initially elected captain-general but quickly turned out to be a poor appointment. After 632 days at sea the ships were now battered, the total complement of men whittled down to 110. It was unfeasible to man three ships with so few. They decided to abandon the worm-eaten *Concepción*; everything of value was transferred to the *Trinidad* and *Victoria*, and they left the ship burning to the waterline. Gonzalo Gómez de Espinosa was now the captain of the *Trinidad*, and soon Juan Sebastián Elcano of the *Victoria*. They attempted to sail south towards their intended goal, the Moluccas. For a month they wandered aimlessly, zigzagging via the coast of Borneo, bumping into Mindanao, stopping at tiny islands; desperate for provisions but wary of encounters, given to acts of piracy and intimidation. Along the way they spent a month on the island of Palawan, a tropical paradise of turquoise lagoons and brilliant light; they were overawed by the sophistication of the ruler of Brunei. For Pigafetta this world was still exotic and worthy of description. They had little idea where they were and resorted to kidnapping local pilots in the hope of steering a course south. Eventually, with the aid of one of these, on 6 November 1521, they caught sight of a line of dominant volcanoes on the horizon.

Five

Circumnavigators
1521- 2

Pigafetta recorded his first glimpse. 'We discovered four lofty islands fourteen leagues towards the east. The pilot who still remained with us told us that those four islands were Maluco ... we thanked God and as an expression of our joy discharged all our artillery. It was no wonder that we were so glad, for we had passed twenty-seven months less two days in our search for Maluco.'[1] It was an emotional moment. They had reached the land of spices.

With some awareness of the Portuguese disinformation campaign typified by the Miller Atlas, Pigafetta commented that attention should not be given to the assertion of the Portuguese 'that the region could not be navigated because of the numerous shoals and the dark sky as they have imagined'. Instead, the ships eased their way into what must have seemed, on first impression, another tropical paradise: the brilliant light; the scent of the clove trees borne across the water; the turquoise of the lagoons and the brilliant green slopes of the volcanic islands; the chatter and cries of birds in the trees; the island people travelling to and fro in their now-familiar proas – and the plentiful supplies of food: 'Daily so many boatloads of goats, fowl, figs [bananas], coconuts and other kinds of food were brought

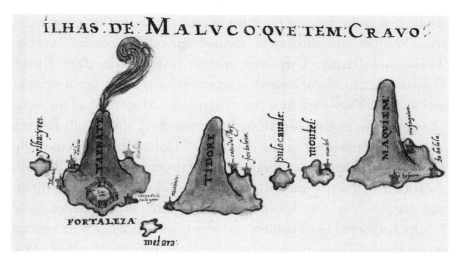

12. 'The Moluccan Islands that Produce Cloves' in an early Portuguese drawing. The most prominent is Ternate, with its plume of fire and substantial fort. Adjacent to it is Tidore, also indicating a fort and the position of the king's residence.

to the ship, that we were surprised.' Another exotic feature was the thermal geology: 'we supplied the ships with good water which issues forth hot [from the ground]'.[2]

On 8 November they docked at the port of Tidore to a further volley of gunfire. They had arrived at a fortuitous moment; there was no Portuguese fleet in the islands. They were welcomed by the king, who claimed he had predicted their coming in a dream, a standard convention, it seems, in the ritual of guest welcome. Pigafetta described him as 'well-built and has a regal presence . . . at that time he was clad in a shirt of the most delicate white stuff with the ends of the sleeves embroidered in gold, and in a cloth that reached from his waist to the ground. He was barefoot, and had a silk scarf wrapped about his head, and above it a garland of flowers. His name is Raia Sultan Manzor.'[3]

There followed an exchange of gifts and the eager desire of the king to ally himself with Spain against Portuguese-backed Ternate. For Almanzor, the Spanish arrivals offered protection in the inter-island feuds. It was the newcomers' introduction to yet another complex of tribal rivalries and allegiances, focused around the contest between Tidore and Ternate. They were anxious to meet Magellan's friend, Francisco Serrão, whose letters had set in motion their voyage of torment and wonder. They were nine months too late. Magellan had not been alone in misjudging tribal politics. Serrão was dead. Siding with Ternate, he had been poisoned in the feud with Tidore. Learning something from past experience, they became wary of invitations to feasts. Beneath the surface of this tropical idyll, there lay an undercurrent of superstition and menace – one in which poisonings were commonplace, dense jungles harboured head hunters and ghosts walked. They were warned by the king of Tidore not to go out after dark, 'because of certain of his men who anoint themselves and roam abroad by night. They appear to be headless, and when any of them meets any other man, he touches the latter's hand, and rubs a little ointment on him. The man falls sick very soon, and dies within three or four days.'[4]

However, in Tidore there was much mutual junketing and the exchange of gifts – so many from the Spanish side, apparently, that 'the king bade us desist. After that he declared to us that he had nothing else except his own life to send to the king his sovereign.'[5] There was one Portuguese merchant, Pedro de Lorosa, who had been in the islands for a decade and indicated that the Portuguese were intent on sending another fleet. He now gave his allegiance to Spain. As usual, Pigafetta set about collecting information on the islands' culture and natural history. He studied carefully the cultivation of the clove tree and the production of ginger and nutmeg.

As the amity with the king of Tidore grew, the two sides settled down to energetic trading. The *Victoria* and the *Trinidad* were able to obtain full cargoes of cloves in exchange for cloth, metal and glass objects, and whatever they had plundered from passing ships on their way from Cebu. By mid-December, they were ready to leave. On the morning of departure, it was discovered that the *Trinidad*, Magellan's battered flagship, had sprung a leak. There was nothing for it but to leave the ship to be patched up, and for the *Victoria* to head for home. At this point there was an invidious choice for those among the crew who had the option: sail on the also ageing *Victoria* and risk the ship foundering or being captured in Portuguese territory, or wait for the repair of the *Trinidad* and hope to be away before a Portuguese fleet arrived. On such decisions fates were decided. Many saw the *Victoria* as a death trap and refused point blank. Ginés de Mafra was among those who opted to stay with the *Trinidad*. The decision now was on the choice of route: west through Portuguese waters, or back across the vast extent of the Pacific to New Mexico? In the event the two ships chose different options. The *Victoria* would sail west through Portuguese waters. The vessel was heavily laden with all the spices it could carry, but, made wary by the leaking *Trinidad*, Juan Sebastián Elcano, as captain, thought it wise to reduce the weight of cargo. Among the other things they took with them as presents for the king of Spain, Pigafetta recorded the bodies of two birds of paradise which were 'extremely beautiful ... these birds are as large as thrushes, and have a small head and a long beak. Their legs are a palm in length and as thin as a reed, and they have no wings [sic], but instead long feathers of various colours, like large plumes. Their tail resembles that of the thrush.'[6]

On 1 December, the *Victoria* prepared to go. Departure was slightly delayed by those left behind writing letters home to be entrusted to the ship. From its deck, Pigafetta observed the moment of casting off.

> When that hour came, the ships bid one another farewell amid the discharge of the cannon, and it seemed as though they were bewailing their last departure. Our men [those who were to remain] accompanied us in their boats a short distance, and then with many tears and embraces we departed ... and then immediately laid our course toward the southwest. Juan Carvalho stayed there with fifty-three of our men, while we comprised forty-seven men and thirteen Indians.[7]

Back on Tidore it was estimated that patching up the *Trinidad* would take fifty days. It took a hundred, and even then they were hurrying. Fear of the Portuguese concentrated minds. The wind was now westerly and the decision was taken to attempt to sail the *Trinidad* back across the Pacific to New Spain (Mexico). On 6 April, the ship went on its way, commanded by Gonzalo Gómez de Espinosa, an experienced soldier but no seaman, and laden with 50 tons of cloves. They made it out just in time; a month later seven ships arrived, under the command of the new Portuguese governor-general of the Moluccas, António de Brito, armed with orders to expel the Spanish rivals and capture Magellan.

The last voyage of the *Trinidad* was a predictable disaster. Under command of the inexperienced Espinosa, they headed north-east in an attempt to catch winds to carry them across a Pacific whose extent they significantly underestimated. They sailed into ever higher latitudes, where they were hit by the cold and heavy storms. Scurvy again destroyed the crew. Three men deserted on the Mariana islands. Eventually the ship turned back. After seven months of wandering, they returned to the Moluccas.

As they approached the islands, the survivors were too weak to dock the ship. A message was sent to Brito, the Portuguese commander, begging for help. A boat-load of armed men went to capture the stricken ship, but once aboard, they recoiled at the stench. Shouting down into the hold there was no reply. The sources offered different accounts of the subsequent treatment of the crew, but the historian João de Barros gave a Portuguese version of the initial response: 'When they eventually boarded the ship, Duarte de Resende felt great pity for the men. Most of them were so lame that they could barely walk without support, they were so crippled. Thirty-seven men were already dead, the ship was infested with disease, and there were the issues of hunger and their other needs.' Just twenty men were still alive.[8]

Brito's treatment of the survivors was more vengeful. The *Trinidad* was nursed into harbour and stripped of her useful fittings. Charts, papers, astrolabes and maps were confiscated. When a storm hit the ship, it was smashed to pieces. Planking was recovered to go into construction of a fort on Ternate. Brito had already imprisoned four men left to run the spice depot; he executed the Portuguese renegade Lorosa and put the survivors of the *Trinidad* to forced labour. There was no more symbolic statement of occupancy and conquest than the timbers of Magellan's flagship embedded in Ternate's Portuguese fort.

Brito also wrote back to King Manuel about everything that had happened. He gave a concise account of the Magellan adventure based upon close interrogation of the Spanish crew, described his chastisement of the Rajah of Tidore for siding with Spain, and spec-ulated on the likely whereabouts of the *Victoria*:

> The crew of the other Castilian ship, the one that departed first, has resolved to navigate from Maluku straight to Timor with the pilots provided by the king of Tidore. From there, if they can, sail out into the open sea, touching the island of Madagascar, and then follow the course that Your Highness's ships take. In my opinion, Sire, if they get from Maluku to Castile this would be as extraordinary as was their coming from Castile to Maluku, for the ship is very old, and its supplies miserable. Moreover, the men hardly obey their commander – and I'm not even mentioning the various patrols that Your Highness has in the Indian Ocean ... If anyone meets this ship [the *Victoria*], may he deal with it as I've done with the one I've captured [the *Trinidad*]![9]

The possibility of the battered and undersupplied *Victoria* ever making it back to Europe did indeed seem unlikely.

Brito was correct about the voyage to Timor. The *Victoria* threaded its way through the Malay Archipelago, taking on what supplies it could, while Pigafetta continued with his ethnographic studies and gathered outlandish stories:

Our old pilot from Maluco told us that there was an island nearby called Arucheto, the men and women of which are not taller than one cubit, but who have ears as long as themselves. With one of them they make their bed and with the other they cover themselves. They go shaven close and quite naked, run swiftly and have shrill voices. They live in caves underground.[10]

Meanwhile, Elcano had out-thought Brito. He had no intention of taking the obvious route towards Madagascar across seas scanned by Portuguese ships. Leaving the Java Sea on 11 February, the *Victoria* turned south-west. His plan was extraordinarily ambitious: to swing round the ocean in a great southern arc, out of reach of the Portuguese, and clear the Cape of Good Hope without touching land.

The going was always tough: the battling headwinds, the growing cold, shortages of supplies, a suffering crew. 'We subsisted for five months on nothing but corn, rice and water, not going near to any land, for fear of the King of Portugal,' Elcano wrote later.[11] On 18 March they passed the isolated Amsterdam Island, so named later by the Dutch, then suffered tormenting and battering storms. At 35° south, the *Victoria* sprang its foremast; on 8 May they sighted Africa. 'We thought, according to the run we had made, that we had passed the Cape.'[12] In fact they had fallen short. 'Finally, by God's help, we doubled that cape . . . at a distance of five leagues.'[13]

By this time lives were hanging by a thread. They crossed the equatorial line on 7 July. Twenty-two men died of hunger after passing the Cape. They had been 148 days without resupply. It was imperative to find food if they were not all to perish. Now the only option was the risky one of putting in at the Cape Verde islands, Portuguese territory, where they might face arrest. In more ways than one, these islands were a place of destiny for the expedition. They were the point from which all calculations about the position of the indefinable Tordesillas Line were made – the Iberians' Greenwich meridian – the epicentre of all the troubles between the Portuguese and Spanish pioneers. They landed on the island of Santiago with a fabricated tale of being a Spanish ship from the Americas blown off course and managed to barter cloves for food, but their story unravelled. A number of men were detained ashore and the *Victoria* had to flee from Portuguese caravels.

Elcano recounted the final leg home: 'with my company I determined to die rather than fall into the hands of the Portuguese. It so fell to us, overstrained at the pumps, working at them by day and by night, and more exhausted than men have ever been before, that with the help of God and the Blessed Virgin Mary, we continued under sail, and after voyaging for three years, ran into the harbour of Sanlúcar.'[14]

Pigafetta added his own coda.

On Saturday 6 September, 1522, we entered the bay of Sanlúcar with only eighteen men and the majority of them sick, all that were left of the sixty men who left Maluco. Some died of hunger, some deserted at the island of Timor, and some were put to death for their crimes. From the time we left that bay [of Sanlúcar] until the present day [of our return] we had sailed fourteen thousand four hundred and sixty leagues, and furthermore had completed the circumnavigation of the world from east to west.[15]

Sanlúcar de Barrameda was their beginning and their end. Two hundred and sixty-five men had set out; eighteen came back. They still had to coax the leaking ship up the Guadalquivir to Seville, pumping all the way. It had been an extraordinary feat.

On 8 September, the *Victoria* cast anchor at Triana, the mole of Seville. They fired off all its guns. The next day a sight to amaze the city: a procession of haggard, dishevelled figures, more ghosts than human beings, carrying lit candles and walking barefoot to the shrine of the church of Santa María de la Victoria. They were fulfilling a vow they had made in a storm off the coast of Brazil. It was three years and a world ago that the whole crew had been in this church for the blessing of the flag. By chance and destiny, the pitiful survivors had returned on the church's feast day. To fulfil further vows they then processed to the city's monumental cathedral, the largest Christian building in the world, to give thanks at the shrine of Santa María de Antigua.

They had come full circle: 'We have given practical proof', Elcano wrote in a letter to the king on the day of arrival at Sanlúcar, 'that the earth is a sphere: having sailed round it, coming from the West, we have come back through the East.'[16] It also demonstrated that the world was larger than they knew. Given the immensity of the Pacific, it was bigger by thousands of miles than the ocean they had expected to traverse.

The lucky few who returned had witnessed extraordinary things. They had fallen on their knees at the crackle of St Elmo's fire; enjoyed carefree encounters with the Tupi people; survived shipwreck, terrible cold and the immensity of the Pacific Ocean. They had suffered hunger beyond hunger and watched their skin turn blotchy and their gums come away in their hands – harbingers of a death that they had somehow cheated, even as they lowered their comrades into the depths with a soft splash. They had shivered at the utter desolation of the strait. They had met human giants and marvelled at the wonders of the natural world: seen whales and sharks, penguins and sealions basking on the shores of great rivers, birds of paradise and tropical forests.

Above all, they had experienced the hitherto unimagined immensity of the planet's oceans in all their moods – the element that gave and took away: by turns benevolent and sullen, deadly in its placidness, fearful in its rages – an implacable being against which they had offered hundreds of prayers to the Christian god. It was the sea that had carried them and fed them and driven them to delirium. They could attest to the Basque proverb: 'The waters of the sea are vast, and their bottom cannot be seen.'[17]

There had been one more mind-bending wonder in store when they reached Cape Verde. From his meticulous record keeping, the pilot Francisco Albo was sure that they arrived on a Wednesday. When the men landed they were told it was Thursday. 'And so, I believe that we had made a mistake of a day'[18] – but by sailing west around the world they had gained a calendar day.

Elcano's feat was the wonder of the age. Printing presses thumped. Maps were drawn. There were enquiries and interrogations of the survivors of all that had happened. Four more men from the *Trinidad* trickled back to Spain years later, courtesy of Portuguese ships and prisons. Ginés de Mafra did not return until 1527 via Lisbon, only to find that his wife, assuming him dead, had remarried and squandered all his money. And then there was the spice haul from the *Victoria*, the almost-forgotten motive for the whole thing. Despite the cargo's value it barely covered the costs of the expedition.

By the end of September, Elcano was at the royal court in Valladolid, where he had audience with the king. He brought with him exotic proofs of the world's wonders: the bodies of the birds of paradise, samples of spices and 'a species of native bread made from the pulp of palm trees spiced with cloves, and kneaded into the form of a brick'.[19] Pigafetta came too, and presented the king with his account. Soon manuscript versions were circulating in the courts of Europe. On a popular level, the survivors of Elcano's return were themselves objects of marvel. Crowds turned out to look on the circumnavigators with awe when they returned to their home towns, like astronauts back from the moon. The following year, Elcano was granted the right to a coat of arms. It showed cinnamon sticks, nutmegs and cloves and a globe bearing the motto '*Primus circum-dedisti me*' – 'You were the first to circumnavigate me'. The planet had become a character in its own right. It got to speak. And it had been bound by a human chain.

Pigafetta believed that the voyage had been so terrible it would never be repeated. Just a month after Elcano's audience, Charles was

Primus   Circumdedisti me.

13. Elcano's coat of arms.

writing to his aunt, Margaret of Austria, with the news that 'my captains have confirmed that they have sailed all round the world. And in order to take advantage of this achievement, and in further-ance of the Christian faith, I propose to arrange for a second expedi-tion to be sent to the Moluccas.'[20]

Charles, blithely planning to despatch more human fodder across the oceans, had overlooked one detail: the Spanish had no means of getting home without trespassing on Portuguese territory. And if there were ambitions there were also consequences. Elcano's return held the makings of a major diplomatic row.

Six

Cannon Fire on the Pearl River
1514–24

While trouble was brewing back in Europe over 'ownership' of the Moluccas, the Portuguese had continued to push east. If Charles V had 'Further' emblazoned on his sails, King Manuel was encouraged to believe in a pre-eminent God-given mission to 'discover'. 'Among all Western princes God only wanted to choose Your Highness,'[1] wrote the mariner and adventurer Duarte Pacheco Pereira. The Portuguese advance had been so fast. Each new landfall suggested the next. Their worldview envisaged an unending map, forever scrolling up over further horizons. They were voracious in their information gathering and they had been interested in the Chinese from the outset. In 1508, even before his first ships reached Malacca, King Manuel had issued robust instructions to his commanders to learn about the people beyond: 'Item: You shall ask after the Chins, and from what part they come, and how far, and at what times they come to Malacca, or to the places at which they trade ... all other information concerning them, and ... if their country is a great one ... and what customs they observe, and towards what part their country extends.'[2]

Behind this lay the enduring influence of Marco Polo. The first Portuguese translation of his travels was not made until 1502, but

Polo's dazzling descriptions of the wealth and magnificence of the country he called Cathay resonated everywhere. China had been the objective of Columbus when he landed in the Caribbean and it remained the subject of intense curiosity. To what extent had *Il Milione* – the teller of a million tall tales – been inventing Cathay, a place that even he said was beyond belief? The city of Suzhou with its 6,000 stone bridges? The area of Beijing with its 'many beautiful cities, many beautiful castles of great trade and great crafts, beautiful fields, beautiful vineyards and civilized people'? Guangzhou (Canton), to which a hundred times more cargoes of pepper are brought than to Alexandria? A kingdom where people pay with paper money? 'It's impossible to relate the wealth in this kingdom. There was no kingdom in the whole world worth half as much as this one.'[3] Of course the Portuguese were interested. When they came to Malacca they met Chinese merchants in their trading junks, and they asked a lot of questions. Manuel's interest was not entirely innocent. Not only did he want to know 'if they are wealthy merchants' but also 'if they are weak men or warriors, and if they have arms of artillery, and what clothes they wear, and if they are men great in body'.[4] Trade and conquest went hand in hand. This confusion of mentalities would cause the Portuguese great difficulties.

The man who set himself to seek answers to these questions more astutely than anyone was the apothecary Tomé Pires. Pires, though not a man of high rank, was well educated. His knowledge had connected him to the royal court in Lisbon. He was sent out from Portugal on the recommendation of King Manuel to serve as 'scrivener and accountant of the factory [trading post] and controller of the drugs' in the newly conquered Malacca.[5] He was, in the words of Albuquerque, 'a diligent man'. His understanding of herbs, spices and medicinal remedies, their prices and trading procedures, was invaluable. Pires, astute and inquisitive, set himself to learn all he could about the East from the Red Sea to Malacca and beyond – to the new horizons that the Portuguese were now contemplating: the Malay Archipelago,

Borneo, the Philippines, China and Japan. His *Suma Oriental* – a short summary of the knowledge of the East – was probably compiled for Manuel, and it contained a concise account of the world unfolding in front of the Portuguese. Pires had opportunities to quiz Chinese merchants in Malacca and to present the monarch with a digest of all that he had usefully gleaned about their country. A few succinct pages cover sailing distances, culture, political structures, military strength and commercial opportunities. Pires was the first European to record that the Chinese 'eat with two sticks, and the earthenware or china bowl in their left hand close to their mouth, with the two sticks to suck it in',[6] something that he would have observed at first hand in Malacca. He echoed Polo's belief that 'the things of China are made out to be great, riches, pomp and state in both land and people and other tales', before adding, with a dangerous sense of Western superiority, 'which it would be easier to believe as true of our Portugal than China'.[7] Above all, he identified the city of Guangzhou (Canton), 'where the whole kingdom of China unloads all its merchandise, great quantities from inland as well as from sea',[8] the trading conventions involved and he noted that 'those who take merchandise from Canton . . . make a profit of three, four or five in every ten'.[9] There was also a response to Manuel's questions on the possibility of conquest: 'China is an important, good and very wealthy country, and the Governor of Malacca would not need as much force as they say to bring it under our rule . . . with ten ships the Governor of India who took Malacca could take the whole of China along the sea-coast. And China is twenty days' sailing for our ships.'[10] It was a dangerous assumption.

Portuguese interest in China arose at a potentially fortuitous moment. The Ming dynasty, in the wake of the Mongol invasions and rampant Japanese piracy, had turned inwards. In 1371 it had banned all foreign maritime trade, and people were forbidden from going to sea and contacting foreigners. This inflicted serious damage on coastal cities, such as Canton, where the appetite for trade remained and illegal commerce continued. There was a mercantile vacuum waiting to be filled. At the same time, the Middle Kingdom operated through high levels of centralised bureaucratic protocol, of which the Portuguese were blithely unaware, and its dominance in eastern Asia was unquestioned. Only a few formal tributary states, such as Malacca, that recognised their submissive position in the relationship, were licensed to trade. The Portuguese had ruptured Chinese suzerainty of Malacca. They also thought they could talk to the emperor, king to king, as equals. The encounter with China was to prove the collision of two incompatible worldviews.

It was not until 1513 that the Portuguese made their first modest attempt to penetrate the Chinese world and assess its commercial potential. A trading expedition undertaken on Malay or Chinese junks, aiming for Canton, landed on the island of T'un-men at the mouth of the Pearl River and erected a stone pillar bearing the arms of King Manuel. Such monuments were the calling cards of Portuguese exploration. They both commemorated 'discovery' and hinted at appropriation. The Europeans were not allowed to land on the mainland but they sold their goods profitably on T'un-men, known as 'the Island of Trade' to the Portuguese. Enthusiastic accounts of the potential of contact with Cathay were conveyed by Italian merchants in Portuguese service. 'They have discovered China,' wrote one of these, Giovanni da Empoli, 'which is the greatest wealth that there can be in the world ... there come from there amazing things.' He mentioned the enormous profits to be made (thirty to one) and the demand for Indian pepper. He was overwhelmed by the abundance of other goods brought to the Pearl River: 'ginger, mace, nutmeg, incense, aloes, velvet, our gold thread, coral, woollen clothes, robes ... the great things are so many that come from there, that they are amazing; so that if I do not die, I hope before I leave here to take a leap thither to see the Grand Khan, who is the king, who is called the king of Cathay'.[11]

The following year another Italian, Rafael Perestrello, a distant cousin of Columbus, was despatched by Albuquerque to 'discover

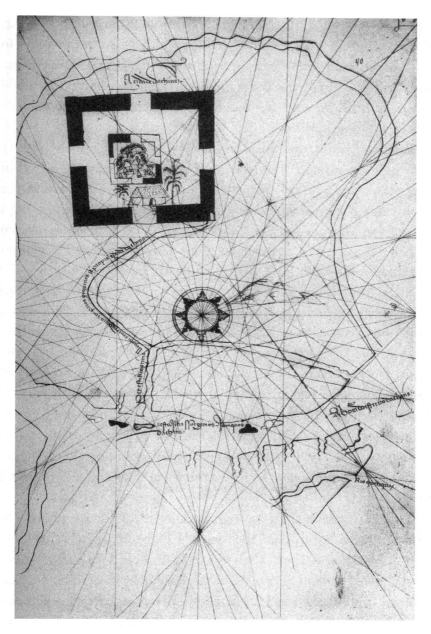

14. An early map of the Pearl River delta and a fictional representation of the city of Canton by Francisco Rodrigues – the site of Portugal's first landfall in China.

China'. He travelled on a Malay junk up the 30 miles of the Pearl River to Canton itself, disposed of his goods at a profit of twenty to one and returned with the positive view that 'the Chins desired peace and friendship with the Portuguese, and that they were very good people'.[12] Both these probes had been conducted under the radar of official Chinese authorisation.

Back in Lisbon, the king's enthusiasm for making 'the discovery of China' continued to grow and, with the encouragement of Perestello's voyage, an official embassy was prepared, under the command of Fernão Peres de Andrade. In June 1517, eight ships sailed from Malacca carrying Chinese pilots. On board was Giovanni da Empoli to act as a commercial agent, as well as Tomé Pires. Pires had now been in the East for five years and had become personally wealthy from spice trading. It had been his intention to return home. Instead, perhaps driven by curiosity to visit the land about which he had sought to learn, he agreed to go as Portugal's ambassador to the Chinese emperor. This was a highly unusual appointment. It says much for his abilities that, 'although not a man of very much quality [that is, not an aristocrat], being an apothecary . . . he was the most skilled for that mission and the best fitted for it; for besides his distinction and inclination to letters, according to his ability, and his liberality and tact in negotiation, he was very curious in enquiring and knowing things, and he had a lively mind for everything'.[13]

The Portuguese ships were guided by the Chinese pilots. On 15 August they approached the island of T'un-men, where they were shot at by Chinese ships. Only formally approved foreign missions were allowed to land and the Europeans, whom the Chinese called *Folangji* (the Franks), had no such authorisation. Everyone else was a pirate. Undamaged, Andrade's ships landed and sent a message to the local officials that 'the principal reason of his coming was to bring an ambassador whom the King of Portugal, whose captain he was, was sending to the King of China with letters of peace and friendship, and he asked for pilots to take the fleet to the city of Canton'.[14] Delay was built into the system: the matter had to be referred to higher officials. It was the Portuguese introduction to Chinese bureaucracy. Waiting was part of the protocol. Andrade waited. It was now late September. Eventually impatience got the better of him: he would set out up the Pearl River without permission. At this the local authorities wavered and pilots were forthcoming. Hit by storms, the ships took three days to sail the 30 miles to Canton. They went 'all very well prepared for peace as well as for war'.[15]

As they anchored, the Portuguese committed a further faux-pas. They celebrated their arrival by flying flags and firing an artillery salute. This caused immediate offence – cannon were only to be used in anger – and a flurry of consternation among the city's officials. The regional viceroy, Ch'en His-hsien, was away from the city. In the meantime, what to do with these insistent and unauthorised visitors, ignorant of protocol? Pires was a careful and tactful man. He apologised over the burst of cannon fire. The Portuguese had been intending it as a mark of respect and thinking it a Chinese custom, as they had been greeted in Malacca by Chinese merchants with such salutes. Mollified, the officials sent word to the viceroy. In the interim Pires forbade any of his men to go ashore.

The Portuguese recorded the arrival of the viceroy:

The river was jammed with small boats bedecked with flags and silken awnings . . . In a huge square, next to which stood a beautifully ornate stone quayside where he came ashore, it was striking to see the variety of colours, costumes and numbers represented by the officials of the sundry departments of public finances, military affairs or matters of justice and the state. Some had to go on foot, others on horseback, bearing strangely ornate baggage, with more patterning and tassels than in Portugal we use in great ceremonies. On this day the ramparts were covered in silken banners, while on the towers reared flagstaffs from which hung silken flags, so huge that they could be used on a vessel with a rounded prow. Such is the wealth of that country, such is its vast supply of silk, that they squander gold leaf and silk on these flags where we use cheap colours and coarse linen cloth.[16]

It was a sobering display for the Portuguese. With the viceroy's arrival, they were instructed in the ceremonies appropriate to a meeting. They did the best they could. On the appointed day Empoli, 'accompanied by men splendidly dressed, and preceded by trumpeters, went with the greatest ceremony'[17] to meet the viceroy with the message that the Portuguese were 'wishing to know and establish friendship with such a great Prince as the King of China'.[18] There was no precedent in the Collection of Ordinances – the Ming rule book – for Folangji being granted access to the Middle Kingdom, nor for the tone of a message that assumed parity between the two rulers, but the dignitaries agreed to send a report to the emperor. In the meantime, the Portuguese were to be allowed to land and granted a house near the water to carry on trading activities.

Pires, as ambassador, stepped ashore in style, to a fanfare of trumpets, and was lodged in a house with a retinue of eight men. Meanwhile, trading went on, and Andrade used the opportunity to undertake some strategic information gathering. Men were despatched secretly to spy out the city. One, António Fernandes, taking advantage of a festival of lanterns, climbed up the city wall, ran round on top of it and counted ninety defensive towers, learning much about its defences.

Empoli achieved his desire to see China but did not live long enough to enjoy the experience. In September or October cholera hit the fleet. He was among the nine who died. It was time for Andrade to depart, leaving the small Portuguese delegation to await word from the emperor. Before he left he sent a public crier to announce 'that if anybody had been injured by or had anything owing to him from a Portuguese let him come to him to obtain all satisfaction;

which was much praised by the natives, and had never before been seen amongst them'.[19] There may have been an element of self-congratulation in this note, but the tactful Andrade, after the initial blunders, had left affairs in China in a promising state. Unbeknown, the Portuguese had arrived at a lucky moment – the emperor, Zhengde, was more open to foreigners and international exchanges than his predecessors. Andrade arrived back in Malacca 'very prosperous in honour and wealth, things rarely secured together'.[20] From there he returned to Lisbon and reported to the king. Interest in China was intense and follow-up initiatives were ordered. Yet all Andrade's good work was destroyed by the next mission. It was led by his own brother.

Exploration and conquest were closely linked in the mindset of the Portuguese nobility, and in Simão de Andrade they were personified. He brought with him the aggression that the Portuguese had employed on the coasts of Africa and India. Touchy, short-tempered and imbued with the spirit of the conquistador – 'so full of self-confidence, so pompous, arrogant and spendthrift' in the words of one Portuguese chronicler[21] – he simply lacked the patience and cultural awareness to cope with the Chinese way. By the time he arrived at the mouth of the Pearl River he expected to find Pires returned from the embassy to the emperor. He hadn't even set out. The deeply encoded rituals of China's centralised bureaucracy proceeded at their own pace. It was becoming clear that 'the majesty [of the emperor] is such and the affairs of this kind so slow, mainly when foreign people are involved, for all is cautions and subtleties, that much patience is needed on the part of whoever has to wait for their dilatoriness'.[22] All through 1519 Pires and his little retinue sat waiting in Canton for word to proceed. Meanwhile, the irascible Andrade took the law into his own hands. Concerned about piracy, he set about constructing a fort on T'un-men island as a secure base for Portuguese trade. This alienation of Chinese territory was simply unacceptable. Andrade then compounded the offence by setting up gallows and hanging one of his sailors – again, only the Chinese could pronounce a death sentence in their own land. When an official came to collect custom dues, he assaulted him and knocked off his hat. Further, he barred other Asian merchants from landing their goods before the Portuguese had sold theirs. Monopoly trading remained a Portuguese fixation.

Stories of their behaviour multiplied and rippled outwards: they were said to have kidnapped children – or possibly bought them. In wilder versions, to eat. The *Ming Shih* – the official history of the Ming dynasty – certainly believed they went 'so far as to seize the children for food'.[23] It was also claimed that they roasted and ate dogs. Andrade's expedition destroyed all his brother's good work: 'within a few days their wretched behaviour earned them the reputation not of friends and allies but of vile pirates and enemies'.[24] The Folangji now became reviled as *Fangui* – barbarian devils – and Andrade's assumptions of European superiority were soon to receive a severe dent.

Pires was still waiting at the start of 1520. Finally, he was given permission to attend on the emperor at Nanjing. 'In the year 1520, on 23rd of January, we set out for the king of China,'[25] wrote a member of his suite, Cristóvão Vieira, at the start of a long letter that would chart the misfortunes of Pires's embassy. They travelled up-river in Chinese galleys decked with silken awnings and sporting Portuguese flags, and climbed mountain passes. One man died on the way. It was May before they reached Nanjing, but by this time tales of the misdeeds of the Folangji had preceded them. Complaints about the abuses of Simão de Andrade were coming in from various quarters – from both the ex-sultan of Malacca and the mandarins in Canton. The Portuguese mission was informed that the emperor would not see them in Nanjing: they were to proceed to Beijing. They set off north, covering the 1,200 miles by horse, on foot and then by the Grand Canal, the country's astonishing 1,000-mile artificial waterway, with its sequence of pound locks – a Chinese invention for lifting ships over steep gradients. It was September before they arrived to await Zhengde, who entered the city in February 1521.

Even beforehand, the misunderstandings were piling up. These began with the letters of accreditation. Pires came with a sealed letter from King Manuel, accompanied by another composed by Fernão Peres de Andrade. The interpreters had rendered these into Chinese in tributary terms 'according to the custom of the country ... to beg, according to custom, for a seal from the lord of the world, the son of God, in order to yield obedience to him'.[26] But when Manuel's letter was opened it did not tally with the other and, furthermore, it assumed a parity between rulers. To the punctilious court officials this was all suspicious. 'It therefore appeared to them that we had entered the country of China deceitfully,' remembered Vieira, 'in order to spy out the land, and that it was a piece of deception that the letter to the king was written differently from the other letters. The king therefore commanded that we should come no more to his palace to do reverence and soldiers and a guard were placed over us.'[27] Vieira said that the interpreters attempted to excuse themselves and the foreigners, explaining that 'we were from a far country, and did not know the custom of China, which is great; that in future we should know it'.[28]

Zhengde himself was inclined to take a lenient view of these uncultured barbarians: 'these people do not know our customs; gradually they will get to know them'.[29] At this point two senior court officials weighed in with volleys of accusations: that the Portuguese had seized the subject city of Malacca and must restore it; that their intentions were dishonourable; that they were 'cruel and crafty'[30] and came as spies with formidable weapons; that unregulated trade was against traditional precepts and 'prohibition and precaution having been neglected, the *Folangji* became more and more familiar with our fairways [ports and harbours] ... all foreign junks in our bay and the foreigners who secretly live in our territory [must] be driven away ... so that part of our country will have peace.'[31] An ambassador from the deposed sultan of Malacca arrived in Beijing to reinforce these arguments: 'the ambassador of the King of Portugal who is now in the land of China is a sham. He does not come in earnest but to deceive the country of China.'[32] Pires was not even permitted to perform the preliminary ceremonies required of ambassadors – prostrating himself full length on the ground 'five times before a wall of the king's palace with both knees on the ground and head and face flat on the earth'.[33] The final blow came on 21 May when Zhengde died, allegedly as a result of falling out of a boat into the Yellow River while drunk. The death of an emperor required a ceremonial period of mourning and the departure of all foreigners from the country. The next day Pires and his embassy were packed off on the long road back to Canton, their gifts undelivered. The interpreters were beheaded. On 22 September the now weary Pires was back where he started. He had traversed southern China from end to end twice – a distance of some 2,600 miles. Another of his party died on the return journey. The rest were ordered to be detained until Malacca was restored to its sultan. Pires had been in China for four fruitless years.

In his absence from Canton, the stock of the Portuguese had fallen even lower. Back in Malacca the good news of Fernão Peres de Andrade's embassy had encouraged a volley of new trading initiatives over the spring and summer of 1521, just as the order was being given, in the wake of the emperor's death, to ban all foreigners from China. Time lags in communication had led the Portuguese to believe that Fernão's venture would ensure a welcome in China. A fleet that arrived at the island of T'un-men in the spring, under the command of Diogo Calvo, found itself hemmed in by a fleet of Chinese junks. Those who came into Canton to trade were seized. These included Diogo's brother Vasco. For forty days the Portuguese were detained on T'un-men. Three ships managed a breakout on 7 September. It was just a fortnight later that Pires returned from Beijing to face the wrath of the city officials. Among the prisoners now being held, including some from his retinue, were Cristóvão

Vieira and Vasco Calvo, who lived long enough to recount the deteriorating situation.

While those captured in these encounters were imprisoned, Pires's party was still being shown some respect. 'They treated us like free people,' remembered Vieira; 'we were closely watched in places separate from the prisoners.'[34] They still maintained some of the kudos and privileges of a diplomatic mission. Pires was evidently being held as a hostage against the return of Malacca, under constant pressure to write to Manuel requesting its return. He resolutely refused, saying that 'he had not come for that purpose, nor was it meet for him to discuss such a question'.[35] The interrogator was insistent. How many men were there in Malacca? How many in the Portuguese fort at Cochin? Why could he not answer? 'With these questions,' recalled Vieira, 'he kept us on our knees for four hours; and when he had tired himself out, he sent each one back to the prison in which he was kept.'[36]

Unaware of any of this, King Manuel was planning further expeditions. Behind this lay a model of expansion that had served the Portuguese well in the Indian Ocean: establish trading relations and create fortified coastal positions from which to conduct profitable business – either with permission or by force. This had become something of a rigid mindset. The Chinese, informed by ambassadors from the deposed sultan of Malacca, understood that this was potentially a strategy for conquest, and that information gathering was key for the Folangji. The collision between the centralised Middle Kingdom that only acknowledged outsiders as supplicants and the assumptions of the Europeans was growing more intense.

While Pires and his dwindling retinue remained under tightening house arrest yet another Portuguese fleet was on its way. Four ships left Cochin on the west coast of India in April 1522 under Martim de Melo Coutinho. The royal instructions from faraway Lisbon repeated the request to establish a treaty of friendship and gain permission to build a fort on T'un-men. To this end the expedition carried a second ambassador to foster relations with the emperor. It was only when it reached Malacca that Coutinho learned the true state of affairs from those who had escaped the naval confrontation the previous year. He decided to press on. The four ships, together with two junks laden with pepper and carrying 300 men, sufficient to garrison a fort, departed in July. When they showed up at the mouth of the Pearl River in August, a patrolling fleet of Chinese junks was awaiting them.

The Portuguese had misjudged the nature of the Ming empire. They had arrived blithely expecting to foster relations and secure a trading post. Instead, they found themselves in a sharp maritime engagement off the shores of T'un-men, in which both sides suffered casualties, and the Portuguese the loss of two ships, before withdrawing to Malacca. The Chinese took forty-two prisoners. They had also captured some of the Europeans' superior bronze cannons, which they copied and installed for coastal defence. Whatever the material damage, after the battle of Trade Island, as the Portuguese named it, all their hopes of amity with the Ming empire vanished. It shattered the prospect of legal trade with China for years.

The consequences for Tomé Pires were immediate. On 14 August, Vieira recorded, they 'put fetters on the hands of Tomé Pires and on those of the company fetters, and irons on their feet, the fetters riveted on their wrists, and they took from us all the property that we had'. They were led through the streets with chains on their necks to the house of detention.

> There they knocked off our fetters and put on us stronger chains, on our legs riveted fetters and chains on our necks; and from there they led us to this prison. At the entrance to the prison Antonio d'Almeida died from the heavy fetters that we bore, our arms swollen and our legs cut by the tight chains . . . Before it was night they put others once more on Tomé Pires and conducted him alone and barefoot without a cap amid the hootings of boys to the Canton prison.

The request was made to the mandarin 'that we had come to spy out the country and that we were robbers, we should at once die'. They were told they had two days to live. The following day brought a surprise. 'They struck off our fetters, which if we had borne a day longer we should all have died; and they brought Tomé Pires back once more to this prison.'[37] The mandarin had ordered their release: the execution of ambassadors required the authority of the emperor. It had been a narrow escape.

The fate of those taken in the sea battle was different. A few, such as Vasco Calvo, managed to claim they were part of the official embassy. 'The others were all seized and put into prison. Some of them died of hunger and some were strangled. Simão the interpreter and the Balante Alli were imprisoned; and Alli died here in prison: they struck him on the head with a mallet, and so they killed him; Simão who was in the Canton prison died of beatings.'[38] Others perished from hunger and cold. On 6 December some were paraded through the streets carrying boards with the message: 'Petty sea robbers sent by the great robber falsely; they come to spy out our country; let them die truncated as robbers.'[39] By this time only twenty-three of the forty-two captured in the sea battle remained alive, awaiting the formal pronouncement of the death sentence by the city's officials.

They were executed on 23 September 1523 with great public show in various parts of the city:

in the streets, outside the walls, in the suburbs ... at distances of one crossbow shot from another, that all might see them, both those of Cantão and those of the surrounding area, in order to give them to understand that they thought nothing of the Portuguese, so that the people might not talk of the Portuguese ... each one cut into pieces – heads, legs, arms, and their private members placed in their mouths, the trunk of the body being divided into two pieces round the belly ... and their heads and private members were carried on the backs of the Portuguese in front of the mandarins of Canton with the playing of musical instruments and rejoicings, were then thrown into the dunghills. And from henceforward it was resolved not to allow any more Portuguese into the country nor other strangers.[40]

This very public display was designed for the local population, to deter them, whatever the temptation, from trading with the Folangji.

The retained embassy was kept alive but succumbed one by one. Vieira recorded the attrition.

> We came in thirteen people. Some had died on the way to and from Beijing. Also, three or four lads in this prison by reason of the heavy fetters ... Cristóvão d'Almeida, also Jorge Alvarez, both Portuguese (the scrivener of the prison being fuddled with wine killed him with lashes, and he died in six days) ... Pero de Freitas [died] in this prison and Tomé Pires died here of sickness in the year 1524 in May ... so that of all this company at present there are only two here.[41]

These two survivors, Cristóvão Vieira and Vasco Calvo, wrote long letters that were smuggled out to Malacca, probably by Malay merchants, and intended for the Portuguese king. These not only detailed the fates of their compatriots, but provided lengthy descriptions of the country, its customs and its strategic strengths and weaknesses. Calvo's letter contains an extraordinary analysis of how to conquer Canton and coastal China. In this there was probably an encoded hope that they could persuade a spirited rescue mission. Calvo's voice fades into silence:

> Because these mandarins are afraid of us, Sir, that we know the country, that is the reason why they do not release us and keep us in this prison ... I am not able, Sir, to write more fully because my hand is painful with wounds that keep opening, and because Cristóvão Vieira does not fail to describe everything else.

Done in this prison . . . in the tenth moon and on such a day of October. Praying our Lord to guard You and to carry You in safety wherever Your Honour desires.

The servant of Your Honour, Vasco Calvo[42]

Both men were thought to have died in custody sometime in the 1530s. No letters of Tomé Pires from China survive but there is a curious after-story about his fate. Despite Calvo's claim, it is possible that Pires did not die in a Cantonese prison and neither did Calvo. In 1543, a worldwide Portuguese wanderer called Fernão Mendes Pinto was in China. Pinto had something of the Marco Polo about him, a teller of lively stories in which truth, hearsay and complete invention have become so entangled that the Portuguese pun his name as 'Mentes' – 'Are you lying?' Nevertheless, much of the Liar's story-telling has been verified and a reasonable case made that somewhere in China he met a Chinese/Portuguese Christian woman whose name was Inês de Leiria. She had a cross tattooed on her arm. She spoke just a little Portuguese and she had a tale to tell. Her father was Tomé Pires. Both her father and Calvo had been banished to inland China. He had married her mother many years previously and lived in exile, dying about 1540. At the time of the meeting Calvo was still alive.

The fates and fortunes of adventurous Europeans scouting the world were many and various. They drowned in shipwrecks, were enslaved on Pacific islands, went native in the Moluccas, intermarried in Goa, became pirates in the Mekong Delta and mercenaries of the kings of Siam, left traces of their DNA in Polynesia. Between the silences, astonishing stories survive of discovery, fate and adventure.

The Portuguese were learning all they could about China. The historian João de Barros was the first European to mention the Great Wall. The spying in Canton had been purposeful. There was a notion, proposed in Calvo's letter, that it might be feasible to conquer southern China, an idea that would persist in Portuguese and Spanish dream schemes for the rest of the century.

PART II

COMPETITORS:
THE BATTLE FOR THE MOLUCCAS
1522-46

Seven

The Spanish Reply
1522-26

Back in distant Lisbon, the return of the *Victoria* to Seville on 6 September 1522 had provoked a furious response. On 28 September 1522 a frosty letter from the recently crowned John III ordered his ambassador:

> to present his complaint to the Emperor Charles V, because a ship of the fleet of Fernão de Magalhães had arrived at Sanlúcar with a cargo of cloves taken in the Moluccas, then entered territory that belonged to Portugal, and to request the punishment of the ship's captain and the handing over of the cloves . . . and in the case that the Emperor does not give a definite and favourable response, claiming that his captains had not acted unreasonably . . . refrain from discussing the matter further.[1]

4 February 1523: a lengthy and carefully crafted reply; a blocking manoeuvre by the emperor. Wrapped in amicable language ('You know of the love that I have had and do have for the Most Serene King' etc.),[2] it suggested that a commission be sent to the Moluccas with learned 'astrologers, cosmographers, notaries and pilots'[3] to

determine the demarcation between the spheres of influence; that neither should send fleets to the Moluccas during this enquiry; and anyway the counter that 'we claim that Malacca and many other islands leased by him are within our territory and demarcation and he should refrain from sending his ships and fleets to these parts during the time of the demarcation, and I will do likewise in the islands of Maluco and other islands discovered by me in those parts that he claims to be in his demarcation'.[4] It was a clumsy and unworkable proposal designed to slow the Portuguese advance. Charles was pre-empting any commission by stating that these areas were within his sphere anyway, and his discovery claim was absurd. Meanwhile he was already planning a follow-up fleet to Magellan's – the expedition that he claimed shouldn't be sent. It was calculated to pressurise the Portuguese.

The notes of endearment revealed how deeply the two Iberian kingdoms were entwined. Diplomatic relations were complicated. Charles was soon to enter into negotiations to marry John's sister, Isabel. In 1525, Charles V's younger sister, Catherine of Austria, would marry John. The marriage of Charles and Isabel followed a year later. Notwithstanding, the Portuguese response was fury at Charles's claims. There was a great deal at stake and they were not going to let Spain pocket the proceeds of years of effort in reaching the Spice Islands. The Moluccas were potentially the flashpoint for imperial war. The Portuguese demanded discussions. The emperor was preparing a fleet.

To defuse the controversy both sides agreed to a joint commission to determine the demarcation line on the other side of the world. On 11 April 1524 they met on symbolically neutral territory: the bridge over the Guadiana, the frontier river separating Portugal from Spain, halfway between Elvas and Badajoz. Each party came with its own Olympic team of expert cosmographers, cartographers and navigators, equipped with globes and maps demonstrating to its own advantage how the antemeridian (the Tordesillas demarcation line on the other side of the world) included the Moluccas within its rightful territory. Sessions were held alternately in the towns on either side. The Portuguese were at a disadvantage in that some of the maps they had previously produced had been falsified to push the Spice Islands further east in an attempt to demonstrate to potential interlopers that sailing there was immensely difficult – a strategy that had never previsioned Magellan's voyage from an easterly direction. The defection of skilled pilots to Spain had also increased the leakage of sailing charts and valuable information. The Spanish could accuse their adversaries of forging evidence, while they on their side made wild claims that the antemeridian was so far west that 'it cuts through the mouth of the Ganges, so that Sumatra and Malacca and the Moluccas fall within our demarcation'.[5] Their claim was based on a belief – one that proved to be wrong – that the circumference of the earth was quite small. Christopher Columbus's son, Hernándo, and Juan Sebastián Elcano attended, using a globe to demonstrate how the Moluccas lay in the Spanish zone. All these claims were refuted by the Portuguese. Three sessions of the enquiry were held in April, eleven in May. In the event, the impossibility of defining the issue resulted in stalemate.

The apparent absurdity of this attempt to neatly divide up the world was summarised in a story that went the rounds in Badajoz. Some of the Portuguese delegates at the commission were walking beside the Guadiana when they came upon a small boy guarding his mother's washing. 'He demanded of them whether they were those men that parted the world with the emperor and as they answered, "yes": he took up his shirt and shewed them his bare bottom, saying: Come and draw your line here through the middle.'[6] It kept the citizens of Badajoz amused for months.

In the very long view of history, the Portuguese claim that the Spice Islands and the Philippines lay on their side of the fictional Tordesillas Line would be vindicated, but the impossibility of determining longitude in the spring of 1524 rendered the whole exercise futile. On 31 May the talks were suspended. Only possession could resolve the issue. Two months later Charles's fleet was ready to sail. What was at stake were the huge profits to be made from the spice trade.

'Monday, the seventeenth of the month of July, 1525, we departed from the city of A Coruña for the islands of Maluco, where the clove grows, with seven ships, and in them four hundred and fifty men, more or less. And the ships were well armed, both with artillery and munitions, as well as with many other weapons.'[7] The opening of an account of Charles's follow-up expedition by a 17-year-old Basque boy called Andrés de Urdaneta.

The intent was clear: only possession could resolve a cartographic squabble. The fleet that Charles had assembled was considerably larger than that with which Magellan had set sail. The *capitana* (flagship), the *Santa María de la Victoria*, was a sizeable vessel of 300 tons. The second in command, the *Sancti-Spiritus*, of 250 tons, was followed by other ships of descending size: the *Anunciada, San Gabriel, Santa María de Parral, San Lesmes*, down to the tiny 50-ton pinnace, *Santiago* – a light sailing vessel for tendering and scouting duties. The size of this fleet indicated Spanish intentions.

The commander of the expedition, García Jofre de Loaísa, was an experienced seaman. His second in command, Juan Sebastián Elcano, co-opted for his knowledge and pilotage skills and now in command of the *Sancti-Spiritus*, had volunteered for a second attempt on the Strait of Magellan. The crew of 450 included a number of experienced Basque seamen from among his kinship group and region, including the youthful Urdaneta, as page. The young man was literate, intelligent, observant and highly resourceful. His journal was to provide the fullest account of a venture that was to change his life. Amazingly, three other survivors of the first navigation also volunteered for a second pounding on the high seas. Others, with no say in the matter, included some indigenous people abducted on the first voyage, who might be useful as interpreters.

Loaísa was provided with a tightly defined list of fifty-three instructions, drawing on the experience of Magellan's expedition and covering all aspects of decision making, discipline, sailing procedures, routes, treatment of native peoples, trading strategies and the succession of command in the case of the commander's death. This time there were no Portuguese on the ships to divide loyalties, but experience showed that the punishing conditions of the westerly route were always liable to test group morale and stoke dissension, and the failure to resolve the demarcation of territories left Loaísa's instructions riddled with contradictions. They were 'on no pretext to discover or touch on lands within the [unresolved] limits of the king of Portugal'. They were to shun armed conflict – unless they could win without risking the fleet – while at the same time avoiding direct contact with the Portuguese in the Moluccas at all: 'the landing should be to the north, to avoid meeting the Portuguese whose station is on the south side. But if it should be found that the Portuguese have arrived, the landing should not be abandoned on that account.' They were also ordered to hunt for the *Trinidad*, whose fate was as yet unknown. All the unsolved issues at Badajoz remained. Underlying the document was the explicit aim to possess: Loaísa's titles included that of 'Governor of the islands of Moluccas and its dependencies'.[8] If they reached the Spice Islands conflict was inevitable. The Iberians were exporting their conflicts to the other side of the world.

Relying on Elcano's knowledge, the July departure was aimed to dodge the fierce Atlantic storms that had hammered Magellan's fleet off the coast of Patagonia. The problem with this timing was that they would hit the strait in the depths of a southern winter. A first stop was made at the craggy volcanic island of La Gomera in the Canaries to replenish supplies. Here some soldiers deserted: already the prospect of the voyage ahead was causing doubts. From there, 'sailing with a prosperous wind',[9] the going was at first easy, but shortly after, on 18 August, the fleet got its first taste of the ocean's moods. The sea roughened. A blast of tempest shattered the capi-tana's mainmast. Elcano despatched two carpenters in a small boat to try to reach the damaged ship. It was a hair-raising venture. The sea was rearing violently. The rain battered down. They made it aboard but not without intense suffering. The fleet proceeded, using only its foresails. Despite the repairs, Loaísa's ship was evidently now more cumbersome. In the heavy seas and ferocious rain, it rammed the *Parral*, damaging its poop and mizzen mast.

On 6 September, off the coast of Sierra Leone, they came across a ship believed to be French. With Spain and France at war, the *San Gabriel* and the *Santiago* went in pursuit. When the *Santiago* chased it down, the vessel turned out to be Portuguese. The *Santiago*'s captain, Guevara, ordered it to return to the capitana. At which point, the commander of the *San Gabriel*, Acuña, fired a shot at the Portuguese now under Guevara's protection. A furious row broke out between Acuña and Guevara. They were on the point of bombarding each other. The Portuguese were treated honourably by Loaísa and sent on their way, but the stresses were already apparent.

The going was getting tougher. 'All these days the wind was against us, then we languished in very large calms, so that in a month and a half we did not progress more than 150 leagues,' recalled Urdaneta.[10] As calm followed storm and the wind died in the sails, dissatisfaction grew. On Elcano's ship a group of officers was becoming restive. Possibly spooked by the challenging conditions, they demanded that the ship should abandon the crossing of the Atlantic and proceed east, past the Cape of Good Hope – in direct defiance of the orders.

All this came to a head when the fleet reached the island of Annobon, which the Spanish called San Mateo, in the bight of the Gulf of Guinea. Here they found good watering and an opportunity to patch up the damaged vessels. Urdaneta recalled that there was 'very good fishing and many palm trees. We also came across some hens and evidence of pigs, and there are many foolish birds. We killed a large number of these with sticks. We found many eggs in their nests.' The diet was not without its dangers. 'From the capitana they caught a very beautiful fish, they described as beaked.' Loaísa invited all the officers to dine on this. 'All who ate this fish developed such terrible diarrhoea that they lost consciousness and we thought they were going to die, but our Creator wanted all of them to survive.'[11] Having recovered, Loaísa handed out punishment to the two squabbling captains, Acuña and Guevara, and set about getting to the bottom of a potential mutiny on Elcano's ship. He was preparing to put the mutineers to torture to get at the truth, when the *Sancti-Spiritus* was seen to be dragging its anchors and proceedings were hastily curtailed. The island, despite its tropical beauty, was a sinister place. 'We came upon the skulls of two men who had been killed and on a tree some words in Portuguese that read *"Here died the wretched Juan Ruiz, because he deserved it."* '[12] They were probably glad to get away.

The attempt to reroute the expedition had been scotched, but a groundswell of discontent persisted. However, the turn west towards the Americas 'brought us abundant wind that was good for our voyage', Urdaneta recalled.[13] He was astonished by the wealth and drama of marine life: the flying fish, 'the most beautiful I have ever seen', sailing through the air, 'with wings like a bat', a rifle shot from the ship; and other large fish as big as tuna leaping out of the water half the length of the ship in pursuit; then birds also swooping to snatch the flying fish out of the air. In attempting to avoid one or the other, 'they came crashing onto the ship, and as they landed on the dry deck they couldn't get up and so we caught them'.[14]

On 5 December they sighted the coast of Brazil – Portuguese territory – and swung south without landing. On Christmas day the fleet was becalmed; but that night the weather shifted. Loaísa's fleet was about relive Magellan's torments in the southern Atlantic, only it was now winter and the conditions were even worse. At 40° south, they encountered strong headwinds. They found it was impossible to go forward; on the 29th the ships were hit by more violent storms. The capitana vanished. After two days of fruitless searching, the rest of the fleet headed south to the Santa Cruz River, where Magellan had holed up for seven weeks. It was the agreed meeting point in such an eventuality. Still no sign of Loaísa's ship. At a meeting on the *Sancti-Spiritus* it was resolved to push on to the strait, leaving a message in a bottle marked by a cross. Two days later Elcano thought he had reached the opening of the strait and signalled to the fleet to advance. However, doubts soon set in. A ship's boat was despatched. Two of the men, Bustamante and Roldan, who had been on Magellan's voyage, were confident it was; others were less certain. It seemed more like a river. The rising tide demonstrated that it wasn't a seaway. Urdaneta was critical. 'Truth to say, it was a great blindness of those who had been in the Strait previously, especially Juan Sebastián del Cano.'[15] They sailed on.

By nightfall they had reached the Cape of Eleven Thousand Virgins, the hooked promontory at the mouth of the strait, and the *Sancti-Spiritus* anchored. By ten that night a fierce onshore wind hit the ship. 'After dawn, we thought we should sail out but could not. The wind was very strong. The four anchors that we had secured began to drag because the sea was so high that many times it rose higher than the middle of the mast. No man could move from where he stood. The sailors were dismayed. They knew we were lost. The soldiers were unable to keep their footing.'[16] The situation was worsening by the minute. Elcano gave the order to release the cables, lower the sails and beach the ship. The *Sancti-Spiritus* was completely grounded. By now the waves were breaking high over the beach and some soldiers and sailors began to jump. They tried to time their leap as the undertow drew back. 'Of the ten . . . only one escaped. The sea caught them and hurled them under the ship. Most of them were torn to pieces, the others, unable to help themselves, drowned.'[17] The one who made it ashore was the saviour of the crew:

We threw a rope, tied to the lateen yard, to land to the one who was saved and with the aid of this we managed to cross over the yard to land and all of us got out with the help of God, not without exhausting work and great danger, drenched in our shirts as we were. And the place where we emerged is so cursed that there is nothing there but pebbles. It was bitterly cold and we would have died if we hadn't set ourselves to running up and down to keep warm.[18]

The storm abated and the shipwrecked crew managed to rescue boxes and provisions, but later that night it returned with renewed force, sweeping away everything they had saved.

The expedition was coming apart at the seams with the battering of winter in the south Atlantic. The *Sancti-Spiritus* was wrecked beyond repair, leaving Elcano marooned on the shore. The capitana had vanished. The other ships had weathered the storm out to sea but now wanted to shelter within the strait – and for that they needed Elcano's past experience, only he was now stranded elsewhere with the other shipwreck survivors.

When the storm lulled, a boat was despatched to take Elcano off. All the men on the shore were desperate for rescue but the boat was too small to accommodate more than a couple of people. Urdaneta recorded that 'only I embarked with the captain and we went to the *Anunciada*'.[19] The young man was apparently already valued. At the mouth of the strait, they encountered the lost capitana and the *San Gabriel*. The storm returned, lashing the vessels, sweeping away their ships' boats. The *Anunciada* started to drag its anchor. 'We were dashed against some steep banks, from which none of us would escape alive.'[20] The men started to cry out pitifully. Elcano ordered the captain to force the men back to work. The ship was saved, put out to sea and entered the strait again. And there they found the two missing vessels. 'God knows how much pleasure we had finding them there, because we thought them lost.'[21]

The landscape of the strait that Magellan experienced had been devoid of humanity. Now it was otherwise. 'We saw people on the land. They seemed to be dressed in red. To see what people they were, we sent a skiff ashore, and found that they were Indians. Of whom they brought one, who was very big, a cubit taller than anyone on the ships. He wore the skin of a "zebra" [a guanaco, a llama-like animal] and on his feet some sandals of the same skin. When they brought him on board, he was astounded.' They gave him some wine 'which pleased him very much' and a mirror which puzzled him – 'believing that some other Indian was behind the mirror . . . he was very happy and danced for a long time and made signs to be taken ashore'.[22]

It had become important to rescue those from the shipwreck still marooned on the beach, and to that end Urdaneta and a party were landed to trek back to them. As soon as they got ashore it was apparent that the generous treatment of the visitors had sparked the interest of the other Patagonians. As they set out, thirty of them, both men and women very tall, followed them.

> And they began to ask us for something to eat and drink. We gave them some of what we had in our knapsacks and then went to see their settlement. It consisted of huts made of the skins of zebras where they had their wives and children. When they want to go somewhere else, they take up their huts and put them on the backs of their women, while they march only with bows and arrows. About ten of them followed us for a day and a half, but when they saw that our knapsacks were getting empty, they turned back.[23]

They walked on. The sun was hot. Deprived of water they became intensely thirsty. Urdaneta resorted to drinking his own urine. 'I drank seven or eight sips of it, and came to myself as if I had eaten and drunk.' They eventually found a stagnant puddle but the trek was descending into nightmare. Walking along the seashore below steep cliffs they were trapped by the rising tide. 'We could go neither forward nor go back, nor to the land behind because the cliffs were very high. Finally, the water reaching up to our knees, and there being no other remedy, we decided to climb the cliff.'[24] It was tough going but they made it. 'We thanked God for the favour he had done us.' That night when they made a fire to roast some ducks and a rabbit, a gunpowder flask caught fire. Urdaneta was badly burnt 'which made me forget all the past work and dangers'.[25] It was so cold they buried themselves in sand but the night brought no rest, with the barking of unknown animals and the fear that the Patagonians might kill them. 'We stayed like that all night, anxious and without sleep. The next day we again walked forward along the shore.'[26] It was on the fourth day that they reached the shipwrecked sailors who were relieved and delighted to see them.

From the beach there was better news. They could see, off shore, the arrival of the lost capitana, together with the *San Gabriel* and the *Santiago*, the small pinnace. They lit fires to attract attention and the *Santiago* was despatched to assure them that rescue would come.

Following the first bout of storms, Loaísa attempted to regroup his battered fleet, rescue the men stranded on the shore and salvage whatever he still could from the carcass of the *Sancti-Spiritus*. It was brutal work. On 5 February the fleet was again hit by violent storms. Some of the ships were able to find shelter in the Magellan Strait. The *San Lesmes* was temporarily swept away to 50° south, to some islands off the very southern tip of the Americas – further than any European ship had been before. The capitana ran aground and was badly damaged. With great difficulty she was refloated, but only by throwing much of her cargo overboard.

Morale was sinking. The captain of the *San Gabriel*, Acuña, was so despondent that he contemplated giving up. On 9 February the *Anunciada's* captain, Pedro de Vera, sent a signal, according to Urdaneta, that he 'did not wish to come to us. Finally, she disappeared, sailing out of the strait and we never saw her again.'[27] De Vera left without a ship's boat, cables or a pilot, declaring that he would attempt to reach the Moluccas via the Cape of Good Hope. The ship was never seen again. At the suggestion of Elcano, Loaísa ordered the remaining ships to regroup in the Santa Cruz River, where the capitana could be repaired, but it seems Acuña too had had enough. The *San Gabriel* also disappeared – possibly not deserting but driven north by high seas. It was destined for a remarkable survival of its own.

Nursing the capitana into the river was arduous. They had no option but to patch her up. 'We began to unload the ship to drain out the water . . . there was so much water that it took two pumps to try to keep her afloat . . . we had very hard work repairing the capitana as it was winter. We were working in the water and we found three fathoms of her keel broken. We applied a remedy the best way we could, first with boards, and then with sheets of lead.'[28]

The repairs took weeks. There was ample time for Urdaneta, a keen observer of natural history, to take in what was around them. Amidst infinite salt flats, there was a small island inhabited by flightless ducks (penguins) and basking sea lions. 'And one day forty comrades decided to go out in a boat to see if we could kill one of them . . . there were a good hundred sea lions . . . we could hear them bellowing from more than half a league away.' To get to the animals they had to wade through the penguins, 'and since they could not fly, we stepped on them . . . to reach the sea lions'. Up close they faced fierce resistance. 'They are so strong that it was no use grabbing them with hooks, nor hitting them with other weapons. If they seized a spear with their teeth they would break it to pieces. Only one died, we opened it up and found many pebbles in his crop which he broke up. Tonight, we ate the liver and the spleen.'[29] The beast was so heavy that it took twenty men to haul the creature aboard with tackle. Urdaneta claimed that the head and neck fed 140. They were severely ill.

The river was rich in fish; they netted thirteen barrels worth – enough to provide the whole fleet with fresh food. Along the shore they found and killed ostriches, and discovered an animal 'like a tortoise . . . that with its shell looked like a cloaked horse'.[30] They also collected semi-precious stones, 'and I found a topaz for which I got forty ducats . . . In all the time we were in this river we saw no Patagonians. The tide here rises very high.'[31]

By late March they were ready to go. They had endured three months of torment on the Patagonian coast. On the 22nd or the 29th of March 1526 – accounts differ – the four remaining ships set sail. The wind was still strong, although in their favour, and there was a heavy rolling sea. 'On the eighth of the month of April, we entered the strait.'[32] They had been at sea eight months. They now had to tackle the 350-mile labyrinth, with its series of narrows, bays and inlets that twisted and turned around the sharp angles that had so baffled Magellan's fleet. This time they had the charts and pilots' log of their predecessors – and Elcano's previous experience – but the season was shifting into winter. Days were shortening, the winds fierce, the cold biting. The little *Santiago* went ahead to scout.

Inside the first wide channel, Loaísa sent men ashore to gather edible greens and also to see if they could capture a Patagonian. An attempt to snatch one was met with a shower of arrows and they had to withdraw. Accidents continued to stalk the fleet. A cauldron of pitch caught fire on the capitana. 'We were in great danger. While some of us were trying to put out the fire others were scrambling to get in the ship's boat. They wanted to kill each other to get into it. If we had all done so, we would have been in a terrible situation.' Fortunately, the fire was extinguished. 'The Captain-general tongue-lashed all those who had got into the boat.'[33] Keeping in touch with each other remained tricky. The *Santiago* vanished for a while, then reappeared.

The Magellan expedition had given names to the capes, bays and narrows of the strait and these provided familiar reference points for Elcano on his second voyage. Urdaneta recorded their passage through the maze, while the pilot Hernándo de la Torre maintained a scrupulous log. On 12 April they reached a bay they called La Concepción, 'where we stayed four days because the wind was against us'.[34] Two days later they were at the point of Santa Ana, which they called the Strait of the Snows. They were continuously battling aberrant seasonal winds. 'The mountains were so high they seemed to reach the sky. The sun did not enter there almost all the year. Night lasted more than twenty hours. It snowed regularly and the snow was very blue – because of its antiquity – without melting, and the cold was extreme.'[35] 'On the eighteenth we entered the haven of San Jorge, where we got firewood and water, and wood to make a couple of dinghies.'[36] The toll of the voyage was starting to tell – 'the factor Diego de Covarrubias died here' – and there were glancing

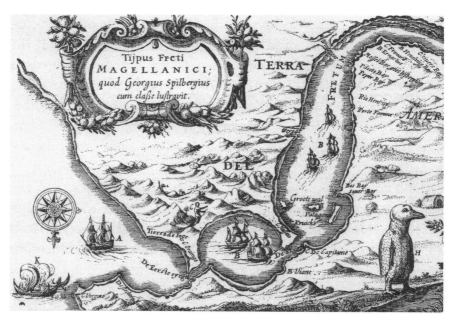

15. *Entering the Magellan Strait: a vivid seventeenth-century panorama, again orientated to the south, with an exotic outsized penguin. The ships approach via the Cape of the Virgins, pass through the bottleneck of two narrows and into the Broad Reach. The decisive right-angle turn takes place at Cape Froward. Tierra del Fuego lies beyond.*

encounters with native people. Two canoes approached in the dark; the sound of shouting. 'Since we could not understand them, they did not come to the ships but turned back.'[37] Thinking that there was something more to it, the men on the ship stood to arms. A boat sent out next day failed to locate them. By night they saw fires reflected in the water, and found a canoe whose ribs were made of whale bone, but the people remained elusive.

Their next stopping place was the aptly named Buen Puerto – a source of ample firewood and a 'red fruit like sour cherries, without stones, and we ate it'. They also found mussels with pearls inside, and a tree whose bark tasted like cinnamon – 'everyone in the fleet ate it'.[38] The vitamin C from the cherries would prove necessary but insufficient.

16. *Leaving the Strait via the long narrow channel leading out to the Desired Cape and the Pacific, 'the Sea of Chile'. This Dutch expedition is shooting birds for food and seems to have struck up friendly relations with the indigenous people.*

119

They had negotiated the sharp north-west turn at Cape Froward and reached another harbouring point, which they called St Joan de Portalina. It was a desolate region, 'very snowy and cold', Urdaneta remembered, 'no clothes could keep us warm'.[39] Under towering mountains, the wind raged, the sea roared turbulently. Conditions on board were wretched. On deck, cold ate to the bone. Holed up below, the stench was unbearable and they were plagued by lice. 'We couldn't escape them.' An ailing Galician sailor was said to have been suffocated by the lice. His shipmates cleaned him, and put him in an open cask in clean clothes. 'When I saw him on the third day, neither he nor the cask were visible, they had both become completely covered by very large lice, and so he died.'[40] When they tried to sail on, they were beaten back by the gale. The ships got under way again on 13 May and a south-westerly wind carried them out of this zone of torment. The sea now teemed with marine life: whales, tuna, bonito sharks, hake, large quantities of sardines and anchovies, oysters and mussels. Finally, they reached the furthest tip of the strait – Cape Deseado – the Desired Cape. 'On Saturday morning, 26 May, the capitana, the two caravels and the pinnace came out of the Strait,'[41] was Urdaneta's terse conclusion to a hellish transit. It had been another test of endurance. Despite all the knowledge gleaned from Magellan's navigation, it had taken them forty-eight days – ten longer than their predecessor's spring-time passage. Now they were in the Pacific Ocean, the calm sea. Except that it wasn't.

Almost immediately the fleet was hit by a violent storm. Loaísa's ship ran before the wind with all sails lowered. When the wind eased, the other three vessels had vanished. He never saw them again. The *Santa María de Parral*, the *San Lesmes* and the *Santiago* were all destined to have astonishing adventures of their own. The *Santa María de la Victoria* was now alone on a vast sea. Despite repairs, the ship was in a parlous condition, and still leaking. It required the crew to continuously man two pumps to keep her afloat. A north-westerly wind prevented them making a course for the Moluccas. 'Each day we expected the end to come,' remembered Urdaneta. 'We had to reduce the rations by reason of additional men who had come aboard from the ship that was wrecked. On the one hand we worked hard, on the other we were insufficiently fed. We passed through much misery, and some perished.'[42]

With nothing in sight day after day, spirits dropped. Malnourished after months at sea and without adequate vitamin C, the ghastly symptoms of scurvy once again took hold. 'All of those whom we lost, died through the swelling of their gums that prevented them from eating anything at all, and I saw one man whose gums were so swollen that he would pull out flesh as thick as a finger.'[43] They were battling to hold a course until early July when they picked up the north-east trade winds. The deaths continued to pile up. 'Sunday 24th June, Rodrigo Bermejo, pilot of the flagship died. It was a great loss for our navigation because he was a very good pilot ... Friday 13th day of July, Álvaro de Tejada, accountant died ... on the 30th of July the Captain-general died.'[44] With each death there was a shuttling of responsibilities, but that of Loaísa was particularly significant. One survivor suggested that he had lost the will to live. Because of acute depression caused by the loss of his fleet he 'grew weak and died'.[45]

According to instructions laid down by Charles, in the event of the captain-general's death there were secret orders to be opened. These named Elcano as overall commander. He lasted a week, long enough to dictate a will. On 6 August the circumnavigator, who had seen as much of the world as anyone who had ever lived, was lowered with a splash into the depths of the Pacific Ocean. 'At the same time the treasurer died.'[46] Another captain-general was appointed, Toribio Alonso de Salazar. He too did not last long.

It is apparent from Urdaneta's testimony that Elcano had planned to take the expedition to the Moluccas by way of Cipangu (Japan), against the stated instructions of the emperor. Evidently the temptation to ignore orders was not confined to Magellan. However, 'at this time', Urdaneta remembered, 'we were overworked and worn out, being in 14° or 15° north, seeking for Cipangu. As the people were so exhausted from much work at the pumps, the violence of the sea, the insufficiency of food, and illness, some died every day. We therefore agreed to make the best of our way to Maluco.'[47] They drifted past an island they named San Bartolomé, but were unable to land. Twelve days later they reached Guam, the Island of Thieves. When canoes came out to inspect the ship, the new arrivals were hailed in Spanish. The man addressing them was an extraordinary sight: 'he was naked except his genitals were covered with a piece of mat and his hair was bristly and came down to his buttocks'.[48] His name was Gonzalo de Vigo, a Galician, a castaway from the Magellan voyage. He was one of three who had deserted from the *Trinidad* because the crew were all dying. The other two had been killed on the island. He had been there for three years. 'He came on board and was of great use to us, as he knew the language of the islands.'[49] Urdaneta was able to gather a detailed picture of the anthropology of the Ladrones and their people: 'The natives of these islands go naked, not wearing anything. They are well made men wearing their hair and beards long. They have no iron tools and work with stones. They have no other arms than slings, clubs hardened in fire, and a sort of knife made out of the shin bones of dead men, and fish bones.'[50]

'Monday, the 10th day of September. We left these islands to go in search of the islands of Maluco.'[51] The Galician came with them. They were now so short of able-bodied men that they either co-opted or kidnapped eleven islanders to work the pumps. Meanwhile the deaths continued to mount. 15 September: the new captain-general, Alonso de Salazar, was taken by the sea, then Juan de Huelva, master of the ship, then its bosun, Chimigo de Loriaga. The ship was divided over who should succeed Salazar. After a dangerous division another Basque seaman, Martin Íñiguez de Carquizano, was appointed and all were called to swear loyalty to him.

On 6 October they reached Mindanao, the largest of the southerly Philippine islands. Gonzalo de Vigo, who knew a little Malay, was able to converse with the some of the people. They managed to barter for food supplies, but relations soon deteriorated. The local people 'thought we were *faranguis* [Portuguese], thieves and robbers, wherever we went'.[52] It was the first mention of their Iberian rivals. Urdaneta again compiled a detailed description of these people, their dress, their religious and sexual practices, their skills in boat building. They were evidently more warlike than the people of Guam, armed 'with bows and arrows and cutlasses and assegais, daggers and shields'.[53] There was talk of gold and cinnamon and evidence that the Chinese came to trade in these islands, bringing two junks a year.

There was antipathy on both sides. When the Spanish raided a village for supplies, the people abandoned it and retreated into the forest. Urdaneta, for his part, claimed that 'they are a treacherous people, and intended to seize the ship by treachery. But we were on our guard, and their plan did not succeed. They often came at night in their very light row boats to cut our cables, but we kept a good watch and they were never able to do any harm. We were in this port ten days, but never succeeded in buying any fresh provisions.'[54] To escape the toil of working the pumps, the men taken from Guam absconded in their canoe. When they landed they were all killed. The *Santa María de la Victoria* departed on 15 October.

The intention was to head to the island of Cebu, where Magellan had died and his officers had been murdered at a banquet, with the hope of finding survivors, but the monsoon season had begun and a northerly wind prevailed. Instead, they turned south, sailing straight for the Moluccas. On 22 October, they arrived at the island of Talaut, one of a spatter of islands south of Mindanao, where, to their relief, they were well received. They sighted the island of Gilolo, the principal island of the Moluccas on the 29th and approached it on 2 November.

Some people from the small adjacent island of Rabo paddled out to greet them 'and they spoke to us in Portuguese, of which we were very happy'.[55] After all the travails of the voyage, there was a joyful homesickness in hearing even the language of their rivals. 'On Sunday the 4th of the said month we went to enter the port of Zamafo . . . through a chain of small islets crowned by very small trees.'[56] They rejoiced to have reached the goal of their voyage. It had taken 440 days of storms and calms, terrible cold and malnutrition. Seven ships had departed from A Coruña, one had made it. The cost in human life had been enormous. Of the 450 who set out 'we were now a company of one hundred-and-five, forty men having died since we left the Strait'.[57] They were completely exhausted.

Now they had to face the Portuguese.

Eight

Microwars
1526- 8

When the Portuguese first reached the Spice Islands, they came with a set of strict instructions from the crown that framed peaceful intentions. Where they had sought to monopolise the spice trade of the Indian Ocean, on this outer periphery they recognised that they had turned the corner into another world – one that was beyond the reach of central control. Now a modicum of wisdom prevailed: they no longer had political or military ambitions. The royal spice ships made regular voyages to load up with nutmeg and cloves, but private trade was also permitted, albeit not without causing friction. Merchants and armed fleets were not to attack other ships nor to impede their loading, wherever they came from and whatever their religion; they were to study and follow closely the example of other indigenous merchants, participate in their trading systems and respect local customs as inviolable. The Portuguese were adapting. These were perhaps lessons learned the hard way on the Pearl River.

This more conciliatory approach might have gone on indefinitely were it not for the arrival of the *Victoria* and the *Trinidad*. The irruption of Spanish rivals via the Pacific changed the game. Tidore's acceptance of the suzerainty of Charles polarised local rivalries in the Moluccas. A European competitor for spices raised prices for the

Portuguese. By the 1520s Lisbon had changed the rules: more ships and men; a nominated governor; the building of a fort on Ternate; destruction of the town of Tidore and the Spanish trading post; the attempt to monopolise the Moluccan spice trade. The Moluccas became an imperial project, but one that, in practical terms, was too distant to be effectively managed or supported. The sultan of Tidore saw in the new arrivals a counterweight to the Portuguese presence, lighting the fuse of a more intense rivalry with Ternate. Each now had its European champion.

All this came into play when the *Santa María* reached the town of Zamafo on the island of Gilolo. Here the Spanish learned, through the invaluable services of their interpreter Gonzalo de Vigo, the true situation – and something of the tribal complexity of Moluccan politics. The Portuguese had destroyed the town of Tidore; its sultan had just died and the royal family had fled into the dense and inaccessible recesses of its volcanic mountain. The Ternate fort commanded the strait between the rival islands; the Portuguese had ships, men and guns. To the ruler of Gilolo, as a vassal of Tidore, the arrival of the Spanish was providential. The formal alliance with Castile in 1521 was to be resurrected. The newcomers were welcomed with open arms but it was necessary to proceed with caution. 'As soon as they knew of us,' Andrés de Urdaneta was told, 'Dom Garcia Henriques, the Captain presently in their fortress with a large fleet of the King of Portugal, would come and capture us.'[1] To avoid Portuguese surveillance, a canoe was quietly despatched to Tidore by night carrying word of the arrival of the *Santa María*. The news came back that its present sultan – a boy of 8, under the direction of the queen his mother – would warmly welcome them. On Gilolo the famished sailors were feasted; 'they sent us a great deal to eat and drink, enough to feed a hundred men'. The islands promised a tropical abundance: 'pigs and goats and rice and chickens, coconuts, bananas and many other fruits'.[2]

Despite the secrecy, news of the *Santa María* could not long be concealed. On 30 November, St Andrew's Day – the pious Urdaneta ticked off the religious calendar as the days passed – a messenger ship approached with a letter for the Spanish commander from his opposite number, Garcia Henriques. It was brought by the chief bailiff of Ternate, Francisco de Castro: the Spanish were encroaching. 'All those islands were in the demarcation of the king of Portugal.' He required them to proceed to Ternate 'where much honour would be done to him'.[3] If not, they must leave the islands and return to Spain, in effect by the way they had come. From Carquizano a robust reply: 'Write and go on writing, but we are coming not going'[4] – and the automatic counterclaim: the Moluccas were in the demarcation of the Emperor Charles V – and, for that matter, another 400 leagues beyond. 'For which [Henriques] was required to go and leave the said islands and land and not stop until he leaves the demarcation of His Majesty.'[5] Thirty-two years after the Iberians had first carved up the world at Tordesillas, they were reiterating the fruitless claims made at Badajoz. Only occupation could decide. What was at stake was not just honour and imperial possession. It was dreams of unimaginable wealth, the 1,000 per cent mark-up on spices.

In an almost comic gesture of prickly aristocratic protocol, Carquizano's formal letter of reply was deliberately left unsigned because the one he received was without signature. This was taken by Henriques, who had simply forgotten to sign his letter in the rush to get it off, as an affront to his honour. A few days later, a second messenger from Ternate, Fernando de Baldaya, clerk of the trading station, came with the same demand – and received the same reply. The Portuguese were trying to winkle out their opponents without bloodshed.

On 23 December, Carquizano landed with the crew on an uninhabited island to hear mass. Here they considered their position: their backs were against the wall, they were alone, and threatened by a superior force. After all the suffering they had endured, how should they now respond? There was open discussion. 'All jointly and individually replied to the captain that we were all ready and prepared to

127

serve His Majesty and to die in his service and in no way should we give up going to Molucca.'[6] There was talking up: they had plenty of artillery and ammunition and were well armed and as numerous as their opponents. 'On the ship we constituted a hundred and five people of whom there were more than ninety fighting men, gunners and crossbowmen, and everyone [somewhat unbelievably] was as tough and strong as the day we left Spain.'[7] Above all, they evoked the belief that discovery was a God-given national mission and recalled the emperor's heraldic device – a pair of columns that flanked the end of the Mediterranean world inscribed with the motto 'Further'. And so Carquizano, 'seeing in their response the fighting spirit of his men, boarded the ship, distributed the crews into teams ready to fight, had the ship fitted out and prepared with everything necessary and we set out for war'.[8]

On the equatorial line – the point zero of latitude – that cut straight through the tiny chain of clove-bearing tropical islands, two miniature colonial armies were destined to fight an intense and dirty war that dragged in the tribal loyalties and rivalries of the Moluccan islanders on one side or another. Distances between the protagonists were tiny: Ternate and Tidore, each with its dominant volcano curling puffs of steam, faced each other across 1,000 yards of strait, though the swirl of currents and winds could be baffling. Scattered islands with their creeks and coves fringed by transparent seas and backed by jungle provided ample opportunities to launch guerrilla raids, ambushes and surprise attacks. It was a war that was both modern and primitive: European artillery and gunpowder, of which both sides seemed to possess a surprising amount, alongside the Moluccans' weapons – wooden throwing spears with fire-hardened points and iron fighting tools. Its primary vehicles were the light and fast proas – outrigger canoes, equipped with sails – and its variant the kora-kora, traditional to the Moluccas, a war canoe used for raiding and enslaving enemies, that could be rowed by up to a hundred men.

17. The Moluccan kora-kora, a hulled boat with double outriggers, propelled by large numbers of rowers, was used by sultans for ceremonial display, trade and warfare.

Urdaneta was astonished by the first sight of one of the king's fighting proas, intricately made without nails, with stabilising outriggers, a large rowing crew, and a platform for fifty or sixty fighting men. Three hundred years later the British naturalist Alfred Russel Wallace similarly marvelled at the skills of these Moluccan boat builders, working with simple tools, producing wonderful boats using no iron or nails, 'so well done that the best European shipwright cannot produce sounder or closer-fitting joints'.[9]

For all their apparent superiority, the Portuguese position was not as strong as it seemed. Nor was the solidarity exhibited by the Spanish at their rallying mass durable. Fear and uncertainty lingered in the camp. Carquizano soon learned of an attempt by the ship's accountant, Francisco de Soto, to stir up dissent. His resolution to behead the dissident was only staved off by the pleas for mercy from many of the crew.

On 28 December, the *Santa María* set out from the island of Rabo to make its way to Tidore in the company of the royal proa of the king. The Portuguese were watching. 'Two Portuguese galleons and a fusta [light galley] and other vessels and eighty *proas* from Ternate came to fight with us.' It was a feint. Nothing happened. 'They let us pass … Monday 31 December,' Urdaneta wrote in his diary, 'we awoke in sight of the islands of Ternate and Tidore.'[10] On New Year's Day 1527 they rounded the southern tip of Tidore and docked in the bay of its now demolished town, where they were met with heartfelt joy by the boy king and the local populace. 'In truth the Indians wept with pleasure at seeing us, as if we were their cousins or brothers.'[11] The Spanish undertook to defend the people and their island, to build forts on Tidore and Gilolo and to contract for spices. Both sides swore loyalty, on the Qu'ran and the Bible respectively, to the sound of trumpets and gunfire. Carquizano's men then set about building wooden bastions on which to mount artillery, and local people constructed walls and huts to repopulate the derelict town. Preparations were made against attack. A few days later, another visit from Fernando de Baldaya under safe conduct, repeating the request for the Spanish to leave. Polite words had failed. It was now clear from Ternate that only force would shift the stubborn incomers. The Spanish readied their cannon and allocated men to their stations.

Warfare broke out in earnest after the New Year. On 17 January, a midnight attack from Ternate in canoes and fustas, hoping to catch the Spanish off guard. Their objective was to capture or destroy the *Santa María*. 'Thinking we weren't keeping a good guard, they rushed to get towards the ship,' Urdaneta recalled. 'We bombarded each other ferociously. The combat lasted until Friday at noon.'[12] An attempted surprise landing was repulsed. The artillery duel continued throughout the afternoon. As if their intentions were not clear enough, a Portuguese fusta approached sporting a red flag from its fighting spur – the red rag to the bull – 'representing a war of fire and blood'.[13] The next day the bombardment resumed. Volleys of heavy

fire were directed at the *Santa María* from the spur of the fusta 'and
they returned to Ternate thinking they had left the ship in a shape
unfit to sail. The truth is they did us much damage,' Urdaneta
recorded.[14] In fact the real damage to the *Santa María* had been self-
inflicted. Returning fire, the recoil of the cannon had proved too
much for the battered ship that had sailed for a year and a half across
two oceans. The vessel burst its seams and started to sink. All attempts
to pump it failed. The ship was written off and burnt. The Spanish
were now effectively trapped: all they had was one small boat.

The war spread. A counterstrike by canoes from Gilolo, accompanied by Spanish gunners, hunted down a large proa bound for
Ternate, laden with cloves belonging to Garcia Henriques. There
were twenty-three islanders on board and one Portuguese. The
Gilolo men threw themselves into the sea with their weapons and
swam towards their prey. 'The Portuguese raised his hands to us
asking for mercy,' remembered Hernándo de la Torre, the *Santa
María*'s pilot. The Castilians tried to save him but by this time the
swimmers had climbed aboard and thrown him into the water. In his
armour he went to the bottom, 'which our men did not like because
they could not save that Christian'.[15] Twenty-one men were decapi-
tated. One, a Christian convert, killed six of the attackers with a
dagger before they finished him off. The Indians in their proas
returned triumphant, to the beating of drums and blowing of horns.

In the regret for the drowned Portuguese there was a recognition
that the Iberians were a brother people, Christians, and that the
Moluccan islanders, whom they referred to by the generic term
'Indians', were of another world. Urdaneta was repulsed by what he
had witnessed: 'these Indians are absolute butchers and cruel in war
and they cut off the heads of the men they kill and hang them on
poles in the proas and take them to the towns from which they come,
and when they arrive they hold great festivities honouring the
warriors for being brave men. Whoever cuts off a head in war gets a
reward from the king.'[16]

The fighting reached the island of Gilolo. Crippled without any sizeable vessels, the Spanish started to build fustas there and on Tidore with the help of local carpenters, though the work on Gilolo was frustratingly slow; the workforce frequently downed tools on days considered inauspicious by the sultan's astrologer. The canoe raiding and slaving increased. Twenty Spaniards and 300 native warriors attacked the island of Moti; then Urdaneta, scouting another island, attacked a village that refused them supplies, burnt the place and captured a hundred or so men and women, whom they sold elsewhere. The raids and killings were tit for tat. On Shrove Tuesday, Urdaneta and his Gilolo warriors were ambushed by their opponents 'in such a way that a good forty Indians were wounded on our behalf and six were killed, and a companion was also wounded'. Then open warfare in the strait between the Ternate and Gilolo led to a mass engagement – 'we fought until neither they nor us had any ammunition left . . . on one side and the other there were many Indians dead and wounded'.[17]

18. Tidore from Ternate: the arena of war across the narrow strait.

Such encounters were risky but Urdaneta led a charmed life. On 27 March the appearance of two Portuguese proas menacing Tidore demanded a response. Carquizano ordered Urdaneta to put them to flight. In the mêlée a barrel of gunpowder caught alight in his canoe.

[It] burned many of us, and finding myself near the barrel of gunpowder, I jumped into the sea unarmed. By the time I surfaced our proa was fleeing, because the Portuguese, seeing the powder on fire, attacked us. Nothing I shouted nor the blows of the Castilians could persuade the Indian rowers to rescue me and they fled leaving me in the water. Seeing this I began to swim towards the Gilolo proas, and from time to time, putting my head above the water I clapped my hands so that the Castilians in the canoes got to come and help me. The Ternate canoes were bearing down on me firing *berzazos* and shotguns. It pleased our Lord that that those of Gilolo arrived just in time and rescued me so that the enemy didn't harm me. Swimming well that day helped me a great deal. I was very badly burned so that I stayed a good twenty days without leaving a house of the Gilolo Indians.[18]

For ten of those days, he was unable to speak. Seventeen others were burnt, and most of the Castilians among them died. Urdaneta's face was scarred for life.

The warfare was a stop-start affair. A few days later the Portuguese captain-general, Garcia Henriques, asked for a truce. It lasted a month, with a changeover of command in the Portuguese camp. In theory the Portuguese had the resources of Malacca to call on for men and materials, but the fort on Ternate was always under-resourced. The lure of the spice trade had a malign influence on the agents of the crown. Those sent to command in the Spice Islands generally had a greater interest in private gain than defending a royal monopoly. Corruption and lawlessness, and internal jealousies, were rife. The handover from one commander to the next was always tense. It took place in an atmosphere of mutual suspicion. The new appointee risked being kidnapped and having his goods confiscated, while the displaced commander feared lest his replacement invoke a judicial inquiry against him on charges of corruption and arrest him, in which case *his* goods would be sequestered by the new appointee.

All this was in play in May 1527 with the unexpected arrival at Ternate of Jorge de Meneses, appointed commander in place of Henriques. This immediately provoked factional conflict in the Portuguese garrison as Henriques refused to relinquish his post. The discord allowed the Spanish a breathing space. They were able to establish an outpost on Gilolo. In time the circular negotiations went round again: Meneses asking the Spanish to leave and offering to ferry them home; a Spanish delegation, including Urdaneta, countering with their own right to the island and a symmetrical demand. In the midst of this, two Spaniards, Francisco de Soto the Contador (accountant) and one other, defected to the Portuguese. They had decided to take the offer of a way out. Meneses was waiting to strike a decisive blow.

There were accusations of truce breaking on both sides: 'peace with the Portuguese was not concluded', Urdaneta remarked.[19] The dimensions of the contest created much collateral damage and spread well beyond the control of the Europeans into score settling between the island peoples. In May, during the period of truce, two proas with Portuguese on board attacked some fishing boats off Gilolo and killed their crews. Furious at this, Urdaneta himself set out in a canoe with a white flag, asking for a safe conduct to discuss the matter. The native rowers were too frightened to approach the aggressors. Under guarantee of safety, Urdaneta swam over to interrogate them. The Portuguese reply was that they had been going elsewhere for provisions but the vessels had been diverted by the local chiefs to settle a private feud. The enterprising Urdaneta asked who was involved, swam back and recorded the names on a palm leaf.

The attack on Gilolo had killed many locals, whose freedom to go about their business under the terms of the truce had been guaranteed. A knock-on consequence was that the sultan of Gilolo was enraged with the Spanish: they had guaranteed the safety of his people during the truce but instead they had been massacred. He demanded a response. The sultan set out personally for revenge, with Spanish support, intent on ambushing Ternate proas loaded with supplies from other islands in the chain, 'and we intercepted them and killed and captured many Indians and so avenged the past injury', Urdaneta recalled.[20] Urdaneta then found himself at risk of being beheaded by his commander, Carquizano, for truce breaking, but managed to clear his name. The cycles of violence became increasingly bloody and convoluted.

The arrival of Meneses introduced a new level of bitterness. According to Urdaneta's Spanish take on events, it was the Portuguese who were the serial truce breakers. The new governor tried to bribe the sultans to kill the Spaniards. An attempt to poison a well on Tidore stirred the conscience of the Portuguese chaplain, who revealed the plot to his opposite number, 'so we were on our guard for that time, closing the well, and thus being in no danger whatsoever'.[21] Unverifiable accusations of poisoning continued. 'At this time Captain Martin Íñiguez (de Carquizano) sent me to Gilolo to take command of the Spaniards who were there, and to push forward the building of the vessel. While I was there some Portuguese came to Tidore, pretending to want to make peace with us, and they gave some poison to Captain Íñiguez in a cup of wine, of which he presently died.'[22] Elsewhere this was attributed to hearsay. Either way his death was protracted: it took a month.

During periods of uneasy half-truce, there was a to and fro of emissaries and negotiations. Meneses had multiple strategies. In July a Portuguese spy, pretending to be a deserter, showed up in Tidore. 'He was well received and given clothing and a salary like any in our company.'[23] Fifteen days later Meneses sent a delegation across the

strait to negotiate certain things. They brought with them gunpowder grenades which they gave to the 'deserter' to sabotage the
almost finished fusta the Spanish had laboriously constructed. On a
prearranged night he planted the explosives, crept down to the sea
and fired a signal shot. A waiting boat took him off. Shortly after, the
grenades exploded. Urdaneta claimed that the sound alerted the
people, the fire was quickly put out and no real damage was done.
Later it emerged that the boat proved unseaworthy anyway, because
of the Spaniards' ignorance of local timber. The planks of the ship's
sides were unsound and it could not be kept above water. He noted
ruefully, 'Thus, all our labour was lost and in vain.'[24] But clearly the
attack rankled: 'and this is how the Portuguese had behaved with us
during the truces, because they could not achieve the things they
wanted through war; and from our side we preferred a good war to a
bad peace. The result was that one side and the other keeps breaking
the truce.'[25] But this was just the Spanish version of events. The
Portuguese believed, with some justification, that their neighbours
were trespassers across the Tordesillas Line.

Command structures began to fray. The death of Carquizano,
however it happened, was a serious loss. 'We buried him in a church
we had, and God knows how much we missed him for being a very
skilful and courageous man in the position that he held,'[26] wrote
Urdaneta. There was the inevitable leadership crisis: discord and fear
of armed violence as two individuals put themselves forward:
Carquizano's brother and Fernando de Bustamante, a survivor of
Magellan's expedition, who resorted to bribery. Voices became stri-
dent. Finally, the majority demanded a neutral candidate, the reluc-
tant Fernando de la Torre, the pilot who had guided the Santa María.
An oath of loyalty was sworn by all the company on Tidore and
Gilolo.

Increasingly, both sets of Europeans, who had been so eagerly
greeted by the sultans of the Moluccas, were coming to seem the
agents of discord, ratcheting up tribal and inter-island conflict, ampli-

fying grievances between the native peoples. The canoe raids, in which only a handful of heavily armed Spanish or Portuguese participated, led to heavy losses among the indigenous population.

For fifteen months the Iberians attacked and killed each other. Each aggression prompted a response. The miniature sieges, raids and counter-raids seemed interminable. Urdaneta's diary becomes a blur. 'On many other occasions that I haven't set down here we clashed with one another. There were dead and wounded Christians – Castilians as well as Portuguese – and many Indians. If I had to record all the encounters that we had with the Portuguese and their Indian allies and the destruction that we wreaked on the settlements of their allies there would never be an end to it.'[27] Gunfire, bloodshed and double-crossing. The fighting dragged in all the clove-bearing islands, the settlements on Gilolo and other outlying communities, whose inhabitants chose their allegiances variably. Urdaneta travelled widely, conducting canoe raids and defensive operations. Sometimes full-scale battles broke out, in which he routinely claimed Spanish victories.

Particularly fierce was the contest for the clove-bearing island of Makian, which had been a tributary of the king of Tidore. The Portuguese had sacked the island. Its ruler, Quichil Unar, appealed to Tidore. Aware that the Portuguese intended to attack the island again, the Castilians mounted a defence. Two small fleets of canoes met off the coast of Gilolo.

Because there was a great rumour that the Portuguese had a large fleet to destroy Quichil Unar, we Castilians found ourselves in a fierce encounter at sea, together with the men of Gilolo, against the Portuguese and the people of Ternate. We had nineteen proas, the enemy thirty-seven, we clashed two leagues off Gilolo . . . we began to bombard each other in such a way that the engagement lasted more than four hours. With the smoke from powder of artillery and handguns we couldn't see what was going on, nor did the Indians stop hurling great missiles – so many that they fell as thick as rain . . . there was a proa that carried forty archers of these missiles . . . each Indian who fired these carried a hundred of them and the fighting didn't stop until both sides had used up all their ammunition. We wanted to grapple with the enemy hand to hand, but they fled and we pursued them for a long time. Then we turned back to recover the missiles that both sides had fired, and so we returned to Gilolo highly triumphant. There were many dead and wounded among the Indians on both sides, and also wounded Castilians and Portuguese. In this episode Quichil de Roebes, the governor of the island of Ternate, the bravest and most feared among all the Indians, was wounded. He was wounded three times – by a gun, an arrow and a blow on the head.[28]

Despite Urdaneta's claims of successive Spanish triumphs, the situation remained a stalemate. The Portuguese could not dislodge their rivals; the Spanish could never win.

And then, sometime around 20 March 1528, a new twist. The Spanish and supporting tribesmen were attacking a dissident settlement on Gilolo when they spied a European ship approaching from the north. 'We fired two musket shots to see if they responded, but because it was nearly nightfall they turned back out to sea.'[29] From this they deduced that the vessel was Spanish; if Portuguese, the ship would probably have proceeded, as the wind to Ternate was favourable. The next day the guess proved correct. The ship was called the *Florida*, commanded by one Álvaro de Saavedra Cerón. It had come, not via the strait, but from Mexico, at the command of the governor, Hernán Cortés. Behind this lay an astonishing chain of events that went back two years.

Nine

The Voyage of the *Florida*
1526-36

Spain, the summer of 1526. While the Spanish and the Portuguese are trying to throttle each other on the other side of the
world and Loaísa's fleet is being scattered, Charles V, Holy Roman
Emperor and king of Spain, is enjoying a long and rapturous honey-
moon in the Alhambra in Granada. In its fragile Islamic pavilions
with their exquisite abstract geometry, among mirrored pools, the
scent of flowers and the gentle splash of water from fountains and
the mouths of lions, he is getting to know his bride. He has just married a Portuguese princess: Isabel, sister of King John III of Portugal.
It is a political union. They are cousins. This is the dynastic bride
swap: his sister Catherine has been married off to Isabel's brother,
John III – but for Charles and Isabel it soon becomes a marriage of
love. In time workmen will be inserting a coffered wooden ceiling
into one of the pavilions: inset cedar wood squares carrying the
repeating legend '*Plus ultra*' and between, the initials K (Karolus –
Charles) and Y (Isabel) linked by a flower.

At the same time, for Charles the vision of an ever-expanding
empire remained at the front of mind and he was anxious to get news
of Loaísa's fleet and the fate of the *Trinidad*. Given the Portuguese
marriage alliance this was not a tactful moment to be seen launching a

new fleet from Spain. There was now an alternative: despatch ships from the shores of Mexico – New Spain – under the auspices of its captain-general, Hernán Cortés, conqueror of the Aztec empire. In 1521 Cortés' men had reached the Pacific shore. The possibility of forging a route to the Spice Islands from the Americas was already under consideration. Cortés had started shipbuilding on the west coast with this aim. On 20 June 1526, Charles wrote to Cortés, ordering him to mount an expedition, with the repeated mantra, to 'the Moluccas and other lands where spices are found within our demarcation'.[1]

Just as these orders arrived, Cortés received encouragement from another quarter. In the storm that had hit Loaísa's expedition when it entered the Pacific, three ships vanished and were assumed lost. However, one, the tiny pinnace, the *Santiago*, was still afloat but in desperate straits. It had almost no food. Its provisions had been stored on Loaísa's flagship. The *Santiago* had just eight barrels of water, 400 pounds of biscuits reduced to dust and fifty men. There was no possibility of crossing the Pacific alive: food was rationed to 2½ ounces of biscuit a day. The captain then took a bold decision: attempt to sail up the west coast of the Americas in the hope of reaching New Spain. He aimed to keep the crew alive by catching fish along the way. As they worked their way up the coast, they saw signs of habitation. On 12 July they caught sight of people and the curl of smoke, but no contact could be made. By 25 July – after fifty-five days of lone sailing – the crew were starving. There was nothing for it but to get someone to risk his life trying to obtain food from an unknown indigenous people. 'The individual was to take with him scissors, mirrors and other things wherewith to barter with the Indians, so that they might not kill and eat him.'[2] Because they had no ship's boat, the only expedient was to try to get a man through the surf in a large box attached to a rope, so that if the box capsized there was a chance the hapless volunteer might be hauled back alive. The chaplain, Juan de Aréizaga, offered to go. 'Commending himself to God he got into the box in his shirt and drawers, with a sword.'[3]

Halfway to the shore the box upturned. The floundering chaplain was rescued half-dead from the water by five Indians.

Their response was a total surprise. They salvaged his possessions, placed the objects beside him and threw themselves on the ground. 'He wanted to give them some of the things, but they would not take them, and they made signs for him to come with them.'[4] He accompanied them, sword in hand, while one of the Indians carried the hamper of trade goods on his head.

Aréizaga's adventure unfolded like a dream. He walked with them over a headland to 'a great town with many towers'.[5] A huge crowd came out to see Aréizaga, 'all armed with lances, bows and arrows, and in front came ten thousand men, cleaning the road by which they passed'. Here he met the Cacique – the lord – who greeted him cordially. On the way they passed a wooden cross. The astonished chaplain burst into tears. 'He worshipped it on his knees, saying a prayer, all looking at him attentively.'[6] It was providential and extraordinary. He had landed in New Spain.

The Cacique promised food for the ship, which was hailed into the town's port. The crew came ashore on rafts, made shelters on the beach and were handsomely provisioned and entertained by the local people. A few days later a local Spanish governor arrived, carried in a hammock by twelve Indians. On 31 July Aréizaga set out to meet Cortés in Mexico City, where he was graciously received.

Almost at the same time, Charles's order arrived. The two events seemed providential to Cortés. He set about marshalling the ships for a voyage to the Moluccas from the Americas. Cortés fitted out three small vessels that had been constructed along the coast and readied them to sail. The *Santiago* itself was now too battered and worm-eaten to risk the voyage; one of the new ships now carried its talismanic name. The expedition was to be commanded by a kinsman of the governor, Álvaro de Saavedra Cerón.

Saavedra's flotilla was to mount the first attempt to traverse the Mar del Sur from the Americas. The ability of the Spanish to construct ocean-going ships on the west coast of Mexico was in itself a testament to the ever-growing ambition and advance of the peoples of Europe across the globe. Even so, the ships were tiny. The *Florida*, its flagship, the new *Santiago* and the *Espiritu Santu* had a total tonnage less than that of Loaísa's capitana, the 350-ton *Santa María de la Victoria*. These ships' total complement was only 110. Nevertheless, Cortés saw this daring new front on the contest for the Moluccas as the chance to turn the Pacific into a province of New Spain – a Spanish lake.

As was customary, Saavedra was furnished with a set of detailed instructions: 5,000 words comprising thirty-seven carefully phrased items for his attention and the order to go to the Moluccas. The document was both prescriptive, vague and all-embracing. It started with a scrupulous checking off of stores and equipment and then worked through an exhaustive set of requirements. The crew were not to blaspheme, and as dice and card games were a major source of blasphemy against 'Our Lord God, His glorious Mother and His saints',[7] these were banned. Nevertheless, the commander was to allow unspecified and carefully supervised recreation. Managing crew behaviour was critical. As voyages got harder, food supplies dwindled and the death toll rose, murmurings of discontent became inevitable. The threat of defection or mutiny remained a constant. The search for lost fleets or their crews – news of the Loaísa expedition and the rescue of castaways – was part of the brief. Saavedra was to discover new lands and gather intelligence on the Portuguese and their fort when they got to the Moluccas; all native peoples were to be treated well, and friendly relations to be established with their kings. To that end, Saavedra was furnished with letters to these rulers written in Latin, because it was considered to be the most widely used language in the world – at least as seen from Europe. Copies were also made in Arabic. Underlying all this was the now standard injunction to compile lengthy and detailed reports. Like the Portuguese, the Spanish were constructing enormous archives – a continuous and expanding body of information – carried forward from one expedition to the next.

Cortés' instructions also included a second method to outflank Portugal in the spice game: 'You will endeavour very secretly to send, via the ships, some (spice) plants in barrels of earth or in any other way that it seems to you they can travel to be planted here, and you will give responsibility to somebody to care for them, so that they arrive in a state to be planted.'[8]

The ships departed from the well-protected bay of Zihuatanejo, on the west coast of Mexico, on 31 October 1527. The route was not completely unknown. Saavedra had copies of Magellan's charts and those from the Loaísa expedition made available to the *Santiago*'s Portuguese pilot, Ortuño de Alango. They were to take a directly westerly course to Mindanao in the Philippines, then hop south to the Spice Islands. Among the crew was an Italian adventurer called Vicente, from Naples, who – perhaps inspired by Pigafetta – recorded the travails of the voyage.

The newly built ships were soon in trouble. On the eighth day the *Florida* sprung a leak. It was necessary to send men below to man the hand pumps, but the source of the leak could not be found. There followed a conference with the other captains: should they turn back? The pilot, Alango, was of the opinion they should keep going. The strongest sailors were sent to the *Florida* to continue the exhausting pumping work. The other captains urged Saavedra to transfer to another ship. 'He answered that in that ship he had sailed, and in that ship he had to be lost or saved. So, he continued the voyage.'[9]

On the twenty-ninth day, the *Florida* would not respond to the helm. There was another leak in the fore-part of the flagship, 'which filled a compartment of the hold with water, wetting 60 *quintals* of bread, all the oil and vinegar, and other things'.[10] Night was falling and the ship's master refused Saavedra's request to go below and investigate: he would do it in the morning. The helm still would not respond 'and as we were between the two other vessels, we could not give way to them nor them to us, so we dropped astern, and encountered a squall. The man at the helm was negligent, and the ship was taken aback and nearly swamped. At last, we got the sail down. The other ships passed on ahead with a strong wind. And were soon out of sight. We showed many lights but they never answered, and so we lost them.'[11] They too were never seen again.

The *Florida* sailed on across the great blank of the Pacific. It was sixty days before they caught their first sight of land: the now-familiar Los Ladrones, the Islands of Thieves. Saavedra called them the Islands of the Kings, it being Epiphany. The natives of Guam came out to see them: 'well grown, rather brown, with long hair, and no clothes except some matting made of reeds ... so elegantly woven that, at a distance, they look like gold ... the men have beards like Spaniards. For arms they have staves hardened by fire.'[12] They remained circumspect and at a distance. Nevertheless, the crew were able to land and obtain water.

As the days went on, Vicente's narrative started to record the familiar list of deaths. 'The pilot fell ill, and the next day he was very bad. We took him below, and he made his will. When he had finished making it he died ... we made 15 leagues and also consigned the blacksmith to the deep. The next day the cooper fell ill, and died after twenty days. Calm for two days.'[13] The loss of Arango, the pilot, was a particular blow: 'we were left without a pilot and without a man who knew how to take altitude'.[14] The going was tough. Landing on an uninhabited island to bury a sailor, they were detained by bad weather for twenty-eight days. 'Searching for something to eat, we found nothing but shellfish.'[15]

By late February they had reached the coast of Mindanao; here they were greeted by natives in canoes, calling 'Castile, Castile!', and there was an exchange of visitors. A large crowd gathered on the beach to watch, among them three captive Iberian castaways. Despite initially cordial encounters, the local people were edgy. An attempt was made to wreck the ship by stealth. One of the three

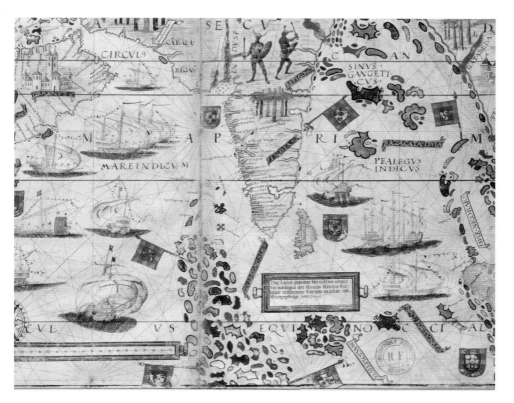

1. In the Miller Atlas, the Indian Ocean is claimed as a Portuguese lake, badged with its flags. The Moluccas are the small group of islands south of India directly beneath the inscription. The maze of fictional islands to their west is intended as a deterrent to rivals.

2. The volcanic Banda islands, the world's only source of nutmeg in the sixteenth century and Francisco Serrão's first landfall on the Spice Islands. A recent lava flow has ripped through the tropical rainforest. The political organisation of the Bandas was unusual; it was governed, with popular consent, by a group of elders.

3. Seville in the sixteenth century, seen across the Guadalquivir River: the gateway to the Americas and the vibrant hub of Spanish exploration. On the horizon sits the tower of the Giralda, once a minaret, then the bell tower of the great cathedral to which returning sailors came to give thanks.

4. The only surviving portrait of Fernão de Magalhães, Fernando de Magallanes, probably sixteenth century. It was painted well after his death, so there is no certainty as to the likeness. Its inscription reads 'Ferdinand Magellan is most famous for having conquered the difficulties of the Antarctic Strait.'

5. The *Santo Niño de Cebu*, the small Christ child figure brought to the Philippines by Magellan, then later rediscovered by the Legazpi expedition, remains deeply revered as a founding image of the spread of Christianity in the islands. It is central to a huge annual religious festival, the Fiesta Señor.

Circulus Aequinoctialis.

Prima ego velivolis ambivi cursibus Orbem,
Magellane novo te duce ducta freto.
Ambivi, meritoq; vocor VICTORIA: sunt mi
Vela, alæ; precium, gloria; pugna, mare.

6. The famous image of the *Victoria*, Elcano's ship, the first to circumnavigate the world, speeding west on the wings of Victory in a map of the Flemish cartographer Ortelius. The ship was extremely small – about 70 foot long, 85 tons in weight – and carried a crew of 55.

7. Richard Chancellor presents his credentials to Tsar Ivan in *The Illustrated Chronicle of Ivan the Terrible*. The Chancellor expedition forged trading links between Russia and England and led to the development of English joint-stock companies that would fund the country's exploration of the world.

8. A replica Spanish galleon, the 500-ton *Andalucia*. Many galleons were much larger, up to 2,000 tons. For 200 years these ships traversed the Pacific between Manila and Acapulco, bringing the high-value goods of the Orient to Mexico and returning with supplies to the Philippines.

9 & 10. Acapulco and Mexico City, links in the chain of global trade. Acapulco (top) was the terminus for ships crossing the Pacific. When the annual galleons arrived from Manila, merchants came for lively seasonal trade fairs. The goods would be carried along tracks and across rivers to and from Mexico City (below). This print of 1700 shows a well-laid-out urban plan, with an aqueduct and many churches. The artist has telescoped into the picture vistas of the Pacific and the lands beyond.

11 & 12. In the sixteenth and seventeenth centuries, silver was the global currency, much of it from Potosí. Its rust red mountain, now hollowed out by hundreds of mining tunnels, rises above the city's colonial period architecture. It produced half the world's silver in the seventeenth century. In faraway Delft, around 1664, Vermeer painted a portrait of a woman weighing silver in a balance, just as the Portuguese missionary Gaspar da Cruz had observed the Chinese doing in Canton. Much of the silver that reached Europe would then be re-exported back to China.

13. Jingdezhen, the porcelain city of China, illustrating all the stages of manufacturing, from raw clay, through forming pots on a wheel, decoration and the firing kilns.

14. Chinese porcelain created for export to the Portuguese market. At the base the coat of arms of the Portuguese king. At the top an armillary sphere, the country's symbol of exploration. Also on the rim the letters IHS – the Latin initials for 'Jesus Christ the Saviour'.

15. Exquisite Japanese painted screens depicted in scrupulous detail the arrival of the Portuguese in their black ships, coated in pitch. To the Japanese the new arrivals were *nanban-jin* – southern barbarians – and these images contain comic perceptions of their strange merchant visitors in outsized ballooning trousers and of the tall black-cloaked Jesuits (on the right).

16. The lure of the volcanic Spice Islands launched the great sixteenth-century European voyages. On the right in the foreground clove bushes with tall clove trees behind. The cloves are being gathered with long poles and dried out on mats – a light, durable cargo, worth its weight in gold.

castaways managed to escape and made it on board. His name was Sebastián, a Portuguese from Oporto, a survivor of a missing ship from the storm that hit Loaísa's expedition, the *Santa María de Parral*, that had been wrecked here. During his stay he had learned something of the local language. Most of the rest of the crew had been killed. He along with two others had been enslaved. Sebastián also claimed to know that eight members of the Magellan expedition had survived the massacre and been sold as slaves to Chinese merchants. Following his orders and his Christian duty, Saavedra determined to try and ransom the other survivors of the *Parral*, who were kept on an adjacent island. Vicente observed the negotiations:

> We reached a port at noon and before anchoring the natives came out to us in a large boat containing twenty persons. They brought with them the two captive Spaniards with their hands tied behind their backs and naked except for a kind of shoes on their feet. The boat came alongside and the Spaniards saluted us in our language. They said that they belonged to the fleet of the Comendador [Loaísa], and had been captives for five months. They entreated the Captain, for the love of God, to ransom them and not to leave them in slavery.[16]

This was accomplished by a gift of gold and an exchange of 'cloths and rich garments of New Spain' for 'provisions, fowls, rice, wine of the country, cloves and cinnamon'.[17] Saavedra had responded to the heart-rending appeal from the two outcasts, but the tale that they told about their circumstances and the fate of the *Santa María* was a fabrication. In time it would unravel.

'We made sail in a southerly course, the wind north,' Vicente went on, 'and proceeded for four days. Always seeing inhabited islands, until we came to the island of Ternate where the Portuguese have a fortress.'[18] This was the ship that the Spanish on Gilolo had seen approach flying the flag of Castile. It was late March 1527. The voyage from New Spain had taken five months and levied the now-familiar death toll: of the 110 who had set out only 30 or 40 were still alive.

As they approached the islands they were met by some Spaniards from Tidore, whom they took on board. Soon after, a Portuguese ship came out to interrogate the *Florida*. Its commander tried to persuade Saavedra that there were no Spanish left in the Moluccas: they had returned to Spain. The appearance on deck of the two Spaniards immediately exposed the lie. The *Florida* continued on its way in the face of Portuguese gunfire. Its arrival in Tidore rekindled the contest. 'From that time on,' Urdaneta recorded, 'the war proceeded with much greater heat.'[19] There was immediate rejoicing in the town from both Fernando de la Torre and the island's king, but reality soon set in. With only these few exhausted men and scant supplies, the *Florida* was in no position to provide ample relief for the beleaguered Spanish, or to tilt the balance of power. It was decided that the ship must sail back and seek help. Saavedra set out in June 1528 with a quantity of spices, taking some Portuguese prisoners with him for questioning, as well as a couple of Portuguese volunteers who had defected. He carried a letter addressed to the emperor describing the Spanish plight and begging for help.

It was the wrong time, the start of the westerly monsoon, and the wrong route. Sailing south and east they made it to New Guinea. There the Portuguese defected, stealing the ship's boat and temporarily marooning the enraged Saavedra on the shore. The winds forced the *Florida* north, past isolated islands where the native peoples were hostile. On Admiralty Island they were showered with arrows; further north, probably in the Carolinas, they were peppered with slingshots and stones. It was increasingly difficult to secure provisions without the ship's boat and the winds remained continuously unfavourable. They turned back. By 19 November the *Florida* had reappeared at Tidore, baffled by the winds and currents, to find that the Portuguese deserters had preceded them. They got their come-uppance and were summarily executed. Another deception also came to light at Tidore. The two Spaniards ransomed by Saavedra on the way across were not the innocent victims of shipwreck that they claimed. They were mutineers who had thrown the captain and senior officers overboard, commandeered the *Santa María de Parral* and wrecked it on the coast of Mindanao. They were also hung and quartered.

The Spanish plight remained desperate. What could they do? They were short of lead, cannon balls, medical supplies – and men. The *Florida* was in poor shape. 'The ship herself was leaky and worm eaten,' recalled Urdaneta. 'We made a sheathing of planks for her sides, with a kind of bitumen which they are accustomed to use here for ships.'[20] De la Torre was insistent that the only way out was west through Portuguese waters; contrary winds would prevent a return to Mexico. But Saavedra was determined. The man who had refused to transfer from a leaking ship on the way out was not to be deterred. He would try a second time by the way he had come. The *Florida* was patched up and set off again in May 1529.

In the Moluccas Spanish morale was at a low ebb. They had been away five years and while Saavedra was attempting a second return crossing, the balance of power shifted decisively towards the Portuguese. In the tit-for-tat fighting the Spanish contingent made a strategic mistake. Half their fighting men set out to attack another island; their departure was probably leaked to Ternate by Fernando de Bustamante, a survivor of Magellan's fleet who had evidently had enough. A quick swoop by their rivals led to the capture and destruction of Tidore. Some surrendered. Others got away to Gilolo and holed up, resolving to fight on. In December 1529, the *Florida* was back again, defeated by the winds for a second time; Saavedra was dead, another body committed to the ocean. The Spanish survivors were slowly being whittled down; more defected to the Portuguese. Yet Urdaneta and a small band still held out in the dense jungles of Gilolo. 'The consequence was that we suffered much misery and anxiety,' Urdaneta later wrote in his report to the emperor:

all for the service of your Majesty, for if we had chosen to go over to the Portuguese we should have been very well off. But we believed that your Majesty would not fail to send a fleet to Maluco, and that we, being there, could be of use to the fleet and of service to Your Majesty. We never thought of joining the Portuguese, but resolved to wait in spite of all risks and hardships, holding it to be our duty to be ready to sacrifice our lives in the service of Your Majesty.[21]

Such loyalty was not to be reciprocated. Towards the end of 1530 they were aghast to learn, from Gonçalo de Periera, the new Portuguese commander, that the emperor had sold his claim to the Moluccas to the Portuguese king for 350,000 ducats. One condition of the Treaty of Zaragoza was that this was only to be a mortgage. The Spice Islands could be reclaimed by returning the money. In reality Charles was always short of cash and he was preparing for war against his rival, Francis I the king of France. Furthermore, there seemed no practical way of maintaining a position on the Moluccas. Charles had effectively bullied the Portuguese into paying for what was rightfully theirs. The redrawn line was now well east of the Moluccas and the Philippines and cut through New Guinea. The news was met with astonishment and disbelief by the Spanish on the ground, after so much suffering and pain. De la Torre initially refused to accept the facts. It took the arrival of another Portuguese governor with official documents to convince him that it was all over.

In the interim, the patience of the local people of both Ternate and Tidore had worn thin. The flashpoint came in Ternate when the Portuguese captain-general Jorge de Meneses ordered a local Muslim man to eat pork as punishment for stealing a pig. A plot was hatched to destroy the Portuguese. Getting wind of it, Meneses beheaded the local governor and several other rajas. There was now a determination to destroy both groups of Europeans. For a while the Portuguese were besieged within the Ternate fort 'so that they could not go more than an arquebus shot from it'. The Spanish also feared for their safety. Driven to extremities, the embattled Europeans came together in mutual recognition and common cause: they signed a peace pact and an alliance. Portugal could maintain its position with support from Malacca; the Spanish could not. All attempts at seeking reinforcements from New Spain had failed and the emperor had cut the ground from under their feet by selling his claim. There was nothing for it but to seek repatriation on Portuguese ships. By 1533 only seventeen Spaniards were left alive. They sailed home in small groups. The Portuguese were determined they should be split up for fear of trouble. They travelled via the Cape, landing in Lisbon and then overland back to Spain.

Urdaneta was among the last to leave. He stayed on to try to secure a shipment of cloves. He reached Lisbon in June 1536, returning with a daughter by a Moluccan woman. He had been away eleven years. He was 17 when he left Spain, 28 when he returned, rich in experience and knowledge. He had seen the world, fought wars, learned local languages, negotiated with tribal leaders and Portuguese governors on behalf of his commanders and travelled widely through the archipelago and beyond – to the nutmeg-bearing Banda islands and Java. Along the way he had garnered invaluable information – cultural, commercial and meteorological. He had made endless canoe trips through the Moluccas and experienced the beauty of the deep tropics. In all vicissitudes he had remained resolutely loyal to an undeserving imperial cause but none of this experience would be wasted.

Arriving in Lisbon, he was stripped of his charts and carefully written reports. On the advice of the Spanish ambassador he made a rapid departure on a borrowed horse over the frontier to Valladolid before the Portuguese could detain him further, leaving his daughter behind in Lisbon. There he rewrote his report to the emperor from memory. Despite having sold his claim, on which the mortgage potential remained, the emperor was urged by Urdaneta not to give up on the Moluccas and to make a treaty there to corner all the trade in cloves, mace and nutmeg for Spain. 'Your Majesty should know that in no other part of the discovered universe are there spices, but only in these islands. So that your Majesty would derive much profit from these islands of Maluco and Banda, for only from the spices there would be a yield of more than 600,000 ducats, not counting the ginger and cinnamon. A treaty for the trade in pepper with Java would also ensure a large profit.'[22]

There would be another large geostrategic gain from maintaining this foothold: 'there are many rich and valuable conquests to be made round Maluco, and many lands with much trade, including China, which might be communicated with from Maluco.'[23] Yet the question remained: it was straightforward to get there but how to return? For the Spanish the Pacific was a dead end: they could sail west from New Spain but they could not get out again without being caught by the Portuguese. It was a problem that would haunt Spanish dreams of expansion for decades. For Urdaneta it was a problem to solve. His reward for a decade's service to the imperial cause was a paltry 60 ducats.

Ten

'End the Suffering'
1542- 6

How big was the Pacific? What were its possibilities? Urdaneta's detailed report had spoken of discovery and subjugation. Charles's motto, 'Further', had been internalised. In the onrush of the conquests of the Americas there was the expectation that there would always be more world to fall into his lap. The new ocean was a space onto which the Spanish projected their imaginings and fantasies. It attracted conquistadors, adventurers, fortune seekers, mystics and missionaries. It was the golden key to the Spice Islands and Marco Polo's China. There were islands that loomed out of its flat expanse and vanished, that could not be verified a second time, mystical prophecies that somewhere in the great ocean lay the biblical lands of Tharsis and Ophir, where King Solomon gathered his treasure. More pragmatically, Cortés, the ruthless plunderer of the Aztec empire, saw the sea as a potential personal fiefdom.

The Pacific had checked the Spanish. They had crossed the Atlantic and established a reliable there-and-back route, via its fixed wind system, so why not this ocean? In the first decade after Magellan's voyage ten ships had sailed west from New Spain; only one had returned – and that through Portuguese waters. Very few who sailed saw Spain or New Spain again. The death count had been staggering. The three expeditions to date had tracked multiple path-ways across an ocean that seemed to offer nothing. Its eastern half was empty. When they had landed on islands to the west they met with unpredictable responses from the native people: sometimes friendly, more frequently with hails of arrows and stones. Deserters and castaways were scattered across the ocean, ships vanished, leaving trails of legend and supposition.

It was straightforward to cross the ocean by sailing west but its extent was hard to assess, given the speed of travel. The difficulty in measuring longitude rendered judgements variable but the voyage was always punishing. The attempt to sail back – *el tornaviaje* – had repeatedly failed. The Pacific was a lobster pot: easy to get into, impossible to back out of. Knowledge of its winds and currents was partial. Saavedra, who had providentially caught the trade winds by sailing at the end of October, had constructed the best outward route, avoiding the snare of dangerous atolls that could rip a ship open; his attempt to return, trying to make it back through low latitudes, had been just one more failure. Henceforth a modicum of wisdom prevailed: there would be no more expeditions launched from Spain via the Strait of Magellan. The route was too punishing. Two further attempts in the 1530s ended in disaster. Henceforth all forays across the Mar del Sur would be from the coast of New Spain.

The Pacific remained European cartography's largest blank, its last great frontier. Spanish acceptance of the Zaragoza treaty had been grudging. It was widely considered a sell-out. Charles and many of his subjects still convinced themselves that the Moluccas were lawfully theirs. Even though the claim had been leased, the belief in their right and the expectation of endless expansion cancelled any scruples. The sober, factual reporting of Urdaneta had been influen-tial. For Spain, the Pacific remained the key to the wealth of the Orient, and the key to the Pacific lay in the trick of getting back. Any hope of pioneering the return journey rested on the creation of a secure and well-provisioned base where their battered ships could be repaired and their sailors nursed back into health. Urdaneta had identified the archipelago to the north of the Moluccas, dubbed by Magellan the Islands of the West (the Philippines), as the ideal place to establish themselves. These had not been settled by the Portuguese, but, though not mentioned by name in the Zaragoza treaty, they lay definitively within the Portuguese zone – an inconvenient detail it would be best to ignore. It was on the Philippines that the Spanish now pinned their hopes.

When Urdaneta was in Valladolid reporting to the Council of the Indies, he encountered the aristocratic Pedro de Alvarado, conquistador of much of South America and governor of Guatemala, a man of legendary cruelty. Alvarado was planning a new expedition to the Islands of the West and the coast of China. At enormous expense he had assembled a fleet of thirteen ships with 550 men, for which the material had been portaged from Vera Cruz on the Atlantic Coast over the isthmus. He offered Urdaneta the position of chief pilot. Urdaneta sailed back to the Americas, but Alvarado's expedition never happened. In a native uprising, in which Urdaneta fought, Alvarado was crushed to death by a bolting horse. Urdaneta did not sail. In 1552 he joined the Augustinian order and retired into a monastery.

Instead, in the jostling for position and wealth among the conquistadors and nobility, another carefully structured expedition came into being at the behest of the first Viceroy of New Spain, Antonio de Mendoza. He recruited his brother-in-law, Ruy López de Villalobos – family connections always played a part – to lead a new venture across the sea. It had well-defined aims: to establish a secure base in the Islands of the West and, after three failed attempts, to solve the problem of the tornaviaje once and for all. At the same time, another expedition was to sail north up the coast of America to China, in the belief that the two were conjoined somewhere to the north-west. This latter, under the command of Juan Rodríguez Cabrillo, made it up the coast of California but was beaten back by the winds. Cabrillo died during a skirmish with the native people and the mission was aborted.

The Villalobos expedition was to be a *Mayflower* venture, an ambitious project with a tightly defined purpose. Villalobos was titled governor of a fortified settlement to be created in the Islands of the West. Supplies included wheat seed for a new colony to plant. As per usual, the commander was hedged in with detailed and exhaustive instructions that contained counsels of perfection covering all aspects of provision and ship management, and the by now obligatory command to treat indigenous people with kindness and not to infringe on Portuguese territory. All crew members were to swear oaths of loyalty – the threat of mutiny was always uppermost in mind – and men who fell asleep at their post were to be keel-hauled. On a second offence they should be thrown overboard. The mission had a strong religious dimension: to convert native peoples, but with the utmost sensitivity. There were four Augustinian friars and four other clerics on board: Villalobos was instructed that the main purpose of his journey was to extend the Christian faith. Every man had to provide a certificate that they had confessed and taken communion before stepping aboard. Blasphemy would result in imprisonment and reduction of rations. Above all, there was the insatiable demand for knowledge that drove the European advances across the globe: the injunction to be endlessly curious. Those who returned to New Spain by the anticipated route were to report on all aspects of the voyage. They were to bring samples of the things they had discovered, deliver accounts of native clothing and customs, religious practices and political relationships. There were extraordinary levels of remote micro-management.

Seven ships were to go, drawing on the original fleet of Alvarado and commanded by Villalobos in the capitana, yet another *Santiago*, with 400 soldiers and seamen, and including a contingent of noblemen – 'Knights, Sons of Someone'[1] – who brought their own servants from New Spain. There were several survivors of previous

Pacific voyages, some who went back years: Ginés de Mafra and the German gunner Anes had circumnavigated the world with Magellan two decades earlier.

The fleet departed from the coast of Mexico on the morning of 1 November 1542, All Saints' Day. The intention had been to spend some time in the coastal fishing grounds of California stocking up, but finding the winds against them they decided to press on. It was the first of a series of mistakes. Food supplies were to be a constant issue.

The voyage unfolded in a familiar way. Small islands were discovered or rediscovered and named after saints' days or physical features. The ships were pushed forward by currents faster than the pilots could calculate, so that they would grossly underestimate the distance to the Philippines, convincing themselves that these islands indeed fell within the Spanish claim. Along the way the litany of accidents: near groundings on unsuspected shoals that caused temporary panic; ships that collided; one that was attacked so violently by a whale that its bow was almost lifted clean out of the water, leaving the great wounded beast to swim away trailing clouds of blood; storms that caused the sailors to beseech God's mercy; ships that vanished only to reappear weeks later. They passed on through belts of islands, striking up conversations with indigenous people as they went, searching for castaways from previous expeditions. Approaching the island of Fais in the Carolines they had a sense that they were nearing their goal when they were met by islanders with the greeting 'Buenos dias, matalotes'.

They reached Mindanao on 1 February 1543. The crossing had taken a rapid ninety-three days. The goal of the expedition had been the small island of Limasawa, set in the strait between Mindanao and an island in the chain further north, Leyte, but they had misplotted their course. Their landfall on Mindanao, at a place called Banganga, proved inhospitable. Nevertheless, Villalobos stepped ashore and claimed possession of the island for Spain. He named it

Cesarea Caroli, in honour of the emperor. Currents and seasonal winds made it impossible to sail north to Limasawa. The problem of feeding the large number of men on this ambitious expedition quickly became a problem. Hunger stalked the fleet. According to one eyewitness, it brought 'a sickness unknown to us, a swelling of the gums and legs, with purple splotches on the skin'.[2]

Finding a reliable food source became the key driver. Villalobos moved the fleet south to the small island of Sarangani, on the advice of a crew member who had accompanied a previous expedition. The villagers refused to sell them food. In desperation, Villalobos obtained a let-out from the clergy regarding the emperor's commandment to treat native people with kindness. The Spaniards attacked the community and drove them from the island. It was first in a series of bloody colonial encounters and, for the Spanish, the start of a slow-motion catastrophe. Whatever they gleaned remained insufficient to feed them all. The crew showed no interest in planting the corn seed: they had come to conquer. They took to scavenging, eating unripe coconuts and worse. 'Ultimately, we ate all the dogs, cats and rats they could find, as well as filthy bugs and unrecognizable plants. All of this was the cause of death for many and serious illnesses for others. In particular many men ate the great lizards – large shiny things – and only a few of those who ate them are still alive. At the end, some ate land crabs and went mad for a day, especially if they ate the intestines.'[3] The expedition was in free fall.

Somehow, food had to be obtained. Villalobos learned that there were good supplies of rice on Mindanao. An expedition there found itself again engaged in bloody conflict, in which many died on both sides. The repeat refusal to sell the Europeans food and the ferocity of the defence was due in part to the presence of the ousted people of Sarangani. In the midst of this, one mislaid ship, the *San Cristobal*, turned up with supplies that provided temporary relief, but at every turn Villalobos took the wrong option. A seasonal shift in the weather provided a window to sail to Limasawa but he spurned it. Instead, he just lengthened the odds: commanding the *San Juan de Letran* to return to New Spain and seek aid and reinforcements was a very long shot.

Meanwhile, an attempt to obtain supplies from another small island, Sangihe, brought more fierce resistance. Worse, several of the ships were wrecked or damaged on the return; precious supplies of armaments were lost. Scouring the archipelago for food sources became increasingly fraught. By this time any injunction to treat the native population with consideration had been totally forgotten. The men were desperate. Further bloody assaults on the Mindanao rice fields only deepened the disaster. A galleon, the *San Jorge*, was lost in a storm on the return. Fifty-six men died and the king of Mindanao captured its guns and arms. 'It was a huge loss,' recorded an anonymous witness, 'partly because the ship was the best in the fleet, and no other remained apart from the capitana, but also the contents. I've mentioned the clothing of the soldiers but there was also heavy artillery, munitions and arms, making it the most heavily armed ship in that entire land. So even if they gathered rice, it could well be said that they paid the price, not just in property and armaments, but in the lives of fifty-six men killed.'[4]

Villalobos was soon feeling the squeeze from another direction. In the midst of all his troubles a Portuguese delegation turned up from Ternate with a written order for the Spaniards to leave Portuguese territory. Villalobos stoutly disputed the claim: it was on the Spanish side of the line. The Portuguese returned to reiterate the demand. The downward spiral continued.

It became essential to establish a more promising base and secure better food supplies. The commander resolved to move his settlement north. The Spanish had turned Sarangani into a wasteland, cutting down 30,000 coconut trees just to get at the fruit. On All Saints' Day 1543, exactly a year after he had set out, Villalobos left the ruined island. He was reduced to one ship and two brigantines – small sailing ships. Again, he had left it too late. Winds forced him back. The expedition was collapsing and the local population had had enough. The men were scattered in different islands. The Spaniards had to fight their way out of an ambush, disguised as a feast. The men were exhausted and starving. There was nothing for it now but to sail south, into Portuguese territory, towards the Moluccas in search of relief. In early January 1544 they reached Zamafo on Gilolo.

Immediately, they found themselves caught up once again in the inter-island politics that dominated the Moluccas. An order from the Portuguese to leave forthwith was again rebuffed. Villalobos replied that his men were sick from pure hunger and on the point of death. He needed provisions and time for ship repairs. The Portuguese demanded that they surrender at Ternate. Villalobos replied tartly. 'It would seem to be the duty of Christians ... to provide remedies with which to cure the sick, rather than make such demands 'without providing the means to put then into effect.'[5] 'Our men were totally disgusted at the lack of charity,' one man reported.[6]

The Gilolo people soon tired of providing them with food, so they moved on to Tidore. In May 1544, the *San Juan de Letran* returned, having failed to sail back to Mexico. There were desperate attempts to patch her up for a second attempt. Unaccountably, Villalobos then sold his flagship, the *Santiago,* to a Portuguese merchant, in the mistaken belief that it was unfit for a long sea voyage. Like a gambler becoming increasingly reckless, the commander pinned his hopes on one more attempt by the *San Juan* to reach New Spain, this time trying a more southerly route. The ship reached a large island, which Villalobos named New Guinea and claimed for Spain, but, with the winds against him, the ship had to return to Tidore.

When a new Portuguese fleet arrived from Malacca it was all over. Although a body of his now diminished crew initially resisted Villalobos's order that they surrender and seek repatriation on Portuguese ships, there was no alternative. Rubbing salt into the wounds, the survivors were to be transported on the *San Juan*, their own ship, which Villalobos had by now also sold. On 18 February

1546, three years after they had set out, Villalobos stepped aboard. Along with many of the crew, he was terribly sick, shaking with fever, and despondent. He called the survivors to him and apologised for the failure of the expedition. Even those who had opposed him were reduced to tears. He died at the port of Ambon on 16 April 1546 and was buried in the dress of an Augustinian friar. According to the Portuguese, Villalobos died of a broken heart. Stragglers of the expedition made it home on Portuguese ships. Out of the 550 who set out, about 117 were alive at Malacca. How many, in their weakened condition, were unloaded at Lisbon is unknown.

Villalobos's doomed voyage had not been completely in vain. They had charted many islands, the failed returns of the *San Juan de Letran* added information about the Pacific winds and the expedition had added new names to the map: New Guinea, and the archipelago that became henceforth known as Las Filipinas. It remained the focus of Spanish ambitions.

It seems likely that in his last days Villalobos was ministered to by the missionary Francis Xavier. Xavier, who was one of a number of priests sent to Asia at the request of the Portuguese king, John III, to spread the Christian faith, was to be an engaged participant in the Portuguese and Spanish exploration of the Spice Islands, Japan and China. In the Moluccas he had witnessed many pointless deaths. He sent a message back to Charles by way of Portugal: end the suffering. Send no more ships. There had been six failed attempts. And indeed, no more ships were sent in Charles's reign. One man who followed all these events with intense interest was Andrés de Urdaneta back in Mexico.

Eleven

'The Infernal Labyrinth'
1536- 40

Even without the Spanish incursions, for the Portuguese the Moluccas were far from a tropical paradise. Antonio Galvão, who came in 1536, was struck with foreboding:

> The shape of these islands is that of a sugarloaf, with the base going downwards into the water, surrounded by reefs at little more than a stone's throw: at ebb tide one can go there on foot. One can put into the islands through some channels in the reef which outside is very high; and there is no place to anchor except in certain small sandy bays: a dangerous thing! They look gloomy, sombre and depressing. That is the way they strike the onlooker at first sight: for always, or nearly always, there is a large blanket of fog on their summits. And for the greatest part of the year the sky is cloudy, which makes it rain very often; and if it does not, everything withers but the clove tree, which prospers. And at certain intervals there falls a dismal, misty rain, which makes the goats become lame and sometimes kills them . . . Some of these island spit fire and have warm waters like hot springs. And they are so thickly crowded with groves as to look like one big mass of them, and they are therefore hiding-places for evil-doers.[1]

The equatorial tropics: dense, rank and dangerous, a place where murder lurked, where the rain falls incessantly, a world of head hunters, crocodiles and snakes large enough to swallow a man, a place 'where nothing may be considered incredible, although we have examples and admonitions that one should not recount sensational things'.[2]

The Jesuit missionary Francis Xavier, who arrived a few years later, was struck by the sheer geological instability of the Moluccas:

One of the islands is almost continually, throughout its length and breadth, shaken by earthquakes, and it sends up flames and ashes. The natives say that the violence of the subterranean fire is so great, that the strata of rocks on which a certain town is built are all on fire. What they say seems credible; for it often happens that large red-hot stones, as big as the largest trees, are hurled into the air, and when there is a very strong wind such a quantity of ashes is sent up from the cavities that the men and women who are at work in the country come home so covered with ashes that you can hardly see their eyes or nose or face. You would think they were rather demons than human beings. This is what the natives tell me, for I have not seen it myself; during the whole of my stay there were no tornadoes. I also heard from them that during these violent winds the ashes are carried up into the air in such quanti-ties that numbers of wild boars are blinded and suffocated by them, and that after the storm they find them dead in the fields. They say, too, that during these tornadoes numbers of dead fish are found on the shores, killed in the same manner – the proof of this being that fishes who have drunk water in which ashes are sprinkled generally die. They asked me what it all meant. I told them this place was the abode of hell.[3]

Xavier's assessment of the islanders was bleak – he described them as 'very barbaric and full of treasons . . . people who poison those whom they don't like, and in this manner they kill one another aplenty'.[4] Missionary work was dangerous and unrewarding.

António Galvão was the seventh Portuguese captain-general of the Moluccas, sent out by King John III on a four-year term with a remit to ensure the royal monopoly on the export of cloves. Where the later settlement in Macau would be the work of freelance merchants, the Spice Islands remained a conquest project, enrolled within the formal Portuguese empire, yet so far away as to render royal edicts ineffective. Xavier reckoned that to send a letter back to Europe and receive a reply involved a three-year wait. Even communications from Goa only came once a year.

What disturbed Galvão was that there was no ethnic, racial, political or linguistic unity. 'These people', he wrote, 'have many and different languages so that the islands represent a Babel ... for not only does every one of them have its own, but there are also towns with different languages.'[5] This splintering of islands, languages, tribal groups and trading interests rendered the Portuguese intention of monopoly trading doomed from the start. Galvão, an educated, intelligent and capable man of unbending probity, had stepped into a hornet's nest of inter-island rivalries and Portuguese corruption – 'the infernal labyrinth',[6] he called it, to which the irruptions of the Spanish voyages had added another layer. He found the island of Ternate 'in a worse and more ruinous state than had been recounted to him; the island depopulated, the town burnt, everything destroyed'.[7] 'This country is always in revolt,'[8] and as for the native people, 'they are intriguers, treacherous, malicious, untruthful and ungrateful'.[9]

The deep tropics had a corrupting effect on the Portuguese. Afonso de Albuquerque, a generation back, had spoken presciently of the nature of his country's colonial adventure: 'Portugal is very poor and when the poor are covetous they become oppressors. The fumes of India are powerful – I fear the time will come when instead of our present fame as warriors we may only be known as grasping tyrants.'[10] The fumes of Ternate and Tidore were literally very powerful. Where some of the captains tasked with securing a spice monopoly attempted to obey the royal command, most just came to line their own pockets and those of their relatives. In a letter back to the Portuguese king, it was clear that the Moluccas were well beyond royal control: 'captains, who, being so far from authority's reach, pursue their own whims rather than Your Service, because we have the kind here who do not follow their orders either in whole or in part, nor allow the other officials to follow theirs – not even their magistrates [to enforce] the ordinances'.[11]

Galvão conjured a world of colonial evil – further complicated by the Iberians fighting their own proxy war – a sort of Botany Bay for the criminalised flotsam of Portugal's imperial project. It was the end of the line: 'the murderers come to India, and from there they are degraded to Malacca, and for the monstrous cases they are transplanted to Maluku, which is the hotbed of all the evils of the world'.[12] It started from the top. One honest captain, Gonçalo de Pereira, was killed by his own men for trying to stamp out the clove smuggling. During the sixty years that the Portuguese clung to Ternate, the behaviour of many of the other captains sent out to manage provided a catalogue of cruelty and avarice. Meneses had Moluccans torn to pieces by dogs. Tristão de Ataide, Galvão's predecessor, cut off hands, noses and ears. He also had the unique distinction of uniting the warring sultans of Ternate and Tidore in an alliance to expel the colonial oppressors. Duarte de Deca had the loyal sultan of Ternate stabbed to death and his body cut up and thrown into the sea to prevent a decent burial.

'These islands', wrote João de Barros, the contemporary Portuguese historian, on the malevolent influence of spices, 'are a warren of all evil, and have no one good thing but the clove; and since it is a thing that God has made, we can call it good; but in so far as it is the material cause of our people going there, it is an apple of all discord. And one could curse it more than gold itself.'[13]

In all the comings and goings of colonial officials, Galvão stood out. He was successful in both stabilising the Portuguese position and winning back some trust among the islanders. He secured the fort on Ternate, cajoled all the resident Portuguese merchants into a spirited defence, waged war on Tidore and its allies, and broke up the league against the Portuguese. He was imbued with unflinching determination but was sensitive to local customs and fair in his dealings, refusing to take vengeful reprisals and forbidding his men to destroy crops and plantations. He engaged in construction work. The Ternate fort was rebuilt. The hazardous channel by which ships approached Ternate was cleared of reefs to create a secure anchorage – 'a very reassuring work, both for the Portuguese and for the native people'.[14] If his third-person account of his time – *A Treatise on the Moluccas* – presents him as a paragon of virtue, he was unique in restoring a modicum of peace to the islands. Even shipwrecked Castilians, no subjects of the Portuguese king, thanked him for calming troubled waters.

In the end Galvão was defeated by circumstances. The Portuguese merchant population had no taste for colonial management and a royal spice monopoly. The aroma of cloves was too alluring. 'Once the Portuguese had got the smell of cloves and peace, he could never again gain control of them,'[15] was his complaint. Galvão's position was completely undermined by an order from Goa re-establishing the right to private trading; his authority now gone, he departed back to Lisbon in disgrace, where he received no thanks and died in poverty, undoubtedly briefed against by his enemies. Distant kings, both Portuguese and Spanish, signally failed to value and support their most loyal and industrious servants.

Only a draft of Galvão's *Treatise on the Moluccas* survives. It was partially a personal defence, written in poverty in the face of critics, and probably in hope of a royal pension. If laced with European prejudice, it also comprised an enormously engaged anthropology and natural history, a description of all aspects of the Spice Islands and their peoples: their flora and fauna, the power structures of the tribal groups, their religious beliefs, foundation myths, sexual practices, warfare techniques, festivities, agriculture and much more besides.

Galvão recorded the cultural complexity of the people and the richness of the islands' natural history: seas amazing in their wealth of fish ('haddocks, barracudas, turbots, mackerels, surmullets, and soles, shads, sardines, turtles'),[16] the vast variety of plants and trees. Above all, those the Portuguese had come to find: the clove ('like a laurel tree') and 'the tree supplying nutmeg and mace ... [like] a pear tree'.[17] These were the products they had sailed the world to trace back to their source and to describe:

As soon as the clove begins to ripen, they gather it; for if they let it attain ripeness, it becomes woody and falls without being of any use. The harvesters climb up the trees and take with them a rope and a pole. They throw the rope down, and those standing there tie a basket to it, and it is hoisted up. And they fasten it with some cord around their shoulders, and thus it stays on their back. They pick the clove with their hands, breaking the ends of the boughs bearing it, and throw it into the *saloi* [basket]. Where their hand cannot reach, they substitute the pole for it; and when the basket is filled, they send it back down the rope ... and they put it out to dry on mats in the sun or on reeds in the smoke as [one does with] chestnuts.[18]

Despite Galvão's gloomy prognosis about the Moluccas, there was much to wonder at and admire. During the Ramadan festival, the Muslim converts lit candles and made them 'float on the sea, where they go burning during the whole night, for they are made of pitch and oil, and the water looks wholly covered with them'.[19] He, like Urdaneta before him and Alfred Wallace long after, commented on the ingenious construction of the many types of local boats, made without nails or caulking, that were reversible, 'so that they can sail forwards and backwards',[20] the quality of their oars ('beautifully worked and light'),[21] and some boats, at the prow, with 'a high snake's neck with the head of a serpent and the horns of a deer'.[22] Large royal galleys were rowed by up to 200 men. 'They carry with them drums, gongs and *sistra*, this being a royal privilege, to the music of which they row and sing rhythmically as the people of Galicia do. [In singing] they mention everything they did or hope to do both in peace and in war.'[23] He noted their boat races and mock tournaments:

They come to these with their swords covered with inlay work . . . and their shields are painted red, with carvings of yellow, and inlaid with cowrie shells. On the head they wear a kind of helmet with green, red and yellow crests of fibres which come from Persia; and on the forehead they wear wide plumes of many-coloured feathers like fool's caps, which they agitate so much to resemble cockatoos. They run and jump from one side to the other with great ferocity.[24]

Their pastimes included chess, bowls, dice, javelin throwing – and the game that was universal even then: 'They play at ball with the foot. They must not touch the ball with the hand . . . [the balls] are made of rattan; they are quite round like those one blows up with air.'[25]

Galvão's treatise was addressed to the Portuguese king and had been compiled at his request: 'I have received the news that Your Highness has written to Your Governor and Captains that they should try to find out the way of life of the countries, their products, in which latitude and climate they are situated, and the customs, costumes and languages of their inhabitants.'[26]

Information, often obtained in dialogue with local people, was gold; it powered the engine that was driving European expansion across the world and ushered in a new era of archival management and data collection. Both the Portuguese and the Spanish were avid for knowledge in the form of maps, pilots' charts, sailing routes, commodity prices, meteorology, languages, geography and ethnology. In this respect, the Portuguese, with their long apprenticeship in exploration on the way to India, led the way. It was a state obligation for ships' captains to draw maps, record latitudes and garner descriptions of peoples and places. A succession of institutions were created to centralise control over imported goods and knowledge gleaned from these voyages. From the late 1400s, the Casa da Guiné da Mina, generally known from 1500 as the Casa da Índia, held the Padrão Real, a master map of the world, continuously updated by information from incoming fleets, the contents of which the authorities aimed to keep secret.

Spain, slightly later in the game, had adopted the Portuguese approach in the establishment of the rival Casa de Contratación in Seville in 1503, with its own Padrón Real, routinely updated to furnish pilots on successive expeditions with the latest navigational information. The Iberian pioneers were Renaissance accumulators of data, constructing virtuous circles of knowledge and capability – powerful feedback loops. It was these formidable skills, developed during an apprenticeship down the coast of Africa, that had allowed the Portuguese, despite the limited horizon that could be scanned from a ship's mast, to work out in a few short years the commercial and strategic structure of the Indian Ocean.

With information came secrecy. The contents of the Casas were classified state documents, closely guarded by royal officials. As early as 1505 King Manuel I of Portugal banned the construction of globes and the reproduction of charts. The competing Iberian monarchs strove to redact and distort knowledge useful to their rivals. Maps such as the Miller Atlas became tools of propaganda, particularly with reference to the positioning of the Spice Islands and the Tordesillas Line, shunted one way or the other to prove ownership. As word of the new discoveries of the world spread across Europe, there was avid interest from merchants and monarchs and thinkers. The Portuguese, who knew most about spices and their origin, published almost nothing in the first half of the sixteenth century. They maintained a studied policy of silence, even if accounts circulated in manuscript form. Galvão's definitive account of the Moluccas never saw the light of day; his one published work on the history of the discoveries never mentioned the Spice Islands; the first volume of the mid-century Portuguese historian Fernão Lopes de Castanheda was withdrawn for 'correction' and the last two suppressed altogether by royal command. The *Suma Oriental* of Tomé Pires, by now dead in China, an informed account of commercial traffic in the East, lacked its chapters on the spice trade. They were not restored until 1944.

And yet, despite their best efforts – and those of their Spanish rivals – it was impossible to maintain a watertight ship. Secrets leaked out. The Portuguese relied heavily on outsiders in their ventures; knowledge was a sellable commodity and Portugal's own intellectual capital had a ready market across the Spanish frontier. Returning sailors could be bribed; maps and rutters could be bought or borrowed; copies could be made; pilots and mapmakers could defect to Seville; spies came to Lisbon. Among those who went over to Spain were the cosmographer Ruy Faleiro, a key organiser of Magellan's voyage, Duarte Barbosa, the knowledgeable author of a book on the East, destined to die in the Philippines, the cartographers Pedro Reinel and Luís Teixura, and Portuguese pilots who were eagerly sought for their expertise.

The Venetian spy Ca' Masser, posing as a merchant, learned a great deal on the Lisbon waterfront in 1504. 'I have seen the sailing charts of the route to India, and how this shows all the places the Portuguese trade and deal in and have discovered,'[27] he wrote back. At about the same time a beautiful copy of a Portuguese world map, the Cantino Planisphere, made it to Ferrara. The sole draft of Galvão's treatise on the Moluccas was acquired by the Spanish royal cosmographer Alonso de Santa Cruz, and was only discovered in the Seville archives much later. Ca' Masser wrote back home in code. The sixteenth century was a golden age of cryptography. Encoded messages passed to and fro among the courts of Europe. In the entangled world of international diplomacy, secrets, plans and plots were disseminated in numbers and tantalising symbols.

Fanning the bushfire of European Renaissance curiosity about the voyages of discovery was the explosion of printing. An increasingly literate public was hungry for knowledge about the world. Marco Polo's *Travels* was widely translated and printed. Illustrated broadsheets of the letters of Amerigo Vespucci, produced in 1505, went through twenty-five editions in a few years – most in the German-speaking world, where merchants were calculating the potential. Trade centres were printing centres: Venice, Lisbon, Seville. Antwerp, Lyons, London. First-hand accounts of new worlds were at a premium and, sensing opportunity, printers obliged, publishing in vernacular languages. In mid-century the Italian geographer Giovanni Ramusio produced *Navigationi et Viaggi* ('Navigations and Travels'), a series of volumes collecting first-hand travel accounts. These included the *Suma Oriental* of Tomé Pires, although Ramusio was ignorant of its author, and it lacked the most secret and valuable description of the Spice Islands. The hunger for maps was intense, and the creation of globes allowed Europeans to survey their planet, to experience it as an entity: a mind-bending realignment of the place of humans in their world. In 1548 Giacomo Gastaldi produced the first 'pocket book' atlas. You could hold the world in your hand; you could spin it round on a globe; you could circumnavigate it with your finger. In the process the furthest reaches of the world were coming into view: Marco Polo's China and the Spice Islands too. Gastaldi's maps were the first to refer to Gaitam (Japan) in place of Zipangu, the name used by Marco Polo. This torrent of mapping was literally reshaping the world – Mercator's world map came in 1569, and Ortelius's *Theatrum Orbis Terrarum*, the first true modern atlas, the following year. Both acknowledged the vast extent of the Pacific Ocean.

The information revolution that began in the first half of the sixteenth century saw the printing of some 10 million books. The second half witnessed a dizzying acceleration. Over the whole century, book production totalled 150–200 million volumes, dwarfing the whole of human history's previous written output. This ever-expanding world of new knowledge opened up by the Portuguese and the Spanish rapidly increased European understanding of the world and the possibilities for discovery and conquest.

The Portuguese had rightly feared espionage and the power of print. In the end their spice monopoly would be destroyed by a spy who wrote a book. Jan Huygen van Linschoten, a Dutch secretary to the bishop of Goa in the 1580s, stole their trade secrets. He surreptitiously copied charts, maps and navigational information that provided a blueprint for voyaging to the East and trading there. His *Itinerario*, published in Dutch, and soon after in English, was the weapon that would launch the Dutch assault on the spice trade. One book was enough to dismantle the Portuguese empire in the Moluccas and the Bandas.

But attempts to outflank Iberian claims on the world started much earlier. By the 1530s northern Europeans in Seville were already eyeing the prize.

PART III

CONNECTIONS:
LINKING THE WORLD

1553-71

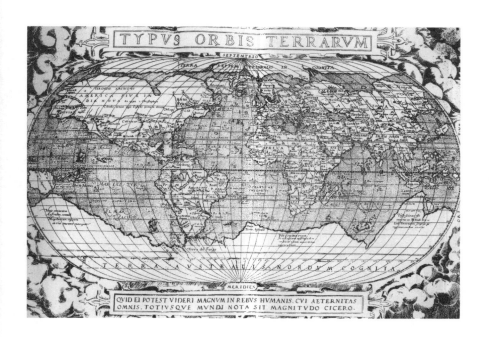

Twelve

The Haven of Death
1553- 6

By the 1520s Seville had become one of the most dynamic cities in Europe, the capital of Spain's burgeoning empire in the Americas and the gateway to the New World. It was from here that Magellan had departed; and here that the ghost crew of the *Victoria* had staggered ashore and astonished Europe. Seville had its disadvantages. It lay 60 miles up the Guadalquivir, but it was safe from maritime attack. It had become a magnet for the ambitious, the adventurous and the needy: navigators, sailors, cartographers, merchants, religious orders, mystics, chancers, thieves and prostitutes – a city of splendour, violence and destitution. The city resounded to periodic bursts of cannon fire, announcing the departure of ships to the Americas. Its wharves saw the unloading of spices, precious metals, wood and enslaved people. The bells of its enormous Gothic cathedral pealed from the Giralda, the converted minaret of the city's great mosque. With the scent of oranges and the whiff of tar and its memories of the lost civilisation of Andalusia it conjured up worlds. 'You are no city, you are a universe,' wrote Fernando de Herrera, the poet laureate of Seville.[1]

At the heart of the city's merchant activities was the imposing Casa de la Contratación – the house of trade for the Indies – from where the commercial and maritime activities of Spain's new empire were regulated. It also functioned as a navigation school, overseen by the royally appointed figure of the *piloto mayor* (the pilot major), an expert in the planning and execution of maritime expeditions. His responsibilities included training pilots and maintaining the *Padrón Real* (the royal master map).

The royal map was a state secret but, in the accelerating world of exploration, secrets were hard to keep. News of the exploits of the Iberian pioneers and the potential wealth of the Americas and the Spice Islands was resounding across Europe. Spain and Portugal's commercial rivals feared being excluded. Venice foresaw the death of her own spice trade and the Genoese complained of the Portuguese 'taking wholly into their hands all the trade of spices to bring the same into Spain, and nevertheless to sell them at a more grievous and intolerable price to the people of Europe than ever was heard of before'.[2] Like the Portuguese, the Spanish worked tirelessly to suppress commercial and cartographic knowledge, but it proved impossible to seal the leaks. Both Spanish and Portuguese ventures were pan-European in nature, dependent on skilled seamen, technicians and commercial agents from other countries. The crews of Magellan, himself Portuguese, had included Greeks, Venetians, Genoese, a German gunner and a sailor from Bristol, while for thirty years, the pilot major at the heart of Spain's enterprise was a Venetian, Sebastian Cabot. Knowledge was valuable: experienced navigators could switch allegiance. No one demonstrated this more vividly than the Cabot family. Sebastian and his father John were adventurers, creatures of the age, flexible in their loyalties, seeking opportunity wherever it presented itself in the heady world of voyages and discovery. John Cabot had brought his family to England in the 1480s, settled in the bustling port of Bristol and sailed for the English kings. He planted the Tudor banner on the northern shores of the Americas, which he christened Newfoundland and claimed for England. Sebastian had also sailed this coastline from Bristol. He established for himself a reputation as a skilled cartographer and navigator. The Cabot voyages had allowed the English to make a claim to these northern shores.

Sometime in 1527, Robert Thorne, an Englishman living in Seville, composed a letter to the English ambassador of Henry VIII, who was visiting the city. Thorne, a Bristol merchant, was a settled resident of Seville, licensed to undertake trading ventures in association with Spanish partners. He knew Cabot well from Bristol days and had invested in his voyages. Thorne had witnessed the world unfolding from the banks of the Guadalquivir. He had been in the city when Elcano returned and seen the stampede to the Americas. He watched closely the conflict in the Moluccas between Spain and Portugal. In his letter to Dr Lee, the ambassador, he wrote 'unto your Lordship of the new trade of Spicery of the Emperor. There is no doubt that the said Islands are fertile of Cloves, Nutmegs, Mace and Cinnamon: and that the said Islands, with others there about, abound with gold, Rubies, Diamonds ... and other stones and pearls.'[3] His letter included a 'card' – a map of the world. Along with another English merchant in the city, Roger Barlow, Thorne was keen to see England break the Iberian monopoly, become a player on the world stage and participate in the opportunities in the East. The map was aimed to demonstrate that there was a route that was a natural right of the English – one that was shorter and bypassed the Iberian gate-keepers. His map cut off the top of the Americas and Asia, whose ends were unknown, but left a promising seaway open due north. In fact, Thorne was proposing three speculative alternative routes to the Indies in that direction: one east 'towards the Orient', round the northern landmass of Asia; a second to the west 'towards the Occident', round the Americas; and a third due north, 'right toward the Pole Antarctike'.[4] Thorne could not altogether dodge the widely held objection that to the north 'the sea is all ice, and the cold so much that none can suffer it',[5] but dismissed this with some complex logic and resounding confidence: 'I judge, there is no land

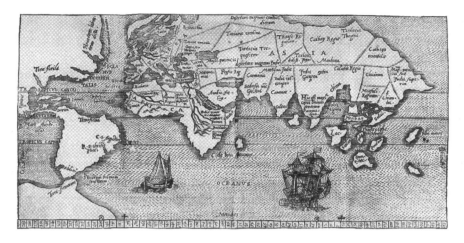

19. *Robert Thorne's card, probably stolen from the Casa de la Contratación by Cabot. The map, conveniently cut off at the top, avoids the awkward question about the feasibility of a north-eastern channel round Asia.*

uninhabitable, nor sea unnavigable.'[6] Furthermore, by one of these routes, 'we should be nearer to the said spicery by almost two thousand leagues than the Emperor or the king of Portugal are'.[7] The lure of incomplete maps. It was the inverse of Magellan's speculative proposal a decade earlier and based on the same kind of unfounded optimism.

Thorne's map was an act of espionage and the letter begged the utmost discretion. 'This card and that which I write is not to be showed or communicated there with many of that [Spanish] court ... none may make these cards, but certain appointed and allowed for masters ... it would not sound well to them that a stranger should know or discover their secrets: and would appear worst of all if they understood that I write touching the short way to the spicery by our seas.'[8]

Thorne and Barlow were clear that competing with the Iberians on a southern route was unviable. Thorne's prompting was to suggest that a northern route to the East was feasible. A couple of years later the two men wrote to the English king, Henry VIII, directly to the same effect: 'there is left one way to discover, which is to the North ... truly the danger and way is shorter for us, than to Spain and Portugal'.[9] The long summer days would make sailing easy, and so 'without doubt they shall find there the richest lands and islands of the world of gold, precious stones, balms, spices and other things that we here esteem most'.[10] Who had leaked Thorne's map and inspired the plan? Probably the pilot major himself.

Sebastian Cabot was complicated: a man moving between worlds – Spain, England, Venice – short of money and eager for a fame to emulate that of Magellan. He told variant and contradictory accounts of his birthplace and voyages. He led a disastrous Spanish expedition to seek a short route to the Pacific through South America in the 1520s, retracing the journey up the River Plate that had killed Solís, but his skills as a cartographer and navigator were widely appreciated.

Cabot was employed as Charles's pilot major for nearly thirty years, but shuttled between Spain and England, seeking preferment and proposing competing plans for voyages. It was clear that the route via the Magellan Strait was punishing. Was there another, shorter way to reach the Indies? A way to outflank the Iberian monopoly? Repeated searches had so far offered no channel through the Americas. But over the decades Cabot continuously proposed versions of Thorne's northern route – one that might legitimately be considered England's prerogative and beyond the reach of the Iberian monopoly – to which he claimed to hold the secret. Despite being Charles's valued and well-paid expert he was not beyond putting out feelers in England. He hinted at secret knowledge that he alone knew. He too realised that because the Iberians held the southern route, the opportunities and potential were greater in states that were locked out of that possibility: England and Venice. To the latter he proclaimed: 'I have the means of rendering Venice a partner in this navigation, and of showing her a passage whereby she would obtain great profit, which is the truth, for I have discovered it.'[11]

The ideas behind the Thorne–Barlow proposal lingered in circulation for two decades and Cabot continued to dangle them before English merchants. In 1548 he was granted temporary leave from his employment as pilot major to join the emperor in Germany for five months. He never turned up. Sometime later, while Cabot was still drawing pay from Spain, the emperor learned that he was living in Bristol and was also being paid by the English king, Henry VIII. For the English this was a coup. Hitherto they had been reliant on foreign pilots beyond their home waters. Here was a man who could train up native pilots and who brought with him the secrets of the Casa de Contratación, which he deployed strategically to whet the interests of new patrons. He brought with him a version of a world map, subtly tweaked for English interests, that suggested the possibility of a north-eastern channel to the Orient. It was his advertisement. Cabot was probably aware that English trade was dangerously over-dependent on exporting cloth. Here was a tempting opportunity to compete in far richer markets.

Charles was furious. In early 1550 he wrote to his ambassador in England, François van der Delft, that Cabot 'must clearly understand that we require his services and claim a right to them'.[12] Cabot played an elaborate game, dropping hints and suggestions before his Spanish paymasters. In a meeting with van der Delft he declared variously that he would gladly return but was restrained by the English, that he had a great secret that he wished to impart to the emperor if he received a safe pardon, on the other hand that he was 'old and does not wish to take up work again, but live in peace and quiet, saying he has come here as a refuge'. Van der Delft 'inclined to entertain a suspicion that Cabot had tried to make a profit out of both sides'.[13] He was probably correct.

The ambassador and his spies were tasked with finding out exactly what the emperor's pilot major was up to. Cabot remained elusive, mysterious, secretive. There were hints and rumours that the English were 'seeking the road to the Indies'.[14] In June 1550 another ambassador, Jean Schevre, wrote: 'Respecting the opinion held by some that the English are seeking a road to the Indies, I have not been able to ascertain anything. It is said that the King wishes to send two of his great ships to the East, but no one knows when. But it is evident, nevertheless, that they have something in their minds ... because they still detain the pilot Cabot, although His Majesty has sent for him several times.'[15]

He had heard that the English had also retained the services of a French navigator, Jean Ribault, 'by all accounts a good navigator and expert pilot ... some say, moreover that the king intends to send a few ships towards Iceland by the northern route to discover some island which is said to be rich in gold'.[16]

Schevre followed up that he was certain that 'Ribault, accompanied by certain Englishmen, experienced in navigation, who have been with Cabot, is to go to discover some islands or seek a road to the Indies, taking the way of the Arctic Pole. For this purpose, five or six ships are being fitted out; and two of them are nearly ready.'[17] The ambassador was not fully correct, but he was getting close to the mark.

In early May 1553, three brand new ships were anchored in the Thames beneath the Tower of London, waiting for the tide to turn. They were stoutly – and expensively – built, their hulls sheathed in lead against destructive sea worms. They had been funded not with royal money, but by the formation of a joint-stock company in which 240 merchants had each invested 25 pounds. 'The Merchant Adventurers for the discovery of regions, dominions, islands and places unknown' was an innovative example of the burgeoning power of European capitalism. England's principal export product was woollen cloth – it accounted for 85 per cent of its foreign trade – and these men hoped to find new markets for their products in China, and to buy spices in the Moluccas. They had been sold the promise of a northern route, analogous to Magellan's strait proposal, by Sebastian Cabot and by unfinished maps, such as Thorne's card, and

20. Sebastian Cabot.

the globe of Mercator, which showed a seaway open to the north-east above the landmass of Asia.

The expedition was to be led by the imposing noble personage of Sir Hugh Willoughby. Tall and courageous, a soldier knighted for heroic deeds in the war against the Scots, Willoughby was a natural leader, a man to inspire confidence among London merchants. What he was not was a mariner. He had almost no nautical experience, though such commands were not unusual at a time when England was lagging far behind its Iberian rivals in the science of navigation. The real trump card was the expedition's pilot major, Richard Chancellor. 'The incomparable Richard Chancellor', as John Dee, the court astronomer, called him, was a modern, intellectually astute navigator: a mathematician, astronomer, pilot and 'mechanician' – a practical man who made innovative astronomical instruments for plotting positions against the sun and stars.

Sebastian Cabot was among the crowd who gathered on the banks of the Thames to see off the ships. Over 70 and now beyond new voyages, Cabot was the godfather of the expedition. Willoughby commanded the flagship, the *Bona Esperanza*. With this went the *Edward*, named in honour of England's 15-year-old Protestant king, Edward VI, which was captained by Chancellor, and the smaller *Bona Confidentia*. They fired a salute as they passed the Royal Palace of Greenwich, where the king lay dying, probably of tuberculosis. Within two months Edward would be dead, and England plunged into religious turmoil.

For the departing ships, time was critical. They knew that they had to be prompt, making the most of the long days of northern light before cold and darkness closed in on their voyage. It did not start well. They were held by contrary winds on the east coast of England for three frustrating weeks. They carried with them letters signed by the dying Edward addressed to 'kings, princes and other potentates inhabiting the north-east parts of the world toward the mighty empire of Cathay'.[18] Their message was friendship and the mutual benefits of trade: 'to seek such things as we lack, as also to carry unto them from our regions, such things as they lack'.[19] This was a commercial venture without any aspiration to claim foreign land for the English crown, or to convert native peoples. They were strictly enjoined in the sailing instructions 'not to disclose to any nation the state of our religion, but to pass it over in silence, without any declaration of it'.[20] Where the Spanish had reproduced their letters to oriental potentates in Arabic translations, these were copied into Greek, and various other languages.

Back in Spain, Charles was anxious for Schevre to keep probing and to determine exactly what they were up to. Just before the ships left, Schevre had the answer, via Cabot, still playing a complicated game: 'the three vessels ... will follow a northerly course and navigate by the Frozen Sea towards the country of the great Chamchina, or neighbouring countries ... they believe the route to be a short one and very convenient for the kingdom of England for distributing kerseys [woollen cloth] in those far countries, bringing back spices and other rich merchandise in exchange. I asked him [Cabot] if the said voyage was as certain as it seemed. He said Yes it was.'[21]

At the same time, the detailed sailing instructions drawn up by Cabot realistically addressed the challenge, risks and reward. Cabot referred to the 'dangers of the seas, perils of ice, intolerable colds and other impediments' that the doubters had talked up, but this was an empirical venture that 'you shall have tried by experience'. He pointed out that there had been similar doubts about 'the Orient and Occident Indies [which] have [been] to the high benefit of the emperor [Charles] and kings of Portugal, whose subjects, industries, and travails by sea have enriched them.'[22]

On 23 June the ships finally got clear of the English coast and plunged into the North Sea. The wind, however, continued to shift, and caused continuous changes of course. Willoughby's log recorded the zigzags. First north then 'north and by west, and north-north-west, then southwest, with diverse other courses, traversing and tracing the seas, by reason of sundry and manifold contrary winds'.[23] Even Chancellor must have found it difficult to determine their position from sightings taken on a pitching deck. They had no idea how far they had travelled, but on 14 July, after twenty-two days at sea, they spied the coast of Norway, and signs of habitation. When they landed the huts were abandoned, the people 'were fled away ... for fear of us'. On the 19th they reached the Røst islands, where the people they met were less intimidated and came down to greet them. It was an opportunity to restock.

They continued north, their progress recorded in Willoughby's log. The coastline was forbidding, a cragged glaciated maze of deep fjords, fragmented islands and peaks dropping sheer into the sea. Behind, a monotonous treeless tundra. They stopped at other inhabited inlets and were able to take accurate readings of latitude. Willoughby impressed on the other captains the importance of staying together. It was also necessary to nominate a meeting point in case the weather separated them: they were to reassemble at the island fortress of Vardøhus – Wardhouse to the English – 'the strongest hold in Finnmark',[24] off the most northern tip of Scandinavia. It was a wise precaution given the North Atlantic weather. On 2 August they neared the island of Senja. When a man rowed out to talk to them, Willoughby asked the possibility of a pilot to take them to Finnmark. He was told, 'if we could bear in, we should have a good harbour, and on the next day a pilot to bring us to Finnmark, unto the Wardhouse'.[25] As they tried to follow the skiff in through rocky headlands, 'terrible whirlwinds' got up.

As Chancellor recalled, 'about four of the clock, so great a tempest suddenly arose, and the seas were so outrageous, that the ships could not keep their intended course, but some were driven one way, and some another way, to their great peril and hazard'.[26] There was nothing for it but to make out to sea. Willoughby shouted across to Chancellor to keep close, but this proved impossible. The *Edward* had struck her sails as the storm approached. Inexplicably to Chancellor, Willoughby's ship was still full sailed and 'was carried away with so great force and swiftness, that not long after he was quite out of sight, and the third ship also with the same storm and like rage was dispersed and lost to us'.[27]

The *Esperanza* and the *Confidentia* had vanished. Chancellor was alone, left 'pensive, heavy and sorrowful by this dispersion of the fleet'. He pondered their fate. 'If the rage and fury of the sea have devoured those good men, or if as yet they live ... I must needs say they were men worthy of better fortune, and if they be living, let us wish them safety and a good return: but if the cruelty of death hath taken hold of them, God send them a Christian grave and sepulchre.'[28] He would never see Willoughby again.

Chancellor had no option but to make for the fortress island of Wardhouse and wait. He sat there for a week. There was no sign of the lost ships. He decided there was nothing for it but to press on, ignoring the advice of some Scotsmen at the fort, who begged him not to continue. Chancellor evidently inspired confidence: he had the backing of the crew. Reciprocally, he felt the weight of responsibility, 'lest through any error of his, the safety of the company should be endangered'.[29] They had now entered the Barents Sea. He held his course tracking the coastline east; it was the height of Arctic summer, so that 'he came at last to a place where he found no night at all, but a continual light and brightness of the sun shining clearly upon the huge and mighty sea'.[30]

Willoughby, however, was not dead. The two ships under sail had been blown north by the force of the wind, so fast that it was impossible to compute distance. When the storm abated, they regrouped. Thinking they were still off the coast of Norway they turned 'to fall in with the Wardhouse, as we did consult to do before'.[31] They found no sight of land. They were now baffled and lost. 'We perceived that the land lay not as the Globe made mention,'[32] Willoughby ruefully noted in his log. Unbeknownst to them, they had overshot the northern cape of Norway and were now out in the middle of the Barents Sea. Willoughby's log records an excruciating saga of maritime wandering, zigzagging back and forth, taking soundings, responding to the changing wind, in an attempt to strike the Norwegian coast. When they did sight land it was unpromising. They were unable to step ashore for ice and shoals and there were no indications of human presence. This was probably the island of Novaya Zemlya, deep in the Barents Sea. Four days later, on 18 August, they turned back, south-south-east, hoping to spy land that they might recognise. The *Confidentia* was leaking and they needed a harbour. On the 23 August they turned west.

The same day, the *Edward* was 200 miles south, running east from Wardhouse, along the shoreline of northern Scandinavia into Russian water. On 24 August, Chancellor arrived at the mouth of a huge bay, 100 miles across, and turned into it. This was the vast expanse of sheltered water that the Russians call the White Sea. A week or two later, in early September, Willoughby must have passed close to this opening now heading west, the other way. Somehow he missed it. On 18 September, having continued along the coastline a short distance, Willoughby also turned into a bay that offered reasonable anchorage. Willoughby's erratic course, searching for an identifiable coastline, had cost him six weeks. Had he known it, he was now not far from the *Edward*.

Although Chancellor could plot the latitude, he had no idea exactly what land he was in. Nosing up the White Sea, the *Edward* spied a fishing boat. Chancellor launched a ship's boat and caught up with it. The fishermen fell at his feet, riven by fear of the strange ship. Reassured, the local people brought them supplies. Somehow he learned that the Russian people were forbidden to buy any foreign commodities without the consent of the king. Piece by piece they acquired knowledge that the king was Tsar Ivan. Chancellor set about seeking trade and connection: 'that they had come from the most excellent King Edward the sixth, having from him in commandment certain things to deliver to their king, and seeking nothing else but his amity and friendship, and traffic with his people . . . whereby . . . great commodity and profit would grow to the subjects of both kingdoms'.[33] He was informed that he needed to seek the authority of the local governors at Kholmogory, a town 100 miles up the River Dvina. Chancellor set out upstream in the ship's boat with a small band of officers and merchants, ten in all, leaving the ship and its crew anchored at the river mouth. He determined to see if he could make an embassy to the tsar.

The regional governors were extremely nervous at their arrival: what to do with these alien visitors? They were not an official delegation; no foreigners should be admitted into Russia without the tsar's permission and nothing could be done without recourse to Moscow, 600 miles away. The Englishmen were compelled to wait and wait as the autumn ebbed away. Excuses were made for the growing delay. After many weeks Chancellor forced their hands: if no permission was forthcoming 'he would depart and proceed in his voyage'.[34] Caught between the tsar's mandate and the possibility of depriving him of important visitors, the governors decided to gamble and let Chancellor proceed.

Meanwhile, Willoughby's ships lay at anchor in the snug bay of the River Varzina, just a day's sailing west of Chancellor's. 'We entered into the haven and there came to an anchor at six fathoms,' Willoughby wrote in his log. The wildlife was extraordinary. There were 'many seal fishes, and other great fishes … bears, great deer, foxes, with divers strange beasts … which were to us unknown, also wonderful'. The thermometer was falling, and 'seeing the year far spent, and also very evil weather, as frost, snow, and hail, as though it had been the deep of winter, we thought best to winter there'.[35] First he sent out three parties of men in different directions on three- or four-day journeys in search of native people. They returned without finding 'any similitude of habitation'. The migratory fishermen had gone. They battened down to see out the winter. Not far away the men on the *Edward* were doing the same. Outside it was stunningly cold. When those left on the *Edward* lifted a hatch to go out on deck, the sudden shock of the cold took their breath away so that they frequently collapsed 'as men very nearly dead'.[36] But on all the ships they had warm clothes, sufficient food and good supplies of wood. They sat tight through the long Arctic nights, awaiting spring. From 25 November to 29 December they lived in total darkness. At this point, with no prospect of sailing until spring, Willoughby's log stops.

Chancellor was also enduring the rigours of winter on his journey to Moscow. The cold was 'very extreme and horrible'.[37] Roads were impassable but the frozen world allowed for rapid travel by sled.

They sped across the snowy tundra, via an organised system of staging posts. Along the way they were met by a royal emissary with a letter from the tsar expressing a desire to see the mysterious ambassadors from a distant king. They were now to be transported at no cost and with all the prestige of imperial visitors. Their status improved instantly, so much so that at each stop there was fierce competition and fighting among the post boys over who should hitch the fresh horses to the sleds.

Chancellor was seeing a new world. He had the opportunity, by observation and whatever could be gleaned across language barriers, to learn a great deal about the country through which they travelled. The land was monotonously flat and extremely wild, a wilderness of huge fir forests, in which roamed bears, black wolves and animals he called buffaloes [bison]: 'they hunt the buffaloes for the most part on horseback, but the bears on foot with wooden forks'.[38] The cold was such that wood laid on a fire could be alight at one end, yet completely frozen at the other. The common people lived in stout square wooden houses built of fir; any cracks between the planks were sealed with moss, the rooms lined with wooden benches on which they slept, 'for they know not the use of beds'.[39] A little light filtered in through narrow windows sealed with translucent animal skin. Their clothes were made of wool. A man's status was denoted by the height of his hat.

He also studied closely, and with a zealous Protestant eye, the style of Russian Orthodox Christian worship, the ordering of their services, their devotion to icons, their monasteries, the ignorance of the common people of the Lord's Prayer and their regular fasts (after which 'they return to their old intemperance of drinking, for they are notable tosspots').[40] His tolerance was finite: 'they hold opinion that we are but half Christians, and themselves only to be the true and perfect church: these are the foolish and childish dotages of such ignorant barbarians'.[41]

'After much ado and great pains taken in this long and weary journey',[42] Chancellor and his men approached Moscow. In fact, the

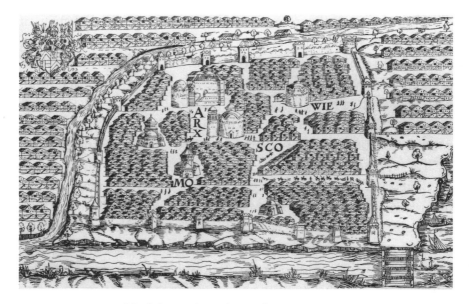

21. Moscow in a sixteenth-century print.

sled transit had been extremely rapid. It had taken two weeks to cover the 600 miles. The city before them was substantial, 'in bigness as great as the City of London', full of 'many and great buildings'. However, Chancellor was struck by the jumble of the place, 'built out of order and with no handsomeness', and made negative comparisons: the tsar's palace and court, built in the form of a square, lacked 'the beauty and elegance of the houses of the kings of England',[43] but the ceremony surrounding their visit was astonishing.

They were housed, and kept waiting on the tsar's pleasure. After twelve days a messenger summoned them to the palace. They passed through the gates into the court; in the first chamber a hundred courtiers sat at benches around the walls, all apparelled in golden robes. Unnervingly, they were so still and silent that they resembled golden statues. What Chancellor did not know was that these were actors – Muscovites impressed for the occasion and fitted out from the royal wardrobe – players in a highly choreographed spectacle.

From there the English party were led gaping into the Chamber of Presence. The tsar looked down on them from a high throne, crowned in gold and wearing a golden robe, in his hand a sceptre 'garnished and beset with precious stones ... There was a majesty in his countenance proportionable with the excellence of his estate.'[44] It was the first encounter with the man the English came to call 'The Terrible'. He was flanked by his chief secretary and the Great Commander of Silence, also robed in gold. His council of 150 were seated on benches. They also were dressed in gold cloth.

Chancellor evidently kept his wits about him in the midst of this overawing spectacle. He delivered the king's letters and presented gifts. Fine English cloth was among these – an important calling card for the trading ambitions of the Merchant Adventurers. The tsar read the letters, asked a few questions and invited them to dinner. They walked out backwards as instructed.

Two hours later the English party were led into the Golden Court, 'for so they call it, although not very fair',[45] in Chancellor's estimation, but the dinner was another presentation of mind-boggling and disorientating ritual. The tsar sat above them on a 'high and stately seat',[46] this time robed in silver and wearing a different crown; the vessels and goblets on display were all gold, among which some were 5 feet long. The other guests wore linen over 'rich skins',[47] the tables were laden with gold vessels, and the 140 serving men, who also wore cloth of gold, changed their 'habit and apparel'[48] three times, during a lengthy ceremonial banquet, in which the honorific presentation of bread by the tsar as a mark of favour comprised a puzzlingly significant feature.

Chancellor's little retinue had arrived in Moscow about 9 December. They remained there three months. In this time, they gathered as much cultural, geographical and financial information as they could. One of the merchants, John Hasse, appraised the commercial opportunities and compiled a detailed report for the Merchant Adventurers on weights, measures, coinage, commodities, promising

22. Ivan IV Vasilyevich, 'Ivan the Terrible'.

market towns and trading rivals. He concluded that 'our merchants may do well to provide the Russians such wares as the Dutch Nation does serve them of'.[49] For Ivan, the English connection also offered reciprocal advantages. He hoped to get munitions and expertise in manufacturing war materials for his ongoing military campaigns.

The English visitors also had the opportunity to observe the ceremonial magnificence of the tsar's diplomatic missions to other coun-

190

tries. They watched the departure of ambassadors to the king of Poland, accompanied by 500 fine horses, the men largely dressed in cloth of gold and silver, 'and the worst apparel was of garments of blue; the trappings of the horses were of gold and silver'.[50] The message that they were intended to covey was one of untrammelled power and majesty.

Chancellor's party finally left on 15 March. By the start of April they were back at the *Edward* to find the crew still alive. If they had made no progress in pioneering a route to China they did at least depart with a letter from Ivan to King Edward with the desire to open trading relations with England. It seemed as if the Merchant Adventurers might get something for their investment. The ice was thawing and, with no sign of Willoughby, there was every reason to depart. The *Edward* made it back across the North Sea. The voyage was not without incident – they were robbed of some of their merchandise by Flemish pirates along the way – but the *Edward* sailed back up the Thames in the summer of 1554 to be greeted by Cabot. The crew returned to find an England turned upside down. Protestant Edward was dead. Queen Mary, a Catholic, was married to King Philip of Spain.

On the southern shores of the Barents Sea, the thaw had also brought itinerant Lapp fishermen into the Varzina River to fish for salmon. There, in the spring light, they saw two strange ships lying anchored by the shore. Drawing cautiously closer, they could detect no sign of life. All was silent. The fishermen, undoubtedly puzzled and frightened by the eerie prospect before them, came alongside. Still nothing stirred. They clambered aboard. The hatches were battened down. Prising them open, they gaped at the scene inside: the frozen bodies of all the crew lying dead on the deck. Exactly what they encountered is not known. When news of the fate of Willoughby's ships finally reached London in 1555, there were wild tales. The Venetian ambassador's report to the Doge conjured up a tableau of gothic horror:

The mariners returned from the second voyage narrate strange things about the mode in which they were frozen, having found some of them seated in the act of writing, pen still in hand, and the paper before them; others at table, platters in hand and spoon in mouth; others opening a locker, and others in various postures, like statues, as if they had been adjusted and placed in these attitudes. They say that some dogs on board the ships displayed the same phenomena. They found the effects and merchandise all intact in the hands of the natives, and brought them back thither with the vessels.[51]

The crew suddenly overwhelmed in some dramatic catastrophe: it was enough to make people shudder. Elsewhere it was reported that they had died 'for want of experience to make caves and stoves'.[52] Yet the crew of the *Edward* had survived intact, and the stores on the death ships contained warm winter clothing and food stocks that had not all been used. Whatever the truth of the ambassador's embroidered tale, it seems that the men had all died simultaneously, not in the slow-motion decimation of a failing polar expedition. The most likely explanation is poisoning by carbon monoxide. Perhaps, having exhausted their supplies of wood, they turned to burning sea coal. With the hatches closed, the toxic vapours could have engulfed the crew with the suddenness of an Arctic Pompeii. Exactly when this had happened is unknown, but Willoughby was still alive in January 1554, because he was witness to a dated will found on the ship.

The frightened fishermen collected all the available material from the ships and returned to the regional governor, where the effects were sealed up. The death ships were sailed back to the mouth of the River Dvina. In 1555, Chancellor led a second expedition to the White Sea in the *Edward* and another embassy to Moscow, in the company of a vessel named after England's new monarchs, the *Philip and Mary*. It was then that he learned of Willoughby's fate.

While working to develop relations with the tsar, Chancellor also continued to try to find out about the feasibility of the northern route to China. The following year these ships sailed out to Russia again, carrying additional crews to bring the *Esperanza* and the *Confidentia* home. When they set out to return that July, they carried with them a Russian ambassador and some Russian merchants, to strengthen commercial and political ties with England. The ships loaded large amounts of valuable merchandise – wax, furs, felt, oil and other commodities. The *Esperanza's* hold contained something else: Sir Hugh Willoughby's body for burial.

Willoughby was destined to die at sea a second time. Off the coast of Norway, the *Esperanza* and the *Confidentia*, now well worn, vanished in a storm with all hands, carrying Willoughby's decomposing body down into the deep. Chancellor again managed to pull clear, but disaster awaited on the coast of Scotland. The *Edward* was being driven towards a rocky shore. Chancellor launched a ship's boat to attempt to get the ambassador to land; pulling towards the beach, the boat was flipped by a huge wave, tumbling all its occupants into the surf. Chancellor drowned, along with his oldest son, brought along to learn the ropes. By sheer good luck the Russian ambassador was washed up alive.

Chancellor's loss, 'the incomparable Chancellor', was deeply felt. He was an innovator in the development of English maritime skills of navigation and cartography. With Cabot's direction and the development of new financial structures for funding trade and exploration, the English were on the threshold of challenging the Iberians' hold on the oceans. The Merchant Adventurers – a privately funded joint-stock company – was reconstituted as the Muscovy Company, which traded solidly, if not spectacularly, in Russia. In the 1570s and 1580s further probes, searching for a north-west and north-east passage around the tips of the Americas and Asia, failed to lead to the creation of a northern sea route, but English ambitions had been fired up. In 1570, John Dee, England's polymath, published a visionary proposal for national maritime expansion: 'General & Rare Memorials pertaining to the Perfect Art of Navigation'. In it he coined the term 'British Empire'. Following on from the Merchant Adventurers, in 1600 another joint-stock company was formed: the East India Company, destined to be a powerful player in global trade and empire, and ambitious for the spice trade. In the short run, however, China and the Spice Islands were as far away as ever.

Willoughby's log was recovered from the *Esperanza* and has survived: the ghostly record of his voyage before the ships' crews were suddenly overwhelmed by carbon monoxide. In the margin of the last page someone has added in a different hand, 'The Haven of Death'.

Thirteen

'Fear Our Greatness, Respect Our Virtue'
1530- 55

The English had been unable to reach fabled Cathay but the Portuguese had, and their early encounters with China had been bruising. They had come with ideas of creating a trading monopoly, through a combination of force and diplomacy, and had been rebuffed. They had failed to understand that the Middle Kingdom recognised no parity with outsiders. There was only submission – kowtowing. Early aggression had led to disaster. Tomé Pires's mission had witnessed the collision between two worldviews. The European interlopers were quite different from all the other tributary peoples that the Chinese had come across and this most centralised of states would be slow to get the measure of the Folangji. In the long run this first contact would prove to be a turning point in history.

The immediate consequence was that the Portuguese were banned from the coast of China. Canton was closed to all foreign trade. When it reopened in 1530 the Folangji remained specifically interdicted and the local population were reminded of the fact. The city gates were inscribed with prominent warnings in gold letters 'that the men with beards and large eyes should not be permitted in this realm'.[1] Kuantung province was too hot a place for the Portuguese to show their faces but at the same time the commercial opportunities were simply too tempting to relinquish: units of pepper that sold for 4 ducats in Malacca fetched 15 in China. The south coast of China, dependent on foreign trade, also suffered, and micro-management by Ming bureaucrats in Beijing was too distant to seal all the leaks. In this climate, illicit trade continued along the coast further east, in the adjacent coastal provinces of Fukien and Chekiang. The Portuguese hid in the shadows. They carried on their activities from a nest of offshore islands, using Malays or Siamese merchants as front men. The trade operated on bribery and the connivance of local officials and mandarins. Temporary seasonal markets – mat sheds – sprang up on these islands and allowed for the exchange of goods. The smugglers were greeted with some sympathy. The records noted that 'the fo-lang-chi who came, brought their local pepper, sappan-wood, ivory, thyme oil, aloes, sandal wood, and all kinds of incense in order to trade with our borderers. Their prices were particularly cheap. Every day they consumed supplies of drinks and eatables which they got from our people ... the prices which they paid for them were double the usual amount, and therefore our borderers gladly provided them with a market.'[2]

This unofficial trade was welcomed on both sides but it was accompanied by lawlessness and violence. There was a thin line between trade and piracy. Alongside the activities of Portuguese smugglers were the ravages of deeply detested Japanese pirates, the *wokuo*, 'dwarf robbers'. Together with Chinese and Korean collaborators, their endemic raiding from islands in the Sea of Japan and the South China Sea was a scourge on China's coastal provinces. The Ming records suggest that the Portuguese smugglers and the pirates sometimes cooperated, and were hard to control: 'the officials in each territory, directly the foreigners entered the anchorage, were unable to restrain the local people from trading. They felt that the court was far away, and they once more took the foreigners' illicit presents and allowed them to moor their ships. The foreigners employed the wicked rascals in the locality and carried on their traffic without restraint.'[3] Activities in this bandit zone allowed the circulation of goods, but patience finally wore out. By 1547 the crescendo of abuses against imperial edict had come to the attention of the government.

The Ming had had enough of disorder and rule flouting in Fukien and Chekiang. A new and energetic viceroy, Chu Wan, was appointed to clear the coast of Portuguese smugglers, Japanese pirates and their Chinese allies. The Chinese were forbidden to have any dealings with foreigners. In the two following years vigorous campaigns were conducted against interlopers and intermediaries. Blockades prevented the Portuguese from carrying out effective trade. Raids took out temporary settlements on the islands. Counter-raids by the Portuguese and their local collaborators ratcheted up the contest. In 1549, Chu Wan's coastal forces rooted out the traders' nests. In these contests a number of Portuguese were captured alongside Chinese. To set an example, four of them were dressed up and exhibited in cages which were toured around coastal towns. The exhibits were labelled with the mocking title: 'the Kings of Malacca'. Others were put to death, together with many Chinese.

Among those swept up in the viceroy's purge and scheduled for execution was a Portuguese soldier of fortune called Galeote Pereira. Pereira was taken to the city of Chuan-chouto to await his fate. Luck was on his side. The officious viceroy had overplayed his hand. As he wryly remarked: 'It is easy to exterminate the robbers from foreign lands, but it is difficult to get rid of those from our own country.'[4] He was pointing a finger at the gentry, 'the robe-and-cap class'.[5] Smuggling was highly lucrative and counter-briefing to the court caused his downfall. He had executed ninety-six men, some Portuguese, in a decisive sweep. He was claimed to have been guilty of exceeding his authority and acting without due process. Along with other dignitaries, he was scheduled for punishment but committed suicide in prison. Galeote Pereira survived. The Portuguese still alive were broken up into small bands and dispersed across the country. This would give Pereira the opportunity to observe China at first hand.

The fall of Chu Wan implicitly signalled an end to a total ban on commercial relationships with foreigners. Overall, China lacked for nothing by way of essentials: it was completely self-sufficient. A Dominican missionary, Gaspar da Cruz, remarked that China's overseas trade 'is so little in comparison of the great traffic of the country, that it almost remained as nothing and unperceived'.[6] Yet the economy along the coast of southern China relied on overseas trade, and that trade was located in luxury items. Spices were in great demand at the imperial court, as well as such items as ivory and aromatic wood, in exchange for silk, porcelain and musk. It was a high-value, low-volume market and, in the wake of the fall of Chu Wan, the Portuguese were in a position to profit. The problem on both sides was how to accommodate the valuable trade with these interlopers who were outside the tributary system without compromising Chinese territorial and imperial integrity.

The solution, worked out pragmatically, came off the coast of Canton. After their effective expulsion from Fukien and Chekiang, the Portuguese moved their activities back west towards islands at the mouth of the Pearl River. Canton was the hub of coastal China but remained strictly out of bounds, the golden edicts still prominent on the city's gates.

The circumstances surrounding the creation of the trading post of Macau remain obscure – even the origin of its name is uncertain – possibly the corruption of the 'Bay (or shrine) of the goddess A-ma'. Initially the Folangji traders held small seasonal markets on some of these islands as they had done before. It was on one of these, Shang-ch'uan, that the Jesuit St Francis Xavier died in 1552, seeking new converts in the East. What the Portuguese craved was a secure trading post: the fort-building complex was hardwired into their model of expansion, but they had learned the hard way that any kind of appropriation of Chinese territory was impossible, and they were still banned from the trade that Canton wanted.

The impasse was overcome by the tactful Leonel de Sousa, captain-major of a Portuguese fleet bound for Japan in 1554, outside any involvement of the Portuguese crown or the Ming court. It was an informal arrangement among merchant communities. De Sousa managed to clinch a trading agreement with the *haidao* (commander of coastal defences of Canton), Wang Bo. This involved bribery, haggling, the agreement to pay taxes (reduced somewhat by sleight of hand) and a great deal of tact. De Sousa, who was not a merchant, saw the problem from the outside and with respect for China. He noted that every other Asiatic trader was allowed to trade, on payment of tax revenues, 'except the European Folangjis, because they were men with dark hearts, thieves and rebels who didn't obey their King ... they do not behave properly in the countries where they travel. They act against China which is a peaceful country and is ruled with justice.'[7] In a letter to the Duke of Beja, brother of King John III, de Sousa explained his countrymen's terrible reputation and his strategy for improving it. 'I took the best care of the ships and told the Portuguese who were with me not to cause any trouble and not to make mistakes, because they [the Chinese] were shocked with the things we had done in the past.' De Sousa won the local mandarins over with an inspection of his ships, an understanding of protocol and hierarchy – and a certain amount of lucrative junketing:

> We had some formal, honourable meetings. One of the Chinese officers, appointed for Admiral, came aboard the ships. We got along very well and with no problems because I knew how to show importance and respect towards their habits and rules of courtesy, which they have in abundance. I welcomed them and offered them a banquet and some gifts which they received secretly, because they can be severely punished if they accept them. They like details and they insisted with me to tell them if I was a merchant's captain or His Highness's captain. If I was His Highness's I should show my credentials and the sign, which they hardly know. Well pleased with this, they were satisfied that I was His Highness's captain and they greeted and saluted me. They

completely accepted my authority not only over the Portuguese, but also over the people of other origins ... because they did not want to interfere and I was in charge of everything.[8]

The local mandarins wanted no trouble: all responsibility was to be delegated to de Sousa and there was no legal contract. The agreement, made at local level, was purely verbal. 'Nothing was written down, lest it become statutory.'[9] 'This agreement put an end to many troubles and difficulties which I cannot describe,' de Sousa concluded with a note of self-satisfaction, but he had indeed opened the door to legitimate – or semi-legitimate – trading, as it was beneath the radar of the imperial edict, an anomaly outside the rules of the tribute system. The European merchants were now able to trade with Canton at the islands at the mouth of the Pearl River. Sometime around 1557, in circumstances that were unclear, they obtained permission to rent the small peninsula that came to be called Macau, joined to the mainland by a narrow causeway. Initially the ground rent went straight into the haidao's pocket, later to the imperial treasury without any explanation of its source.

The small patch of land on which the Portuguese established a footprint had an anomalous status. The Chinese never relinquished the claim on it as part of the Celestial Empire. The city paid an annual ground rent. Its cramped position on a peninsula allowed the Chinese a stranglehold. With no means of food production, it was dependent. The grip that the Chinese maintained on this useful parasite was reinforced in 1573 by the construction of a wall across the isthmus in which there was one gate, known to the Portuguese as the Porta do Cerco – the siege gate. It was opened twice a month to allow food and other supplies to enter the city. When it was closed it was sealed with six paper strips, over its portal an inscription in Chinese: 'Fear our greatness and respect our virtue.' This arrangement was convenient to both parties, and so unofficial that the Ming emperor had no idea that any Europeans were living in his kingdom.

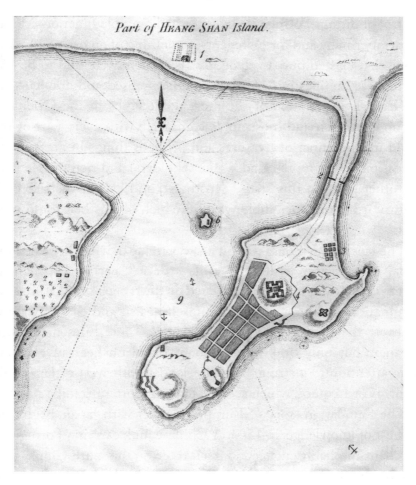

*23. A nineteenth-century British plan of Macau, sited on a cramped peninsula.
China maintained tight control over the Portuguese colony by way of the gate
on the narrow isthmus (marked 2 on the map). Macau had a well-sheltered
harbour (marked 9).*

But Macau was useful, a permeable membrane that allowed goods
to pass to and fro to the benefit of both sides with no concession on
the Chinese side to loss of dignity or terrestrial integrity. Despite a
potentially parlous status that might depend upon arbitrary whims,
the Macau air bubble flourished autonomously, also beyond the

control of distant Portuguese kings. It had one sole function. Macau was a city run by and for merchants, something of an oriental Venice – one that existed only to trade. By 1638 there were said to be 850 Portuguese families in Macau, people naturalised and domiciled in the East, living in 'one of the most noble cities in the Orient by reason of its rich and most noble commerce with every part of the world in all manner of treasures and precious things in great abundance, and it has more casados (householders) and rich people than any other place in this state'.[10] In the second half of the sixteenth century it became incredibly wealthy. Much of this had to do with Japan.

The fact that de Sousa was on his way to Japan when he sealed the initial agreement was due to events a decade earlier. Cipangu, as Marco Polo heard it in China, hovered on the fringes of the European imagination. Columbus thought himself near it and Elcano wanted to divert the Loaísa expedition to visit it. Tomé Pires mentioned Cipangu, but only briefly, his account based on hearsay. He paid more attention to a string of small islands south-west of Japan, the Ryukyus or Léquios, which seemed to be important trading posts.

The foundation story of Europe's contact with Japan, begins, to the best of knowledge, in 1543. A Chinese junk carrying Portuguese merchants probably engaged in illicit trade on the south China coast was hit by a storm, and washed up damaged on the shores of Tanegashima, a westerly Japanese island. The onlookers watched some strange men come ashore. Mendes Pinto 'the Liar' claimed to have played a part but most likely the three involved were António do Mota, Francisco Zeimoto and António Peixoto. To the Japanese they were the *nanban-jin* – southern barbarians – uncouth people who ate with their hands and were reputed not to use cups to drink. They caused a sensation. A prompt report was sent to the island's lord, Tanegashima Tokitaka. Tokitaka invited the men to come to him and ordered repairs to the ship. The Portuguese brought with them something that caught the lord's attention. Via double translation, he enquired what it was. They offered a demonstration. A target was set up a hundred paces away. Lifting the matchlock to his shoulder, one of the Portuguese fired – a flash and a bang. It hit the target. 'The explosion seemed like lightning and the sound like rolling thunder.'[11] Here was a device, the annals recorded, that could break through a wall or iron and smash a mountain of silver. It took a single shot to change the course of Japanese history.

Tokitaka was amazed and impressed. Fifteenth-century Japan was plunged in endemic civil wars between small shogunates and he saw the potential immediately. He bought one or perhaps two of the guns for a large sum of money and set the island's blacksmith, Yaita, a swordsmith, to make a copy. Despite some technical difficulties, he managed it. Word of the nanban-jin's weapon spread fast. Casting difficulties were overcome; essential materials for the manufacture of gunpowder – saltpetre and sulphur – were sourced, along with lead for bullets. Use of the new-fangled weapon, known as the *tanegashima*, spread rapidly across Japan. By the 1560s, firearms were used regularly in battles. There were 3,000 riflemen at the battle of Nagashino in 1575. When Japan invaded Korea in 1592, 40,000 gunners were said to have gone and Seoul was captured in ten days. Along the way, technical improvements were introduced: heavier calibres, devices to protect the firing mechanism from getting wet, and the tactics of gunpowder warfare were refined – volley firing to rain continuous bullets on an enemy, night-firing devices, protective screens. So enthusiastically did the Japanese embrace the gunpowder advantage that, by the seventeenth century, they were possibly producing more guns than the whole of Europe.

In turn, the Portuguese were deeply impressed by the Japanese: people so different from those they had encountered in the deep tropics. The *samurai* culture was comparable in its martial ethos to that of the Iberian Peninsula, with its matching code of glory and great deeds. Francis Xavier was particularly excited by news of the first Portuguese landfall. He saw great potential there for a Christian

24. *The Japanese produced early manuals on the use of gunpowder weapons. Here troops practise night firing.*

mission. He arrived in 1549 and was immediately enthusiastic about the Japanese, although he could not communicate with them directly: 'Of all the newly discovered people among whom I have lived, those of this land are the best: none of the other heretical peoples can compare with the Japanese.'[12] This encounter was to open the country to a century of Christian evangelism.

The arrival of the Portuguese, who came to trade in greater numbers, gave Japan access to the world of Europe. Encounters brought technology transfer. On mainland China they were also crafting muskets and breech-loading swivel guns from Portuguese originals, though their impact on its society was less dramatic. Japan and China, irreducible in the central strength of their cultures, were still attracted by certain ideas and products of the southern barbarians. Astrolabes, observatories and mechanical clocks were objects of fascination and used by Jesuit missionaries to attempt to lead the elite into conversion in both Japan and China. *Nanbangaku* – the science of the southern barbarians – influenced Japan. Ideas about astronomy, geography, navigation and mathematics circulated, via Jesuit Japanese-language printing presses. The incomers overturned their notions that the world was flat and ended at India. In the process merchants and the missionaries broke the country's isolation and marked Japan forever.

During the sixteenth century Jesuit missionaries in Japan were successful beyond their wildest dreams, converting some 100,000 people. In the end, they overreached themselves. Perceived as a threat, their persecution and expulsion coincided with the conclusion of a long period of civil wars and the unification of the country under powerful new shoguns. Ironically, a factor in the success of the Tokugawa shogunate was European knowhow: its overwhelming firepower. The tanegashima helped reshape Japan.

Japan was to prove Portugal's furthest point of exploration and one of its most lucrative, because in 1557 the Ming formally imposed a total ban on direct trade with Japan. This provided rich opportunities for Portuguese merchants, linking up the trade of Goa and Malacca to China and Japan. One of the linchpins would be Macau; the other Manila in the Philippines.

At about the same time, Portuguese travellers were sending back detailed reports from China. One of these was Galeote Pereira, the soldier of fortune caught up in the smuggling crackdown along the south China coast, the other a Dominican missionary, Gaspar da Cruz. Da Cruz, although he was only there for a month, produced the sharpest and most compelling account of China since Marco Polo. To him everything was extraordinary: its magnitude, its ingenuity, its attention to detail. It was a world of wonders, a country where peoples of different tongues could communicate via a shared character-based written language, where cities such as Beijing were 'so big that a pacing horse can scarcely cross the walled city between sunset and sunrise'. Outsiders were astonished by the quality of the workmanship of the stone houses, the fine bridges and the paved roads. 'This causeth us to think,' wrote Pereira, 'that in all the world there are no better workmen for building, than the inhabitants of China.'[13] Da Cruz was struck by the country's 'infinity' – a word that crops up frequently: its shipping, its population, its manufactures, its clever inventions. Given the exhausting labour involved in pumping leaking ships across the Pacific, Chinese technology was revelatory: 'a ship be it never so big, and have it never so great a leak, the pumps are made by such sleight that one man alone sitting moving his feet as one that goeth up a staircase, in a very little space he pumps it out. These pumps are of many pieces made in the manner of water-wheels.'[14]

Da Cruz was also amazed by the country's agricultural fertility and the wealth of produce. 'There is much fullness in the land, and the great abundance of all things necessary for food and sustaining life . . . through every street they sell flesh, fish, vegetables, fruit and all things necessary.'[15] A use was found for everything: 'there is nothing lost in the country be it never so vile; for the bones as well as of dogs as of other beasts, they do use, making toys, carving them instead of ivory . . . they lose not a rag of any quality.'[16] All cultivatable land is nourished with the dung of animals and humans. Astonishingly, fresh sea fish are available far inland, transported on river boats in water baskets lined with oiled paper. Da Cruz was particularly astounded and delighted by these vast inland river

25. The first European book on China, written in Portuguese by Gaspar da Cruz, published in 1569.

systems: 'It is a very pleasant thing to see by the river the multitude of vessels, some going and others coming. And as the rice fields stretch as far as the eye can see, it looks as if many of the vessels under sail afar off, are coming as it were through land.'[17] He observed the life of people living on some of these boats, so arranged that they could keep a pig and hens and have a garden; and other boats where ducks were kept and their eggs incubated buried in warm dung, and the use of cormorants with their throats ringed, to catch fish. There is 'a great abundance of things of every trade and very perfect'.[18]

For da Cruz this was a world of wonders. He found the Chinese 'very ingenious and cunning ... they have many inventions in every kind of work'.[19] There are disquisitions on the quality and manufacture of porcelain, on the clothing of the rich and the poor, on festivals with their colourful paper arches, on justice, foot-binding, executions, the nobility, the civil service examination system, puppet shows, the eating of dogs and civic order. 'It must be noted here with how much care and consideration this country is governed, how great pains are taken to keep it in peace ... this is the reason why China has maintained and governed itself securely for so many years, and is in peace without any internal wars.'[20] His only criticism was the appearance of the Chinese, whom he considered 'ill-favoured, having small eyes, and their faces and noses flat, and are beardless'[21] – just the inverse of the judgement that the Chinese passed on the Europeans: bearded and large eyed.

Like a latter-day version of Marco Polo, da Cruz thought it impossible to exaggerate the marvels of the country: 'I knew I will not be believed ... but this does not sound an incredible thing to those who have seen China.'[22] And he was sage enough to see that Europe had almost nothing that the Chinese might want, apart from a few non-essential luxuries: 'pepper and ivory which is the principal that the Portuguese do carry, a man may well live without'.[23]

But he was wrong about their self-sufficiency. He noted that there was no coinage in the country, only gold and silver by weight: 'wherefore every man hath a pair of scales and weights in his house' for weighing bullion, 'because the common that goeth instead of money is silver by weight'.[24] Silver was king in China, and there wasn't enough of it. It would provide the Europeans with an extraordinary opportunity, and the luck would be Spain's.

Fourteen

Cracking the Code
1557- 71

For the viceroys on the ground in New Spain, the dream of Pacific expansion and contact with China remained. Seen from the shores of Mexico, the echoes of Portugal's advances into the Far East – the foothold in Macau, access to Japan – caused growing concern. They could envisage a repetition of the Moluccas, of losing out. They were haunted by the inability to solve the problem of the Pacific return after five attempts and terrible suffering, and there was resentment against Charles the emperor for pawning the claim to the Spice Islands even if it could someday be redeemed.

Charles was never wholly popular in Spain, to which he under-attended. He remained essentially a foreigner; French was his native language. Through the consolidation of states and the luck of dynastic succession he was the nominal ruler of the greatest empire since Charlemagne. He was talked up as the universal emperor, whose domains stretched from the North Sea to Vienna, from the shores of the Pacific to the coast of North Africa. But this inheritance was a sea of troubles: repetitive wars with France, uprisings in the Netherlands, the scourge of the Lutherans, a titanic contest with the Ottoman empire, endemic raiding of Spain and Italy by Islamic pirates. He spent money as fast as he could get it. The New World was a welcome source – Inca and Aztec gold, silver from the Andes and Mexico – yet there was never enough. Money vanished like water in the sand. The empire was an unsupportable burden: Charles's was the plight of a man juggling an enormous stone ball. In the end he was crushed beneath its weight. In 1556 he abdicated in favour of his son Philip and retired into a monastery.

Philip was a naturalised Spaniard and more closely attuned to his New World empire. Listening to the promptings from Mexico, he brought the Pacific project back to life. In 1557 formal permission was given to its viceroy, Luis Velasco: 'We have decided to send you the authorization to undertake voyages of exploration overseas to islands or countries in your area.'[1] By 1559 Velasco had sounded out experts on the ground and drawn up a new proposal to cross the Pacific. The king was adamant that 'on no account are the ships to enter the Moluccas in contravention of the agreement with the king of Portugal but rather proceed to islands adjacent to that area, for example the Filipinas which are outside the Mortgage Line and are reported to produce spices'.[2] Philip was deluded here – apart from a little cinnamon on Mindanao, these islands were no substitute for the spice riches of the Moluccas, and, although not specifically mentioned in the treaty document, they were in Portuguese territory. However, the principal aim of the expedition, 'after the service to be given to our Lord, is to establish a return to New Spain from the islands of the West'.[3] Without it, no trade and no settlements in the western Pacific were feasible; Marco Polo's China was out of reach. Like NASA scientists trying to solve the problem of re-entry, returning a man from space, this was to be Spain's moon-shot.

The man considered essential to the project, whom Velasco had already consulted, was Andrés de Urdaneta. Urdaneta, always a devout man, had taken holy orders and joined the Augustinians in 1552, yet retained a lively interest in Pacific exploration. The king sent the veteran traveller a highly polite request. Urdaneta's reply was surprised consent: 'While I had hoped to be able to spend the few remaining years of my life in retirement – taking into account I am fifty-two years of age and in failing health after a life of continual hardship since my boyhood – I am nevertheless ready to face the rigours of this voyage, knowing that it has been planned because of Your Majesty's great zeal in the service of God our Lord and for the spread of our holy Catholic faith.'[4]

Urdaneta had had years to study the Pacific return problem. Solving it required two essentials: extremely stout and well-provisioned ships, and correct timing of the return to catch favourable north-westerly winds that would carry them back to Mexico. He had also thought long and hard about all aspects of logistics and outward routes. However, for the monk there was a problem of conscience: the vexed and unresolvable issue of the Tordesillas Line. Urdaneta firmly believed the Philippines to be in the Portuguese zone and was not prepared to countenance a wilful transgression. He championed New Guinea as a goal for establishing a base. Velasco, himself, had similar qualms: 'ask any cosmographer you like . . . if landing in Filipinas is not contrary to the treaty [of Zaragoza]'.[5] There was one small let-out clause. Both men believed it would be permissible to enter Portuguese territory solely for meritorious Christian purposes: rescuing shipwrecked sailors who might be trapped there.

The new venture was seven years in preparation, cost vast amounts of money and drew on huge quantities of human labour. The ships were to be built in the port of Barra de Navidad on the Pacific shore and required raw materials drawn from across the world. In the fledgling new colonies, infrastructure and resources were always a challenge. There was a perpetual shortage of skilled labour. 'We had great trouble', complained one official, 'in finding even the twenty-eight or thirty skilled workmen which now comprises the ship-building band, though as many more died from the strain of overwork.'[6] Many of the industrial essentials could not be created in the New World. Artillery, anchors, arms and sail cloth had to be brought across the Atlantic from Seville to the port of Vera Cruz, then transhipped down the coast and portaged across the narrowest part of the isthmus – a distance of 200 miles – first on river barges then on waggons pulled by oxen. Rough roads had to be hacked through the jungle to the west coast at Tehuantepec. The goods were then ferried from there to Navidad, 650 miles up the coast. Masts were cut from the forests of Nicaragua and shipped to the yard. Gathering supplies was laborious, Velasco explained: 'we had to wait a whole year for the wheat harvest required for making biscuit. Other foodstuffs had to be hauled over long distances to the port of Navidad, and as some had to be kept dry and undamaged . . . we were compelled to wait for this year's dry season before loading them on the ships to ensure they would be fit for consumption over the two years projected for the voyage.'[7] The foodstuffs from Mexico City had to be floated across the Rio de Balsas on perilous makeshift rafts. Then there was the problem of recruiting crews. Probably enough was known of the previous voyages to make this a hard sell. Town criers accompanied by buglers and drums toured the towns talking up the prospects: high pay and the chance to get rich. Even so, it was necessary to resort to pressganging some of the mixed flotsam of Europeans adventuring in the New World. Such unwilling conscripts always posed the threat of mutiny or desertion.

The expedition was a remarkable feat of logistics and as expensive as a moon-shot. The years of planning, preparation and construction cost half a million gold pesos, but Philip still got good value. The fleet had been put together with an unprecedented level of care, based on all the accumulated experience of previous Pacific voyages and the studied advice of Urdaneta. 'They are the best built vessels yet launched in the Pacific, sturdy and well equipped,' reported Velasco.[8] He could justly be proud of the immense achievement of the preparations, though he did not live to see them come to fruition. They were exactly what Urdaneta had specified: two substantial vessels, the flagship the *San Pedro* of 500 tons, the second in command the 400-ton *San Pablo*, then two smaller ships: the 80-ton *San Juan* and a light scouting vessel, the 40-ton pinnace the *San Lucas*. All were well equipped and provisioned.

Like Urdaneta, the man chosen to lead this expedition, Miguel López de Legazpi, was a Basque, and had been recommended by him. Legazpi was something of a surprise choice. He had twenty-nine years' experience of administration in New Spain, yet none in military or nautical matters. He was described by a sneering rival for the post as a man who couldn't tell his left hand from his right, yet he was to prove an excellent commander.

'On Tuesday 21 November [1564] four hours before sunrise, the flagship fired a gun, and flinging her main sails to the breeze, started down the bay of Melesa from Navidad followed by the other ships.'[9] The mood of the chief pilot Esteban de Rodríguez was upbeat. 'I guarantee I shall do everything possible to make this venture a success,' Legazpi wrote.[10] Urdaneta was on board, along with three other Augustinian monks, tasked with spreading the faith in a new world. Evangelism was a key ingredient. The king had ordered the expedition to 'send holy guides to unfurl and wave the banners of Christ in the most distant parts of those islands, and to drive the devil from the tyrannical possession which he has held there for so long'.[11] The course was set to track exactly the route followed by Villalobos.

The overriding task of the venture was to finally solve the problem of the return, for which Urdaneta's involvement was critical. Legazpi was left in no doubt of this:

Father Andrés goes on this voyage on the orders of the king himself. So when the time comes, you or some other officer will select a ship and crew for the return voyage, and you will see to it that Father Urdaneta goes on that ship. For we are convinced he will be chiefly responsible, under God, for the success of this effort, because of his experience and his knowledge of seasonal wind patterns in those parts of the world. Therefore, whatever ship is sent, *make sure Father Urdaneta is on it and with the captain he selects*. No other arrangement will be tolerated.[12]

However, in the grand plan there was an inconvenient detail. The viceroy in New Spain was compelled to point out to King Philip that 'during our discussions . . . the friar Urdaneta gave us notice that if the expedition was sent to Filipinas, he would refuse to go, and with him refusing, all the other Augustinians he said, would follow suit'.[13] And yet, unbeknownst to Urdaneta, this was exactly where it would go, with the aim of trading spices and establishing a permanent base. To this end, Legazpi was sworn to secrecy and given sealed orders that he was not to divulge until the fleet was far out to sea.

The voyage was to be something of a scientific laboratory for exploration. Urdaneta insisted on the pilots keeping impeccable records of their position by celestial observation of latitude, and their best attempts to determine longitude. Urdaneta, passionate about accuracy, checked their work, something of an affront to their self-regard. One aim of this obsessive maritime survey was the hope of finally resolving the problem as to where the line between Spanish and Portuguese territories might lie. There were the familiar disruptions. Eight days after departure the scouting ship the *San Lucas* absconded and was seen no more. This small vessel was invaluable for nosing into shallow waters where the large ships dare not go, with its ability to land and obtain supplies in such situations. It was a serious blow.

They were well out to sea when Legazpi had the unpleasant task of calling the senior officers and priests together and reading them the sealed orders, that they were 'to land at islands bordering on the Moluccas for example at Filipinas and other islands [which] . . . are part of his Majesty's territory and reputed to produce spices . . . you will plot your course directly for those islands . . . to work towards the expansion of the kingdom of Castile through trade and commerce and other lawful means ... you may establish a settlement there if you wish'.[14] Whatever Urdaneta and the other friars thought about this, there was no going back; the betrayal was softened by the knowledge that they would be able to promote the Christian faith wherever they went.

They passed on uneventfully, following in Villalobos's track. They stopped at Guam, the Island of Thieves, where they were variously pelted with stones and traded with, and where the inhabitants lived up to their reputation by trying to dupe the outsiders in their bartering: 'time and again they sent containers filled with sand or grass, and just topped with rice. Even the coconut oil was found mixed with water.'[15] On the eve of departure, they found a cabin boy was missing; when his hacked body was discovered the Spaniards made a punitive raid, burning houses and hanging those they thought responsible.

The expedition had learned from the mistake of Villalobos, who had landed on the hunger coast of Mindanao. 'On February 13 about nine in the morning we saw land come up ahead.'[16] They had arrived at exactly the spot they aimed for: the twin islands of Samar and Leyte, to which their predecessors had given the name Las Filipinas. Initial contacts were reassuring: 'The ship's boats with about twenty men in each rowed ashore next day. We saw small houses which appeared to have been abandoned. Though after some time about fifty men came out to meet us. They were naked except for loin cloths and were tattooed all over. They carried shields and javelins with well-made iron blades: some wore gold bands on their ankles. They were peaceful, trusting and well behaved.'[17]

The abandoned houses, however, told a different story. As the incomers scouted the islands in search of food they were viewed with intense suspicion; sometimes with open hostility. Frequently the people picked up all their food and possessions, abandoned their villages and retreated into the jungle; in other cases there were aggressive stand-offs on the shore. The need to barter for supplies became increasingly critical and they were hindered by the inability to communicate with the local people via their Malay interpreter. Legazpi's approach was to demonstrate continuous goodwill and peaceful intentions but it was proving difficult to restrain his starving men. Finally, he appealed to the friars on board as to whether it was allowable to use force to obtain food in the face of death. Urdaneta accepted this let-out and the raids were made. It was only when they obtained the help of a Muslim translator who spoke both Malay and the local language that tensions eased and the reasons for the outright hostility were explained. A rogue Portuguese band, from whom new arrivals were indistinguishable, had raided, killed and kidnapped the local people. Now able to communicate via double interpretation and the giving of gifts to local chieftains, the tensions decreased. Meanwhile ships' carpenters were at work refitting the *San Pedro* to attempt the return voyage.

When the ship was ready there arose the crucial decision: should they attempt to make a settlement in the islands? The friars were against it on two grounds: first, Urdaneta's belief that these islands were within the Portuguese zone. But they had a second and more profound objection: regard for the rights of native people. They should be able to freely choose to accept or reject the right of entry and settlement. It was a small and seldom-heard objection in Europe's triumphalist century of expansion, a time of staking banners on foreign beaches across the globe and claiming automatic rights of possession in the name of their kings. However, given the royal instructions, the decision was a foregone conclusion. Henceforth Legazpi worked hard to woo local chieftains with gifts and demonstrations of peaceable behaviour. Meanwhile, where was the most suitable site for the proposed settlement? A side expedition was sent to scout the island of Cebu.

Cebu was a place of memory and ill-omen for the Spanish. It was here that Magellan had been killed in battle and twenty-seven other men had been lost at a banquet, but the scouting party reported back favourably. It was thickly populated, fertile and had an excellent harbour. Back history and desire stirred the generally peaceable Legazpi to a post-hoc justification:

> I decided to take the fleet to that island with the intention of asking for peace and friendship with the people there, as well as asking them to sell us food at reasonable prices. Should they refuse, I was determined to make war on them – a step I considered justifiable in their case, because in that very port town Magellan and his ships were well received, and the chief and his people were baptized ... later Magellan and over thirty [sic] of his men were killed ... and the remaining few Spaniards driven from the ground.[18]

Although a pious man and close to the Augustinians, Legazpi's unswerving loyalty to an absolute monarch overrode religious scruples. Another of the friars, Martin de Rada, later continued to object to such tactics: 'any conquest made in these islands by force of arms would be unjust, even if there was good reason for doing so'.[19] The objections were in vain.

On Easter Monday, 22 April 1565, the fleet hove into sight of Cebu. It was forty-four years almost to the day since Magellan's arrival. The local people watching on the shore perceived only threat. Making contact with the chieftain of the island, Tupas, proved a long and complex process. He sent messages from the interior that he would come, but did not appear; that he was afraid to come on board the alien ships; that he was ill. Doubtless he was uncertain what to do with this second visitation from Castile. The memory of Magellan undoubtedly lived long in the memory of the Visayan people. An ultimatum was delivered by interpreters, that Tupas had broken his word, that he should come and pay homage to the king of Spain's representative and make peace. The mood on the shore became more threatening. A large number of armed men gathered to oppose the unwelcome visitors. Now frustrated and apprehensive for their own safety, Legazpi gave orders to bombard the town. The roar and shatter of the cannon terrified the crowd. The people fled back into the forest, taking with them their possessions, food, livestock, women and children. The Spanish landed to find the whole place deserted; and worse for the ravenous men, they found no food to loot. The downbeat mood was however lifted by an extraordinary discovery. Among the contents of one village hut, a soldier discovered an object wrapped in a silk cloth. Inside was 'a statue of the Child Christ lying in a little pine box, dressed in a tiny shirt of Flanders linen and a velvet hat, all perfectly preserved, except the Cross on top of the globe which he held in his hand, was missing'.[20] It was taken as a providential sign that God wanted the Castilians to build a church and establish a settlement on Cebu. It was evidently the statue given by Magellan to a Christian convert, Juana wife of Hamubon. On Cebu they obtained an idea of the valuable trading connections in the region. The island was well placed to receive goods both from China, whence junks came on a regular basis, bringing silk, ivory, jade and porcelain, and from the spice-rich Moluccas.

The Spaniards' immediate priority was food. Raids were conducted to ferret out supplies. Spirits rose among the intruders, but they were hanging on by their fingertips; nocturnal counter-ambushes kept them in a state of unease. The high level of insecurity led Legazpi to order the construction of a defendable stockade on the beach. As the days went by the atmosphere began to thaw. The local people were also short of supplies and they were now unable to fish in the bay. A mixture of strong-arm tactics, gifts and demonstrations of goodwill softened up the chieftain and his people. Legazpi proposed a formal pardon for the murders in Magellan's time – a piece of European legalese probably incomprehensible to the local people. In the end Tupas appeared. Together with another chief, Tamuñan, they performed the blood brother ceremony with Legazpi – each drawing blood from his chest and mixing it in a cup of water from which they all drank. It was the only pact that the Cebu people recognised. There was a major misunderstanding of its significance. For the Visayans it was no more than an allowing of peaceful trade. From the Spanish side, this was not just the giving of permission for a trading outpost. They believed, on the basis of papal decree, that they were given overlordship of the people of the islands, who were rightfully subjects of the king of Spain. The islanders were to be magnanimously pardoned for the slaughter of Magellan and his men. Legazpi was acute enough to glimpse some cultural gap in the proceedings but read their responses as signs of native treachery: 'face to face with one, they agree to everything – never saying "no" to any proposal. But the moment they turn their backs, they never keep a promise and have no conception of truthfulness and sincerity.'[21] Realistically, for the Visayans, Europeans had proved to be a source of repeated trouble and they just wanted them off their patch, but faced with the imbalance of military resources 'no' was not an option.

Despite the ceremony of friendship there was further trouble. In the days following, no chieftain reappeared. Shortly after, a Spaniard was ambushed and slaughtered. In a counter-raid, the Spanish seized local people, including the wife and daughters of Tupas's brother. They were held as bargaining chips and treated courteously.

Their stockade was well fortified but the Spanish long-term presence rested on the ability of the *San Pedro* to make the return. 'Prompt assistance from New Spain is badly needed here,'[22] Legazpi wrote in letters to be carried back. In fact, the whole expedition was hanging by a thread. Could Urdaneta succeed where five previous voyages had failed? If not, the expedition was doomed, either to a slow collapse on the shores of Cebu or another ignominious surrender to the Portuguese in the Moluccas.

On 1 June 1565, the *San Pedro* slipped its moorings. This was the ship that Urdaneta had requested for the job. Now both ship and planner were to be put to the test. The vessel was handsomely provisioned; even during the lean times substantial stocks of biscuit had been held back in readiness. The *San Pedro* was the instrument of survival, the expedition's only parachute, and Urdaneta had reckoned on a voyage that could last up to eight months. All the experience of the past went into improving slim margins. Of the 200 men on board, almost all were sailors. There were to be no supernumeraries. The toll of long sea voyages demanded enough men to survive and work the ship to the coasts of New Spain. Extraordinarily, given this attention to detail, the captain was a 17-year-old. Felipe de Salcedo was Legazpi's grandson: ostensibly this was a piece of foolish nepotism, but the intention was to have someone utterly loyal to Legazpi who could be relied upon to follow Urdaneta's instructions to the letter. Also on board were the two most experienced pilots, Esteban de Rodríguez and Rodrigo de Espinosa, the ship's master. As before, the pilots were ordered to keep detailed daily logs, without conferring, to provide a scientific record of the voyage and a blueprint for future voyages, should it prove successful.

The *San Pedro* nosed its way out of the labyrinth of the Philippine islands and set sail due north, then swung north-east. For Urdaneta timing was everything. His strategy was first to use seasonal south-west winds to gain the high latitudes, then pick up a westerly to sweep them back to the Americas. They caught their last sight of land – an isolated lump of rock fringed with reefs – three weeks out. Thereafter there were no fixed points to aim for, only the pilots' slightly discrepant calculations, with the ship running east over thousands of miles of ocean. They sailed on day after day with no reference points but the sun and the blank horizon, moving still further up the rungs of latitude. At 39° north it was bitterly cold. Everything depended on Urdaneta's unshakeable confidence. On Monday 3 September Espinosa recorded in his log: 'in the evening we had to heave to on account of the overcast and darkness, for some of those who were also keeping a log felt we were close to the coast of New Spain according to their charts'.[23] The sense of anticipation was also a wish: men were growing weaker, the diet was limited and scurvy rife.

On 13 September Esteban de Rodríguez's log ends abruptly. He was a dying man. The same day the second pilot, Rodrigo de Espinosa, recorded 'we held steady on that course as we reckoned we should be close to land'.[24] On the 18th came the great sighting: 'at seven in the morning as I was sitting on the pilot's bench, I saw land to starboard'. It was an island that they christened 'Deseada', 'the long desired', now known as San Miguel off the Santa Barbara coast.

Steering south, five days later they sighted the Americas. They ran south in continuous sight of the coast of California. By this time the crew was at its last gasp. On 26 September the ship's master Martin de Ibarra died and was dropped into the sea; the next day chief pilot Esteban de Rodríguez followed. On 1 October his successor, Rodrigo de Espinosa, recorded: 'Dawn came up as we lay off Navidad. I looked back and calculated we had come 1892 leagues from the port of Cebu to that of Navidad. I then went up to the captain and asked where he wished to anchor ... He told me to carry on to Acapulco.' This was apparently on the advice of Urdaneta, who had realised its far greater potential. It was not a popular decision. 'I followed his orders though at that moment there were no more than sixteen men fit to work the ship, for all the others were sick, and in fact sixteen had died during the voyage. We reached the port of Acapulco on Monday 8 October after a voyage of considerable hardship for every man on board.'[25]

Those still able to work were almost too weak to lower the anchors. The voyage had lasted 123 days, the longest oceanic voyage yet made in the age of European exploration. They had travelled 11,160 miles without a landfall, more than half the distance round the world. The men who crawled ashore at Acapulco with blotched skin and bloody and putrid gums were lucky to be alive. Scurvy – lack of vitamin C – could be expected to start killing men after eighty-four days, to wipe out a whole crew after 111, yet only sixteen had died. The aged Urdaneta himself appeared indestructible. It said a great deal for the planning and the laying in of supplies.

Urdaneta had calculated the voyage would take up to eight months; they had accomplished it in four. In the process he had solved the last great riddle of European sixteenth-century navigation. The pilots' logs and charts contained the blueprints for Pacific returns. The significance of this was recognised almost immediately: it was the final buckle in the belt of circumnavigations that would allow the flow of people, materials and trades in all directions. But for Urdaneta the world traveller the voyage was not over: he had to report personally back to Philip in Madrid.

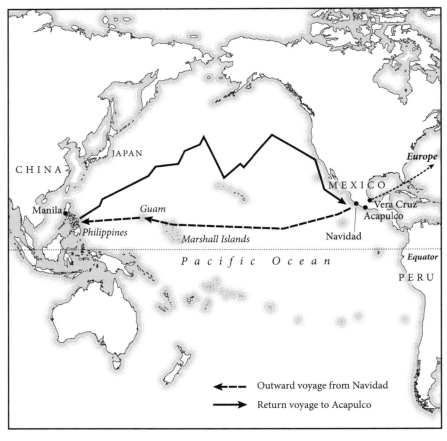

Map 7. Pioneering the galleon route.

Sometime around the end of October he and his travelling companions were saluted into Mexico City by large crowds, triumphant gunshots and the ringing of church bells. 'The people were in raptures at the success of the voyage, complaisantly telling one another that now their city would become the centre of the world.'[26] By January 1566 Urdaneta took ship from Havana; when the news reached Seville with Legazpi's request for support and supplies, the cosmographers conveniently decided that the Philippines must lie in the Spanish zone and authorised the sending of reinforcements and supplies to defend the occupation.

Urdaneta backed out of the limelight. The great and durable traveller, who had seen and experienced as much as any man of his times, who had first sailed out of Seville as a 17-year-old, who had lived wild in the Moluccas for a decade, who had circumnavigated the world courtesy of the Portuguese and had observed and thought and written about the great navigational issues of his time more deeply than anyone else, sailed back to Mexico as an Augustinian friar the following year. He requested permission to return to the Philippines and continue with missionary work. This was refused on account of his age. He would die at the monastery in Mexico City on 3 June 1568 and was buried there. He was 60 years old – remarkable longevity given the toughness of his life.

Unaware of Urdaneta's success, Legazpi and his men were holed up at Cebu, protected by a stockade. His foothold was parlous; his soft touch approach to diplomacy with the local people was compromised by desperation; food was in short supply and depended on raiding villages and adjacent islands. Meanwhile, a mutinous attempt by some of the men to steal a ship and sail away was foiled and its ringleaders hanged.

On 1 October 1566, while scouting the archipelago, they stumbled on a stricken vessel. The *San Geronimo* had made the crossing from Acapulco; its exhausted crew had been without food or water for several days. But they brought with them the news that the *San Pedro*, under Urdaneta, had managed the Pacific return. If heartened by the success, Legazpi was also disappointed – they had brought no supplies and no indication from Spain as to what the king expected of him – and Cebu was becoming an uncomfortable place to be: a cul-de-sac backed by high mountains and no immediate food sources. This became critical when a Portuguese fleet turned up from Ternate and boxed them in. The blockade was total and the Portuguese commander, Gonçalo de Pereira, pointed out that the Spaniards were trespassing. As he had a copy of a letter from Charles V to Villalobos castigating him for entering the islands of the Philippines because they were included in the sale to the Portuguese, the case was clear cut. The blockade went on; the Spaniards starved, yet Pereira hesitated to make a full-frontal attack. After a two-month blockade, he withdrew his ships. But the warning was there: Cebu was a mousetrap.

Legazpi had no idea what the king meant him to do. Philip was 7,000 miles away; the men were famished; the Portuguese might return. He thought they had been abandoned. In a desperate gamble he despatched the remarkable Juan de la Isla to find out. He set sail in the tiny 80-ton *San Juan*, a vessel already frayed and the worse for wear, to attempt a repeat of the Pacific return. It was an adventure that demonstrated the astonishingly lengthy chains of command with which the Spanish kings attempted to manage their far-flung empire. De la Isla made it across the ocean (8,900 miles), journeyed across the isthmus from Acapulco to Vera Cruz (450 miles), took ship across the Atlantic to Seville (3,800 miles), travelled on to Philip's court in Madrid (250 miles), and gave the king a cogent account of the situation: their parlous and endangered plight, the need for a regular shuttle of supplies and soldiers, an overall strategy for a settlement in the islands – if there was to be one – and speed. De la Isla's politely worded plea was 'Do something and do it fast' – otherwise, the expedition would perish.

Philip was weighted down with European wars and the threats of Ottoman piracy but he did at least rapidly authorise supplies and a schooner to carry them to Mexico: 'You yourself go on board your ship on the South Sea and be off to the Philippines without delay.'[27]

De la Isla efficiently collected his shopping list of supplies, sourced a ship to transport them and set sail back across the Atlantic, then portaged the goods across the isthmus to Acapulco. At the end of January 1570, he could write back to Philip that three ships were ready to depart for the Philippines. 'I will be able to sail on February 2. I am bringing one hundred and fifty men, soldiers and sailors [as] reinforcements, as well as married couples, religious, gunners, musketeers, smiths, caulkers and carpenters ... I am taking my wife and children with me to continue in the king's service in that land, as I have always done.'[28] The implication of this was that they were intended to create a permanent settlement in the Philippines. He reached the Philippines in July. The round trip had taken him three years.

Philip's accompanying letter did somewhat clear up the issue of settlement. 'You shall assign and allot villages in the islands that have submitted to us, as you think best, according to the Law of the Indies: provided you do not assign capital towns, or seaports or strictly Spanish settlements – for these are reserved to the Crown.'[29] Legazpi was granted grand titles: governor of the Philippine islands and the more meaningless governorship of the Islas de los Ladrones, plus a fine salary of 2,000 ducats. In practice the latter was an empty promise, as Legazpi was not actually given the money; he had to raise it himself from the subject people. Philip was always strapped for cash and the conquered peoples of the Philippines were to pay for their own subjugation. Remaining just within the bounds of politeness in his returning letter, Legazpi, one of the most judicious and scrupulous servants of the Spanish crown, asked for further help and instructions. Elsewhere he was more forthright: 'Juan de la Isla arrived here from Court without a letter or message of any kind from his Majesty or the Council ... Not one word in answer to our questions. This is a terrible disappointment to us here – not a single directive as to what policy we should pursue. Imagine just one letter from the king in eight years!'[30] The inexhaustible de la Isla had hardly time to turn around before he was sailing back to Mexico.

By the time he had come back from his first three-year round trip, Legazpi, concerned lest the Portuguese should return and anxious about the shortage of food, had shifted his base camp to another island, Panay, described as a place that 'abounds in rice and no one coming by sea could prevent us from going up the river to the mountainous interior'.[31] As they scouted the islands further north, engaging the local people in encounters that were by turns peaceful and hostile, they heard repeated accounts of the island of Luzon, the largest in the archipelago, and the bay of Manila, its most important trading centre.

Manila, 'the place by the waterlilies', was a major hub in an extensive and very old trading network that linked the peoples and goods of Asia. It connected the trading routes of Japan and China, the spice-bearing Moluccas, the sultanate of Brunei, Java and Sumatra, and the seaway to Malacca, another hub, that linked to the Indian Ocean. Muslim merchants had penetrated deep into the Philippine archipelago, bringing with them the religion of Islam and ruling sultanates. Manila was one such sultanate, ruled by Rajah Suleyman, a Borneo Malay, somewhat resented by the local Tagalog people. It was the distribution point for silk and porcelain from China, Japanese silver, cloves and nutmeg from the Moluccas and the Bandas. It despatched gold panned from the mountains of Luzon, sent rice and timber to Malacca. The Spanish were gradually piecing together an understanding of this rich web of trading connections. In their explorations they had encountered Chinese junks, 'loaded with silk, gold thread, musk, glazed porcelain bowls . . . and the decks, filled with earthen jars and crockery', and plundered them.[32] What Legazpi now needed was a secure base with a good defensible harbour and access to local food supplies. As they reached deeper into the archipelago, taking native strongholds by force, enquiry and reconnaissance confirmed to Legazpi that Manila on the island of Luzon was the most promising.

In 1570, a fleet was despatched to reconnoitre. An anonymous eyewitness recorded the first sight: 'The entrance to the port of Manila is from the west, where the sea forms a great basin thirty leagues in extent. Within this bay is Manila and many other towns as well, along the shore. Manila itself is on a promontory between the river and the sea ... the land all round this bay was really marvellous; tilled and cultivated everywhere, smooth slopes cleared of jungle. Nowhere have we seen in these islands such a splendid sight.'[33]

A deputation to the Rajah Suleyman, whose stockade was fortified with cannon, led to a tense stand-off, hesitation and distrust on both sides. When Suleyman bombarded the ships, the Spaniards vaulted the stockade and burnt the town on the promontory. But the initial recce had confirmed that Manila was ideal for Legazpi's purposes. The following spring, he committed to decisive action.

'I left Panay on April 17 1571 aboard a newly build galliot, together with the pinnace *San Lucas* and an older frigate and a *bangka* [a Filipino vessel] and twenty-three native oared boats. We were 210 Spaniards,' Legazpi wrote later.[34] With them went their allies – Visayan and Tagalogs, 'people who live along the river' – who had no love for the intrusive rule of the Brunei Muslims. It took them a month to assemble support along the way. This small strike force disembarked on 17 May. Some of the local tribal leaders submitted on sight; Suleyman did not. Legazpi's men landed on the peninsula they had scorched the previous year, and claimed it for Spain. Two weeks later the rajah launched a counter-attack. Despite having his own gunpowder artillery, it was no match for the more disciplined shooting of the Spanish, supported by their native allies. Three hundred Filipinos were killed, along with Suleyman himself. This crushing defeat was decisive. Tribal chieftains from the surrounding area came to make submission.

On 24 June 1571, the feast of John the Baptist, Legazpi formally founded the Spanish city of Manila. The Visayans and Tagalogs set to, rapidly constructing houses in the traditional manner. The Spaniards had come to stay. It was to be the high-water mark of westward Spanish expansion. At times they were hanging on by their fingernails, only rescued by reinforcement from Mexico, but Legazpi's method of patient if firm diplomacy and restrained use of superior military technology had been effective. By the standards of the conquistadors of the Americas, the conquest of the Philippines, which was only ever partial, had been modest in the application of armed violence. Even so, the voice of the Catholic evangelising mission of the Augustinians was a thorn in the side. The Augustinian missionary Martin de Rada was just one of the voices raised against Spain's conquering projects: 'It is not right to use soldiers to conquer this land, for they have no thought of the good of the country, but to get rich quick and go home. If they fail in this, they just destroy and ravage.'[35] As critical as the gunpowder advantage had been the inherent weakness of the social and political structures of the archipelago. There was no unified authority under powerful rulers, just loose associations of villages. Endemic local conflicts between small communities allowed the Spanish to side with one group and help it to defeat its enemies, thus ensuring the submission of both. It was the tactic that Cortés had employed so effectively in Mexico but on a far larger scale.

The establishment of Manila gave the Spanish a terminus and a base. The summer of 1571 was a signal moment, a pivot of world history. Following Urdaneta's blueprint sailing directions, the Spanish had been able quickly to replicate the return across the Pacific to aid Legazpi, though not without some difficulty. This fulfilled Spanish dreams of linking Asia to the Americas. Manila was set to be a satellite of New Spain and it turned the Pacific into a Spanish lake, at least for a while.

Legazpi died just a year later but he realised what he had done. Manila now provided Spain with an extraordinary entrepôt from which to conduct trade with the massively wealthy Orient. They were on the threshold of great things, Legazpi wrote back to Philip: 'we are at the gate and in the vicinity of the most fortunate countries of the world and the most remote ... great China, Brunei, Java, Lauzon, Sumatra, Maluco, Malacca, Siam, Lequios [Ryukyu islands], Japan, and other rich and large provinces'.[36]

The year 1571 saw a coincidental convergence of forces across the world. As Legazpi was establishing a permanent settlement at Manila, the massed galleys of Philip II were hurtling across the Mediterranean towards an Ottoman fleet for a climactic sea battle at Lepanto. In Japan, the Portuguese were establishing a trading base in Nagasaki. In Beijing, the Ming emperor was instituting a radical overhaul of the Chinese tax system. One single commodity linked these unconnected events across time and space: the use of silver to trade, exchange and wage wars. And it was the luck and curse of the Spanish empire that it happened to be in possession of the world's largest source of this precious metal.

Fifteen

Galleons of Desire
1545-71

High in the remote Bolivian Andes, a barren, treeless alpine wilderness, sits the mountain of Potosí, a rust-red cone rising to 16,000 feet. In the sixteenth century, it lay within the viceroyalty of Peru. The Spanish just referred to it as *Cerro Rico* – the Rich Hill. Here, in 1545, a local prospector discovered that the earth on the mountain was massively rich in silver. What followed was the largest mining boom in history. Hundreds of adits – horizontal shafts with bifurcating tunnels – honeycombed deep into the mountain. It was the cruellest of penal settlements. The work was undertaken by up to 10,000 forced native labourers. They sweated in the humid, oxygen-starved bowels of the mountain, up and down a network of parlous makeshift ladders, digging out the silver ore and carrying it to the surface. Their task each day was to lug up a quota of twenty-five bags of the precious dirt, each weighing 45 kilograms. When they reached fresh air they were hit by the mountain's killing wind and icy cold – as low as 16°C below zero in the winter, when the mountain was capped with snow. Their diet consisted largely of frozen potatoes and coca leaves. 'If twenty healthy Indians enter on Monday, half may emerge crippled on Saturday,' one mining boss noted.[1] The consumption of human labour depopulated the surrounding area. It

*26. Inside the hellish mountain. The Quechua miners hacked away by dim
candlelight. They also tied candles to their thumbs to climb up and down rickety
ladders made of ox hide with heavy loads of ore strapped to their backs. To
occasionally rest their burdens, they carved stone benches into the rock.*

was as cruel an exploitation of native peoples as anywhere in this era
of European expansion. The local Quechua name for Potosí was
simply 'the mountain that eats men'. A bookish European might
have been reminded of Dante's hell.

At its foot – at an altitude of 13,000 feet, as high as Lhasa – a
boom town sprang up. By the early seventeenth century Potosí's
population had mushroomed to 160,000. It was the fourth-largest
city in the Christian world, almost the size of London or Paris, bigger
than Seville and Milan, twice the size of Madrid, the centre of Spain's
empire. It attracted or compelled people from across the Europe and
beyond: Basques, Portuguese, Italians, Flemish people, enslaved

Africans – a melting pot of fates and races. Potosí was an astonishing freak, unlike any other place in the world, the prototype of Californian gold rush towns, yet on a far vaster scale – a crazy boom-and-bust city of extravagant wealth, gang warfare, religious festivities, grand houses, prostitution and murder. By the start of the seventeenth century, it had twenty churches and more brothels per square mile than any city in Spain. It was instantly famous, a by-word for wealth: 'worth a Potosí' was to conjure unimaginable riches. Charles V labelled it the 'Treasury of the World'. Its fame spread as fast as the wind in ships' sails could carry it. A woodcut image of Potosí by an early traveller, Pedro Cieza de León, in 1553, captured the imagination of Europe. His account of the mountain was quickly translated into German, French, Dutch, Italian and English. People, largely men – in the early days there were few respectable women in the place – came from all over the world, drawn by the magnetic pull of this least magnetic of metals.

Potosí was, by turns, an environmental warning, a centre of technological innovation, a melting pot of the world's peoples, a place where men could reinvent themselves, a sinkhole of depravity, a global city. Mercury, mined from the mountain of Huancavelica, 1,000 miles away, with equally disastrous effects on the enforced local people, was transported by llamas to the coast and then shipped south for use in an innovative process to refine the silver ore. There was, it was said, 'no silver without mercury, no mercury without silver [to pay for its extraction]'.[2] Hydro-engineering from twenty-two dams drove 140 thudding mills that crushed the ore; the leaching mercury and heavy metals poisoned the soil; at night the mountain was dotted with the red glow of hundreds of furnaces. This frenzied plundering of the mountain never stopped; the silver kept flowing, stamped into ingots and pieces of eight in the city's mint and carried down to ports on the Pacific coast, or smuggled east down the River of Silver (the Rio de la Plata) through the Land of Silver (Argentina) and out into the Atlantic. From there silver flowed across the world.

*27. The woodcut image of Potosí by Pedro Cieza de León that fed the
mountain's fame in Europe.*

Portuguese merchants carried it back to Lisbon, then exchanged it for enslaved people on the African coast, whom they then re-imported into the New World. 'I am rich Potosí, Treasury of the World, King of Mountains and Envy of Kings', read the city's coat of arms. It was a place of dreams and nightmares, as devouring and implacable as an Inca god.

Potosí would boom and then slowly decline, but during the first century of its operation it produced half the world's silver, and it came on stream at just the right moment. It coincided with the Ming empire's overhauling of its tax system. Overissue of China's paper money currency had led to collapse; taxes were then being paid in an unwieldy diversity of forms, such as rice and labour serv-ices. As Potosí was getting into its stride in the 1570s, the emperor replaced all these diverse payment methods with an efficient central-ising reform: the single-whip system. Henceforward, all taxes were to be paid in silver. China was now hungry for the output of the silver mines of the world; its demand for the shiny metal was insatiable. Potosí produced it and Manila was the pivotal point of exchange.

China had the largest population in the world. In the sixteenth century it accounted for a quarter of the planet's people: by 1600, about 230 million, with cities of a size unimaginable to Europeans. Nanjing had over a million people, Beijing 660,000. London then had 200,000. In the late sixteenth century this 25 per cent of the global population converted to the use of silver and in the process accelerated the creation of global trade. The hunger for silver in China was enormous. It was twice as valuable within the country as elsewhere in the world. Asia had had little interest in the material production of Europe up to that point – only Russia had any appetite for the English cloth trade – and China none, as Gaspar da Cruz had pointed out. The silver revolution changed the game. China became a relentless vacuum pump that sucked in the world's silver in return for its vast and highly desirable range of consumer products. The mines of Potosí, together with those of Mexico and Japan, supplied the silver. The profits to be made from the high value of silver in China were huge. They came back in the form of the luxuries that Chinese industrial production could provide, and both the silver and the goods were largely carried in European ships.

Silver flowed in all directions: some of it from the mines of the Americas across the Pacific from Acapulco, via Manila to China. A great deal went east across the Atlantic from the Americas in the hold of Spanish ships or smuggled in Portuguese ones. In Spain it financed imperial wars. The coin that entered Seville paid for those Spanish galleys at Lepanto and the interminable wars of Philip with the Protestant countries of northern Europe, but, like water, silver found its own level. Given that it was twice as valuable to the Chinese as to the Europeans, much of it just flowed east again, in the holds of Portuguese ships, round the Cape of Good Hope via Malacca, the

Moluccas and Macau – into China. Silver became the currency that facilitated the birth of global trade. Although Europeans, with their competent sailing ships and gunpowder, were the carriers of silver and the purchasers of Chinese produce, the economic engine of trading networks, which spread in all directions, was China. Then as now, the Middle Kingdom produced and Europe consumed. Like a collision of atoms, the ricocheting consequences spread across the world. While Mexico City became a city of outrageous wealth, Philip could finance multifaceted European wars. Silver facilitated the slave trade. Portuguese slavers exported captured Africans to South America in exchange for the smuggled silver that made it to Brazil.

The Philippines themselves had few exploitable resources – a little cinnamon, a little gold, wax and hardwood – but Manila stood at the centre of a network of trade routes and production centres. Legazpi understood almost immediately why occupying this bay was so important. The settlement's function, its only function, was to be an entrepôt, a turntable of commodities from China and Japan, from Portuguese Macau, from the Moluccas, Java and Sumatra, from Malacca, Siam and Cambodia. Manila opened a merchant's chest of desirable commodities, above all those of China – silk and porcelain, rugs, toys, and other products of the consummate skills of its cunning craftsmen; spices from the Moluccas; bronze and copper, amber and cabinet work from Japan; ivory, musk, rubies and sapphires from Indochina; the cotton goods of India; the camphor of Borneo. All in exchange for silver. Manila attracted about twenty or thirty Chinese junks a year and the city boomed. It soon contained a large resident Chinese population, confined to a ghetto outside the city walls.

Urdaneta's route had been critical to the interests of Spain and the global circulation of goods. It connected Spain to the farthest east by way of Mexico and South America, following his blueprint, via a regular shipping line. In 1565, Urdaneta had departed from Manila to the port of Acapulco. And almost every year from 1571 until 1815, with a few notable exceptions, one or two galleons, constructed in

Por Golfos mas procelofos,

efta Nave con fu vuelo.

con valor, a refto, y zelo,

haze gala de Neptuno.

*28. An eighteenth-century copperplate print of a Spanish galleon:
'Through the worst stormy waters, with courage, purpose and zeal,
this ship shows off its sails to Neptune.'*

Manila's shipyard at Cavite from huge quantities of local hardwood,
set sail for Acapulco with the cargoes of the east in June, and would
return the following year, laden with silver to feed the trade cycle,
dependent on the monsoon and the pattern of the trade winds. The
galleons became mythic transports of wealth and desire in the imagination of captivated Europeans – and in the fullness of time, of
interloping pirates.

The galleons were bulk carriers, the container ships of the age,
heavily loaded, but lightly armed. Their cannon were often stowed

below decks so that they could hardly be employed in an emergency: the assumption was of an uncontested sea. The galleons departing from Manila were crammed with the marketable products of Asia, tightly packed into bundles. Hold space was profit and sold as such; every nook and cranny was occupied with merchandise. Sailors slept on deck; the cabins were cells 5 feet square. The temptations of wealth made the galleons vehicles of smuggling, corruption and fraud. Overloading made them dangerous. When an Italian adventurer, Gemelli Careri, on an anti-clockwise world tour, prepared to sail on the Manila galleon of 1693, it was stopped from departing. Instead of its manifest capacity of 1,500 bales of merchandise, it was carrying 2,200. It was the ordinary seamen's chests that were then unloaded. Despite this, the officers wanted more storage space, so the number of water jars the ship was carrying was reduced. Even so, once at sea, some of the 'water jars' were found to be packed with merchandise, which was then thrown overboard. Water provision remained a problem throughout the voyage.

The Spanish crown tried fruitlessly to limit the size of ships for reasons of safety and manoeuvrability, but the galleons just kept getting larger. First 300 tons, then 500, then 700, up to giants of 2,000 tons. The economic rationale for larger ships was clear, yet their reduced manoeuvrability increased the shipwreck threat, and they would later become a prime target for pirate plunder. The passengers on departing ships sometimes felt so unsafe that they demanded the vessel turn back; on one occasion the captain refused and the ship sailed off into oblivion.

On these vessels depended the viability of the community of Manila and the fortune or bankruptcy of the city – and also that of the residents of Acapulco and Mexico City and Vera Cruz. The long-range economic shock waves of a shipwreck or failure to sail could be felt all the way back to Seville. Departure from Manila, usually in June, was a solemn but festive occasion, mingling the commercial and the religious: church bells rang, incense wafted, saints were petitioned, a carved wooden image of the Virgin of Safe Voyages was processed round the city walls then taken aboard, the archbishop blessed the vessel and its passengers and crew – a complement of something between 300 and 500 people. Those with relatives on board or fortunes in the hold repeated the prayer '*Dios llevandolo en salvamento*' – 'God bring the ship to safety' – a prayer also written on the ship's cargo manifest. The galleon departed to a ringing salvo of seven cannon shots – considered to be the lucky number. Its return would prompt a fiesta of fireworks, music and masses.

Despite the advantages of its harbour, the departure from Manila was extremely tricky. Ships had to wend their way out of the islands via the San Bernardino Strait, a chokepoint whose transit wrecked some twenty ships and took two months. From there they set a north-east course to catch the trade winds. The whole voyage could take at least six months and as long as eight. It was 9,000 miles to Acapulco and the galleons required pumping all the way.

Gemelli Careri found the 1693 *tornaviaje* from Manila just awful:

> The voyage from the Philippine Islands to America may be called the longest and most dreadful of any in the world; as well because of the vast ocean to be crossed, being almost the one half of the terra aqueous globe with the wind always ahead; as for the terrible tempests that happen there, one upon the back of another, and for the terrible diseases that seize people, in the seven or eight months, lying at sea sometimes near the line, sometimes cold, sometimes hot, which is enough to destroy a man of steel, much more flesh and blood, which at sea had but indifferent food.[3]

When Careri went ashore on a Pacific Island he carried a flintlock in fear of native ambushes. As the voyage went on, water was increasingly rationed; the situation was only eased by heavy rainfall. Everyone rushed for containers. For Careri the ocean was full of both wonder and dread, sometimes placid, sometimes turbulent: 'I was astonished and trembled to see the sea had a motion like water boiling over a hot fire.'[4] The storms were terrifying:

> A great sea blowing on Tuesday 2nd ... and the sea beating hard upon us, we were forced to lie by the foresail backed, and the waves beating so furiously on the rudder that the whipstaff broke ... the ship was tossed upon vast mountains of water, and then again seemed to sink to the abyss, the waves breaking over it ... about midnight I had like to be knocked in the head by two flint-locks of the guns falling on my head.[5]

When it got particularly desperate the image of St Francis Xavier was processed around the ship and the captain vowed an offering of 200 pieces of eight to calm the sea.

At times the cold was intense; at others they sat in flat calms. Careri was fed encouraging stories by old hands of ships that were wrecked or vanished without trace. It confirmed his belief that 'this voyage has always been dangerous and dreadful'.[6] The insect life was intolerable: 'the ship swarms with little vermin ... bred in the biscuits, so swift that they in a short time not only run over cabins, beds, and the very dishes men eat on but insensibly fasten upon the body'. There was an abundance of flies in the soup 'in which also swim worms of several sorts'.[7] In tranquil times there were diversions and entertainments, such as dancing and acting, to intersperse long periods of boredom.

'The poor people,' he wrote, 'stowed in the cabins of the galleon bound towards the land of desire of New Spain endure no less hard-ships than the children of Israel did ... there is hunger, thirst, sickness, cold, continuous watching and other sufferings ... besides terrible shocks from side to side by the furious beating of the waves.'[8] He considered no prospect of wealth was worth the suffering: 'for my part, these nor great hopes shall not prevail with me to undertake that voyage again, which is enough to destroy a man, or make him unfit for anything as long as he lives'.[9] He calculated this transit of purgatory precisely: 204 days and five hours. Nor was he impressed by the experience of arrival in the promised land: 'as for the city of Acapulco, I think it might more properly be called a poor village of fishermen than the chief mart of the South Sea and port for the voyage to China, so mean and wretched are the houses, being made of nothing but wood, mud and straw'.[10]

In comparison, for Francesco Carletti, another Italian adventurer travelling the other way, from Acapulco to Manila, a century earlier, the experience of the Pacific crossing was quite different: a serene, if monotonous armchair ride, similar to that of Pigafetta. 'In a prosperous and very happy navigation, we made it without ever moving the sails or slackening the yards, and always with a following wind.'[11] It took just sixty-six days. What went principally in this direction was silver from the mountain of Potosí and the mines of Mexico.

At the first appearance of the seasonal galleon, Acapulco came alive. Word was sent express to Mexico City. Careri could report that its city bells rang with joy; merchants hurried to the port for a gaudy seasonal trade fair. For a few brief months Acapulco was transformed into a vibrant market. From there, goods were carried to Mexico City on what was called the China Road; none of this was easy. Crossing the Papagayo River en route was dangerous, as Carletti found:

There is no accommodation for crossing it, neither a bridge nor a ferry, it was necessary for us to do what others did. We placed ourselves on a mass of thick dry gourds bound together with a netting of cane. On that we placed the saddle of our horse, which swam across. On that saddle we sat down. Then four of those Indians, one at each corner of the raft of bound gourds, swam, pushing it and directing it to the opposite bank of the river and breaking through that current of water. This is a thing no less perilous than tedious, and especially for the great quantity and value of goods that pass each year. Nevertheless, it must be done, and even the viceroy passes by there with the same difficulty and danger when he goes from Mexico to embark at that port of Acapulco and pass over to governing Peru.[12]

A proportion of the goods were portaged on, with similar difficulties, to Vera Cruz on the Atlantic Coast, sparking matching trades and festivities. From there, Atlantic galleons carried merchandise back to Spain.

If Careri had no wish to repeat the Pacific crossing, others did: 'Notwithstanding the dreadful sufferings in this prodigious voyage, yet the desire of gain prevails with many to venture through it, four, six and some ten times.'[13] The returns were considerable and people did get rich. He calculated that the profits on the voyage ran at 150

29. The difficulties of travelling in Mexico: crossing the River Papagayo.

to 200 per cent. On top of legitimate trade, taxed by the Spanish crown, there was considerable smuggling, and under-reporting. The level of corruption around the galleon trade was stunning.

The price of trade, however, was high. Of some 400 voyages of the galleons, at least fifty ships never made it, usually with a high, or total, loss of life. Typhoons and shipwrecks on Pacific islands tore vessels apart and drowned their passengers; those who made it ashore were liable to be killed by the local people who salvaged the loot; scurvy ravaged ships; fire from the galley cooking pit or from lanterns and candles was another destroyer. The seabed of the Pacific remains littered with the scattered treasure of Asia. A high proportion of the losses took place leaving or entering the San Bernardino Strait. Some galleons just vanished. In 1657, a year after its departure from Manila, the *San José* was found lifeless off the coast of Acapulco, a drifting coffin laden with corpses and a hold full of silk. Occasional inter-lopers broke into the Spanish Lake. Word of the treasure galleons of Spain soon fired the imagination of northern European pirates. In 1579, Francis Drake captured such a ship bound for Manila on his voyage round the world and made a 4,700 per cent return for his investors. Nearly two centuries later, during war between England and Spain, the English admiral George Anson took the *Nuestra Señora de Covadonga*, en route to Manila. Although the ship had sixty guns, only ten were operational at the time. Anson made off with 1,313,843 silver dollars and 35 tons of silver bullion. It took thirty-two carts to carry some of this legendary booty through the streets of London, watched by goggling crowds. To the English it was 'the prize of all the oceans'.

For Manila and Acapulco, Mexico City and Vera Cruz – the links in the long chain that led from China to Spain – such total losses on the annual galley run were spectacular. In 1638, the 2,000-ton *Nuestra Señora de la Concepción*, the largest Manila galleon the Spanish ever built, struck a reef threading through the Mariana islands, carrying Chinese silk, porcelain, cotton from India, ivory from Cambodia, camphor from Borneo, cinnamon and pepper and cloves from the Spice Islands and jewels from Burma, Ceylon and Siam. The loss was immense but uncalculated: the absence of a manifest of its cargo back in Manila suggested large-scale corruption. Then the returning ship, the *San Ambrosio*, bringing silver from Acapulco, sank off the island of Luzon. To compound the cycle of misfortune, the next outbound galleon went down near Japan. The triple catastrophe crippled Manila. Ten tons of silver had failed to arrive; it was impossible to pay for the goods brought to Manila on Chinese junks. Trade was at a standstill. The result was insurrection by the Chinese colony, a massacre by the Spanish governor and the near destruction of the city.

The volumes of goods carried back and forth were enormous. It is estimated that three-quarters of a million kilograms of silver – some 800 tons – crossed the Pacific to Manila in the first half of the seventeenth century; the real amount was probably double that, allowing for high levels of smuggling. Travelling the other way was, above all, silk. Galleons at the time of the *Concepción* shipwreck would transport something between 30 and 50 tons a time – the demand for luxurious fabrics was voracious.

Silk for silver: a thread running through the dynamic trade developments of the sixteenth-century world. The Portuguese provided another link in the global supply chain. When China banned direct trade with Japan in 1557, Macau was well positioned to profit. Japan had active silver mines; China had the quality silk fabric the Japanese desired. Into the gap stepped Portuguese merchants to facilitate the exchange. They now had regular access to the twice-yearly Canton trade fairs where they could buy and sell. In 1571, hand in hand with the Jesuits, they acquired the use of a harbour at Nagasaki. The Portuguese equivalent of the Manila galleon – the Great Ship from Amacon (Macau) – was a bulk carrier of similar size to the giants of Spanish navigation. Each year it made an annual round tour. Departing from Goa, putting in at Macau to collect silk and other merchandise, it sailed on to Japan. Back came silver for the Chinese market, along with weapons and exquisite works of art – swords and pikes, lacquer ware and gold-leaf screens. The silver went on to China, other merchandise might go to Manila, from which smuggled goods would also come, or on the long seaway back to Portugal. Macau was the turntable of a short-distance three-cornered trade – China–Macau–Nagasaki–Macau–China – and it was immensely profitable.

Sixteen

Going Global

A Chinese official during the Ming era calculated that transport on inland waterways was 30 to 40 per cent cheaper than by land. By sea the advantage was 70 to 80 per cent. Ships were many times more rapid and economical than camels plodding the ancient silk roads. The sixteenth century saw an acceleration of connectivity. By 1600, all the continents could trade with each other, linked by a maritime chain encircling the world and the emergence of silver as a global currency driven by China. Its nodal points: Lisbon, Goa, Malacca, Macau, Canton, Nagasaki, Manila, Acapulco, Mexico City, Vera Cruz, Seville. The discovery of a reliable return route across the Pacific had been the final buckle in this maritime belt.

It had taken the restless Europeans just eighty years to weave the oceans together. From Columbus via Vasco da Gama, Magellan, Urdaneta and the Portuguese voyages to China and Japan they had traversed the navigable seas of the planet. They had probed its waters from 70° north within the Arctic circle by Willoughby and Chancellor to 54° south by Magellan. The foundation of Spanish Manila was the high watermark of this eruption of Europe out of Europe. It was a triumph of maritime communication and transportation technology. In the process the Europeans had drawn maps and replicated the world's spherical reality in atlases and globes. It was possible for humans to visualise their world and grasp its extent.

Almost overnight, Manila became an important entrepôt. Already tapped into traditional regional trading systems, it was now connected to the wider world. By 1620 Manila had a population of 42,000, as sizeable as Marseilles and Barcelona. The city's links were far reaching, its population cosmopolitan, its calendar of commercial activity governed by ocean winds. Manila was well positioned to stimulate consumer desire. From October to April, Japanese ships arrived with lacquerware, silver and finely woven silks. The Portuguese from Malacca came with Indian textiles, Turkish carpets and jewels. Ships from deeply established local Asian trading partners visited – Borneo, Cambodia and Siam – with rhino horns, intricately woven palm mats and black glazed jars. Armenian merchants turned up; above all, Chinese junks with the core commodities – silk and porcelain – plus gold, musk and ivory, taffeta and damasks, rubies, sapphires and live animals. When the galleons from Acapulco docked at Cavite, Manila's port, carrying tons of silver, the population swelled and feverish trading took place. By the end of June, one or two galleons would begin their return to New Spain laden with consumer desirables. Along with raw silk and porcelain went spices (cloves, pepper and cinnamon), ivory, Japanese screens and swords, Persian carpets and luxurious finished fabrics of silk, velvet, damask and taffeta. At the same time the Japanese would also sail home with Chinese silk, deer hides, gold and honey. Manila itself became a place of conspicuous consumption – the use of exotic fragrances, such as camphor, mastic, aromatic resins – and of sartorial innovations: mantillas, perfumed hair, embroidered wraps, Japanese fans, buttons and pockets. Above all, it was about silver for the Chinese market, and it was silver that oiled the wheels of global trade.

The echoes of this process were felt across the world. Everywhere was touched by the silver road and felt its presence. In Mexico City, the wealth was palpable. It had the feeling of a place of global reach.

The city's laureate, Bernardo de Balbuena, called it the 'famous city, centre of perfection, hinge of the world'. An English traveller, Thomas Gage, who visited in 1625, was staggered:

> But for Contratación, it is one of the richest Cities in the World; to the which by the North Sea comes every year from Spain a fleet of near twenty ships laden with the best commodities, not only of Spain but of the most parts of Christendom. And by the South Sea it enjoys traffic from all parts of Peru; and above all it trades with the East Indies, and from thence receives the commodities as well from those parts which are inhabited by the Portuguese, as [well as] from the countries of Japan and China, sending every year two great carracks with two smaller vessels to the islands of the Philippines, and having every year a return of such like ships.[1]

The fabric of the city was magnificent. 'Their buildings are with stone, and brick very strong ... the streets are very broad, in the narrowest of them three coaches may go, and in the broader six may go in the breadth of it.' The coaches themselves were extravagantly decked out: 'they spare no silver, nor gold, nor precious stones, nor cloth of gold, nor the best silks of China to enrich them ... the streets of Christendom must not compare with those in breadth and cleanness, but especially in the riches of the shops which do adorn them'. As a sober Protestant he found the sumptuous displays of the inhabitants quite shocking. 'Both men and women are excessive in their apparel, using more silks than stuffs and cloth; precious stones and pearls further much this their vain ostentation; a hat-band and rose made of Diamonds in a gentleman's hat is common.' Tradesmen with hatbands of pearls hardly raised an eyebrow. He tuts – while describing in great detail – the fabrics, decoration and manner of dress of the women. Even their enslaved black servants were decked out: 'some a dozen, some half a dozen waiting on them, in brave and gallant liveries, heavy with gold and silver lace, with silk stockings on their black legs, and roses on their feet, and swords by their sides'. Then there were the shops in the goldsmiths' street, 'where a man's eyes may behold in less than an hour many millions worth of gold, silver, pearls and jewels'. As to the wealth of the churches he was similarly amazed: 'beautiful buildings, the inward riches belonging to the altars are infinite in price and value . . . jewels belong to the saints, and crowns of gold and silver, and tabernacles of gold and crystal . . . all which would mount to the worth of a reasonable mine of silver'. Gage was both staggered by the wealth and appalled by the flaunting displays: 'I doubt not but the flourishing of Mexico in coaches, horses, streets, women and apparel is very slippery, and will make those proud inhabitants slip and fall,' he notes tartly.[2]

The webbed map of trade expanded and expanded with silver oiling the wheels. It rippled all the way back to Europe. It was the twin elements of the economy of China that dominated the process: the desire for silver and vast manufacturing capacity. Its emblematic product, Chinese porcelain, with its fine translucence, transparent glaze and piercing blues that no one else could replicate, captured the world. In 1573, two years after the first galleon crossing, two Manila galleons landed 22,000 pieces in Acapulco. In the Topkapi Palace Ottoman sultans collected it obsessively. In 1608, when the Dutch East India company entered the market, they placed a bulk order for 100,000 pieces. By 1614 this porcelain was in daily use in Amsterdam and became a staple in Dutch still-life paintings. In half a century the Dutch imports approached 3 million pieces. The use of the word 'china' to describe this ware entered the English language in 1623.

Fragments of Ming pottery scattering the world testify to its ubiquity. Pottery shards have been found at 15,000 feet in the Andes, on the Kenyan coast, in the maritime trading posts of West India, on the shores of the Pacific Island of Saipan where the *Nuestra Señora de la Concepción* went down in dramatic shipwreck. Chinese porcelain was in South East Asia, Syria, Iraq and Egypt. The scale of Chinese manufacturing was vast. By the eighteenth century, Jingdezhen, the porcelain city of China with a population of a million people, had a complex of 3,000 kilns. The Chinese understood markets and were quick to adapt. They produced vessels with quotations from the Koran for the Ottomans, and tableware decorated with his coat of arms for Manuel I, king of Portugal. As early as the 1530s, Portuguese noblemen could order dinner services to their own specifications; at that time the Portuguese were importing 40,000 to 60,000 pieces a year and the nobility were wearing China's other principal export – silk – and drinking Chinese tea. By the 1580s there were at least six shops on one Lisbon street specialising in the sale of Chinese porcelain.

By the start of the seventeenth century there was an emerging world economy, and silver was its currency. In Vermeer's painting of a woman in a Delft house holding a balance, from around 1664, she is weighing silver, exactly as Gaspar da Cruz had observed the Chinese doing a century earlier. When the Jesuit missionary Matteo Ricci produced a world map for the Ming emperor in 1602, *The Complete Geographical Map of Ten Thousand Countries*, it not only showed China the Americas for the first time, it also marked Potosí. The Spanish silver dollar – the pieces of eight of *Treasure Island* – became the most portable form of silver, a world currency. Its descendant would be the US dollar.

At the same time, an extension of the Columbian exchange – the movement of crops and species between the Americas and Europe – also reached China, in what might be called the Magellan exchange. Ships were a vector of plant migration, which came by two routes: from New Spain on the Manila galleons and from the Portuguese via the Indian Ocean. As elsewhere, it brought a changing ecological regime. Cortés' precocious attempt to transplant cloves to Mexico never got off the ground, but plants that travelled the other way were more successful. The Manila galleons brought cocoa, maize, papaya, peanuts, peppers, pumpkins, sugar cane, tobacco and tomatoes into the Philippines. Because of the faster westward crossing from Acapulco, horses and New World cattle were also transported to Manila. Some of the new staple crops were introduced into China and would dramatically alter the country's nutrition. Sweet potatoes, maize and peanuts were instrumental. China's population doubled in the eighteenth century: from 150 million to 300 million. The introduction of faster-maturing rice seeds permitted more crops a year, supplemented by the other new imports from the Americas that supported diet in the intervening periods between rice harvests. Cultivated land increased by 50 per cent. In the seventeenth century, tobacco reached China and Japan via Macau and the Philippines and was widely adopted. The hit of nicotine led to more malign inhalations. Soon after, the Dutch brought opium into the region from India, with social and political consequences that would unfold in the centuries ahead.

The long-distance trades in products, foodstuffs, cuisines and genetic material spread in all directions in a chain reaction. The Jesuits sent Chinese boars back to Portugal. Filo pastry from North Africa led to the samosa in India and the spring roll in China; chillis added new notes to Chinese cuisine; rhubarb came to Europe from south China; satsumas from Japan. Tempura – the technique of cooking battered and fried food – a classic Japanese dish, was introduced via the Portuguese technique for frying vegetables, a more benign gift than the tanegashima. The word is most likely a corruption of the Latin '*tempora*' – the 'times' for fasting from meat eating during Lent, evidence of missionary influences in the country. All these tastes and foodstuffs were speeded on their way by ships.

The Europeans had entered into the deeply established trading patterns of Asia and then extended them. The network of exchanges became increasingly intricate, mixing cultures, visual images, peoples, crops, technologies and diseases: smallpox and astrolabes, syphilis and pilot charts. The historian John Russell-Wood has reconstructed examples of the kinds of intricate trades that took place. A clock made in Flanders might be exported from Lisbon. Carried to the Portuguese hub at Goa, it found no buyers and was taken to Malacca on the Malay Peninsula where it was exchanged for sandalwood (probably from Timor). The sandalwood was shipped to Macau where it was sold for gold. The gold was carried by Portuguese middlemen to Nagasaki where it afforded the purchase of a valuable work of art, a painted screen. This was transported back to Goa and eventually returned to Lisbon. Cloves that would be sold in Morocco made the journey from Ternate via Malacca, Cochin and Lisbon, and would be exchanged for wheat that would find its way to West Africa. Venetian glass beads and Flemish bedpans carried there might be exchanged for pepper, gold and monkeys that would be shipped back to Bristol, Antwerp and Genoa.

There were huge profits to be made. It was the mark-up on spices that had initially fired the sixteenth-century mercantile imagination. Wide-ranging maritime connections demonstrated that it was even possible to make money out of money. The differential in the relative value of gold and silver across the world, and an awareness of this, afforded novel opportunities for arbitrage, prefiguring the money markets of today. Silver was twice as valuable to the Chinese as it was in Europe. A quantity of gold bought in Europe, converted there into silver and carried to China, could be changed back for double the original amount of gold.

Ships not only transported foodstuffs and currencies, they also moved peoples. Like shards of Ming pottery, human DNA was being scattered across the world; in mixed-race communities, in exploitation and in chance encounters. Sailors left their traces wherever they went: the clue to the presence of Basques in the islands of Polynesia may lie in the discovery of bronze cannons on an atoll, in all probability those of the caravel the *San Lesmes*, separated by a storm from the Loaísa fleet. In the sixteenth century, large-scale movement of peoples started to happen by compulsion. Silver from Potosí, smuggled by the

Portuguese via the River Plate, became instrumental in the first wave of oceanic slavery, paying for the export of Africans into the Americas. The enslaved black servants that Thomas Gage had seen in Mexico City, decked out in finery as exotic human toys for their wealthy Spanish owners, were victims of silver's global utility. There were somewhere between 20,000 and 40,000 enslaved Africans in Mexico in the seventeenth century. Many were subjected to more back-breaking forms of exploitation in the forests and plantations of Brazil, while the native Andean tribespeople in the hellhole of Potosí were trapped in an evil loop. They were compelled to mine the silver which fed the slavery machine. Silver rippled through the world, making and unmaking. In Japan, the tanegashima may have helped the Tokogawa shogunate defeat all its rivals and unify the country, but it was control of the country's silver mines that paid for the victory.

Maritime connectivity also allowed the peoples of the world to see each other. If Europeans viewed the Chinese as different – in Gaspar da Cruz's view, ill-favoured, with small eyes and flat beardless faces – the compliment was returned in kind. The Europeans were ugly creatures with round eyes and beards. The Japanese studied the nanban-jin closely. On beautifully painted folding screens they scru-pulously illustrated their ships, their ballooning pantaloons and strange hats in comic detail, lampooning their mannerisms and their large noses, as well as the weird appearance of the tall black-robed Jesuits. Across the trading world, images and artefacts reflected a new trans-hemispheric awareness. Many of the cultures to which the Europeans travelled came to produce hybrid works of art: statues of the Madonna and child that look distinctly Chinese; carved ivory boxes from Sri Lanka that mixed Hindu deities with representations of European kings and images from Dürer; Portuguese nobles in palanquins in Goan art and their ambassadors in Mughal miniatures; Benin bronzes of crucifixes and European soldiers with muskets and crossbows; intricately carved ivory salt-cellars topped with Western sailing ships. The inventiveness of Chinese craftsmen, their ability to

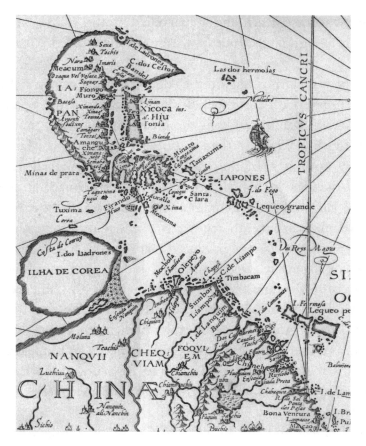

30. *A route map to the East: the coast of China and the seaway to Japan in this map by Jan Huygen van Linschoten, based on information stolen from the Portuguese. Macau is just visible in the bottom right. Korea is depicted as an island. The map indicates Japan's silver mines: 'Minas de prata'. The island of Tanegashima (Tanaxuma) is on the right off the coast of Japan.*

copy and adapt for markets, was already legendary. Much of Manila's religious statuary – figures of the Madonna and child, carved in wood or ivory, gold crucifixes, altarpieces – were produced by the Chinese in the city. Dürer himself was amazed by the artistry of peoples beyond Europe: 'All the days of my life I have seen nothing that rejoiced my heart so much as these things, for amongst them [are] wonderful works of art, and I marvelled at the subtle *ingenia* of people in foreign lands. Indeed, I cannot express all that I thought there.'[3]

Europe was skirmishing on the edge of great continents. Neither the Portuguese with their toehold in Malacca, nor the Spanish in Manila had the ability to dent the great land empires, though the idea of invading China in the late sixteenth century via Manila was touted by optimists. In the end, common sense prevailed. Philip scotched the idea: he had already lost a Spanish armada attempting to invade England and was in no mood to invest in further follies.

Above all, the sixteenth century was an age of information. The printing presses of Europe produced maps and globes, thousands of accounts of adventure, daring, suffering and death; astonishing tales, an ocean of stories, and the sound of human voices. The Portuguese had a whole genre of shipwreck narratives: 'The Tragic History of the Sea'. But despite the noise of exploration, it was China that sat at the centre of the world and around whose needs and industries the Europeans rotated. Until the Industrial Revolution, the European powers were confined to the archipelagos and peripheries of great continental empires.

The Spanish and the Portuguese fought their miniature spice wars and tussled over the imaginary Tordesillas Line for much of the century. What started it, and cranked up the whole machinery of European exploration, was the scent of spices from the shores of Maluco that had so memorably delighted the Portuguese botanist, Garcia de Orta. The Iberian rivalry ended abruptly and close to home on a battlefield in Morocco in 1578, when the Portuguese obsession with crusading against Islam culminated in disaster. On a single day, the young King Sebastião and much of the Portuguese nobility were wiped out at the battle of Alcácer Quibir. In the aftermath, with no direct descendant, there was a succession crisis. In 1580 King Philip became ruler of both Spain and Portugal. The contest between the two was over, although the merchant interests of the two countries in Asia were kept scrupulously separated. In time, the Tordesillas Line – the elusive quark – would shrink into insignificance and vanish, leaving just a ghostly trace on maps. The following year, the Portuguese were ousted from Ternate.

It was the lure of spices that had set the process in motion. They were the first worldwide trading commodity and an ideal one. Dried spices were a lightweight, high-value, reasonably imperishable product with which to stuff a ship's hold on long voyages. The profits were huge. In 1515, the return on a cargo docked at Lisbon was 700 per cent. In the modern world, spice production has itself gone global. No longer are cloves and nutmeg confined, by a quirk of evolutionary biology, to a few tiny volcanic islands in the Malay Archipelago. Both are grown widely in plantations throughout the whole of Indonesia and beyond. Other countries across the tropical belt have seen this plant dissemination started by the Columbian and Magellan exchanges. India and Guatemala grow more nutmeg than Indonesia. Sri Lanka, Madagascar, Tanzania, Vietnam and China also produce some of the range of flavours that stock kitchen spice racks. When we think of them now, spices seem inconsequential. We puzzle over their importance to the peoples of the past. Gaspar da Cruz thought them non-essential luxuries at the time: 'pepper and ivory which is the principal that the Portuguese do carry, a man may well live without'. If they did nothing else, they cheered people as they hauled themselves out of the Middle Ages, the sparser centuries of famine and plague. They provided a glimpse of better lives.

By the end of the sixteenth century, the Moluccans had had enough. When a Portuguese governor treacherously murdered the sultan of Ternate, they rose up, besieged their fort and expelled them. They returned to retain just a modest toehold on Tidore, more as traders than conquerors. When Francis Drake arrived at Ternate in 1579 he was warmly welcomed and hugely impressed by the new sultan, Baabullah, who had stabilised the islands. Unfortunately for both the Moluccas and the Bandas worse was yet to come: the arrival of the Dutch.

DAMAGE

Before maps the world was limitless. It was maps that gave it shape and made it seem like territory, like something that could be possessed, not just laid waste and plundered. Maps made places on the edges of the imagination seem graspable and placeable. And later when it became necessary, geography became biology in order to construct a hierarchy in which to place the people who lived in their inaccessibility and primitiveness in other places on the map.

— Abdulrazak Gurnah

Centuries later. Another ocean.

On 3 June 1844, three men, Jón Brandsson, Sigurður Ísleifsson and Ketill Ketilsson, landed on the isolated rock of Eldey off the coast of Iceland. Their mission was to catch seabirds at the behest of a merchant who wanted specimens. Sigurður Ísleifsson remembered the day well:

The rocks were covered with blackbirds [guillemots] and there were the Geirfugles ... They walked slowly. Jón Brandsson crept up with his arms open. The bird that Jón got went into a corner

but [mine] was going to the edge of the cliff. It walked like a man
... but moved its feet quickly. [I] caught it close to the edge – a
precipice many fathoms deep. Its wings lay close to the sides – not
hanging out. I took him by the neck and he flapped his wings. He
made no cry. I strangled him.[1]

With this act, the world's last great auks died without a whimper.
Ketilsson smashed their eggs with his boot. This great flightless sea
bird, once numbered in millions on the coasts of the North Atlantic,
had been driven to extinction, largely by sailors. Ironically, the last
breeding colony of auks had been betrayed by the planet itself. They
had had a secure location on the tiny island of Geirfuglasker – Great
Auk Rock. It rose sheer out of the sea and was inaccessible to humans.
In 1830 it vanished in a volcanic eruption and the birds moved to
nearby Eldey, where they met their end.

The fate of the auks remains haunting. Along with the dodo, it has
become an iconic extinction, an early warning of what would come,
the beginnings of ecological guilt. To the writer Horatio Clare, their
loss signalled that the oceans were now utterly within human grasp.
The auks' demise came at the end of a long process of the encirclement
of the planet, in which the explorations of the sixteenth century had
been a signal moment – the great acceleration, in the words of the
historian David Abulafia – when European voyages joined up the
world and began to explore and exploit its furthest reaches. Their
narratives are rich in their encounters with a natural world that amazed,
challenged and delighted them, but which they also saw as bounty, a
limitless natural resource. The great auk was already in decline at the
time. In 1553 it received official protection, a precocious initiative that
was to no avail. Its feathers were just too ideal for filling pillows.

The nineteenth-century naturalist Alfred Russel Wallace sketched
out the theory of evolution independently of Darwin during eight
years in the Moluccas and the Malay Archipelago. He studied and
celebrated the astonishing fecundity of this natural world. Even here

31. *Mariners perceived the natural world as a limitless resource. All early European expeditions expected to cull the astonishing wealth of oceans, continents and islands to sustain themselves. Later, larger-scale resource extractions, such as whaling and logging, would become industrialised processes.*

there is an irony: Wallace was not a wealthy man. He had to fund his years in the deep tropics by shooting or trapping specimens to send back to an agent in England to sell to museums and collectors.

With the destruction of habitats came also the destruction of peoples. Adam Smith, the English economist of the eighteenth century who tracked the great silver boom and the expansion of the world economy, was clear about the damage: 'to the natives, however, both of the east and west indies, all the commercial benefits which can have resulted from those events have been sunk and lost in the dreadful misfortunes which they have occasioned'.[2] China and Japan were resistant to the advance of the Europeans with their sailing ship technology and their gunpowder weapons. Others were not. They were picked off individually. The blood brotherhood rituals of the Malay Archipelago and the Pacific islands were misunderstood by the visitors. For the local inhabitants, they sealed an amity between equals that might allow trade. To the Europeans who had come to plant a flag on their soil, they were the first step to subjugation. The islanders' failure to achieve political units larger than that of the village or the immediate tribe, their fragmented cultures and their multitude of local languages, made them easy prey. They were as rarely individuated as the cloves and nutmeg existing on a scattering of volcanic islands, a cultural manifestation of evolutionary processes. 'It seems that God dispersed them in small morsels to be eaten one by one,' was how one Jesuit explained it to Philip II,[3] in a note that suggested that their fate was a rightful design of the Christian God. A few defiant voices spoke up. The Augustinian Martin de Rada objected to the plundering of the Philippines. He demanded that the native people should make their own choices over the coming of the Europeans.

The loudest and most persistent critic of the time was Bartolomé de las Casas, who had interviewed Magellan in Valladolid. He had seen at first hand the atrocities that had already taken place in the Americas: the forced labour, the slavery, the acts of genocide and the destructive diseases. In combination they caused almost total population collapse of the indigenous peoples: 90 per cent in a century. 'I saw . . . cruelty on a scale no living being has ever seen or expects to see.'[4] He put the case for them, that they should not be consigned to some lower rung on the ladder of humanity:

All people of these our Indies are human, so far as is possible by the natural and human way and without the light of faith – had their republics, places, towns, and cities most abundant and well provided for, and did not lack anything to live politically and socially, and attain and enjoy civil happiness . . . And they equalled many nations of this world that are renowned and considered civilized, and they surpassed many others, and to none were they inferior. Among those they equalled were the Greeks and the Romans, and they surpassed them by many good and better customs.[5]

Alfred Wallace, a man of the age of Victorian supremacy, had had sufficient opportunity to study tribal communities in South America and the Malay Archipelago, and made similar comparisons that were not favourable to the inequalities of the industrialised plutocracies of the nineteenth century:

Now it is very remarkable, that among people in a very low stage of civilization, we find some approach to such a perfect social state. I have lived with communities of savages in South America and in the East, who have no laws or law courts but the public opinion of the village freely expressed. Each man scrupulously respects the rights of his fellow, and any infraction of those rights rarely or never takes place. In such a community, all are nearly equal. There are none of those wide distinctions, of education and ignorance, wealth and poverty, master and servant, which are the product of our civilization; there is none of that wide-spread division of labour, which, while it increases wealth, produces also conflicting interests; there is not that severe competition and struggle for existence, or for wealth, which the dense population of civilized countries inevitably creates.[6]

For the Spice Islands, after the expulsion of the Portuguese, worse was to come. The crown-sponsored era of the Iberian presence was frequently cruel but never efficient. It gave way to the more ruthless private merchant companies that had no remit to 'civilise' or convert. The VOC, the Dutch East India company, which replaced them in the following century, looked to get a total monopoly of the spice market through the systematic application of violence. The VOC operated as a state within a state, the forerunner of autonomous multinationals, with enormous power and resources. Its focused and pitiless approach was based on the belief that there was no point in seeking amicable relations with native peoples. The architect of this policy, the ruthless Jan Pieterszoon Coen, put it quite bluntly to his fellow investors: 'You gentlemen ought to know from experience that trade in Asia should be conducted and maintained under the protection and with the aid of your own weapons, and those weapons must be wielded with the profits gained by trade. So, trade cannot be maintained without war, nor war without trade.'[7]

The VOC massacred the Bandanese, uprooted nutmeg plantations on rival islands, punished the indigenous population mercilessly for side trades. With an almost complete monopoly of the spice market, it made huge profits. The Dutch Golden Age, its buildings, its canals, its Rembrandts, its science and its Protestant enlightenment, was paid for, in part, by the suffering of the people of the Malay Archipelago.

Earlier, the Portuguese had set out a more idealistic case for the mutual benefits of long-range trade: 'the principal intention of his king Dom Manuel in making these discoveries was the desire to communicate with the royal families of these parts, so that trade might develop, an activity that results from human needs, and that depends on a ring of friendship through communicating with one another'.[8] It was a claim also made by the Merchant Venturers in their remit to Chancellor. He was tasked with approaching the 'kings, princes and other potentates inhabiting the north-east parts of the world ... to seek such things as we lack, as also to carry unto them from our regions, such things as they lack'. Both assumed matching levels of development and political organisation, neither of which applied to the Spice islanders or the peoples of the Philippines.

The great connection of the world in the sixteenth century certainly carried benefits. The improvement of diets through the movement of crops; the introduction of knowledge, technologies and material items for the greater ease and prosperity of peoples; after the first terrible devastation of the indigenous American peoples an increased resilience of populations through immunity to disease. But these benefits were felt unequally and the transportation technology and global currencies that started with the spice trade would facilitate the next great development of taste. The apparatus was in place to fulfil Europe's sugar craving. The ships, the enslaved manpower, the plantations and the silver to pay for it were all ready and waiting.

Silver ran through the sixteenth and seventeenth centuries like wildfire, an element beyond human control. With overproduction its value fell – by two thirds in a century. Rampant inflation damaged economies. Spain, which produced too little and depended on silver mines too much, faded as a world power. The Ming dynasty, whose taxes were levied in a fixed quantity of silver, was overthrown.

The early European voyagers viewed the Pacific Ocean with fear and awe: 'more vast than mind of man can conceive'.[9] It took centuries to grasp. The island groups into which the sixteenth-century sailors blundered, on which they were wrecked and cast away, were carved up into areas of 'ownership' by world powers in the nineteenth century. In the twentieth, the Pacific saw another great game. The battle between the Allies and Japan has left resonant names: Guam and Pearl Harbor, Guadalcanal – the Pacific's Stalingrad – Midway and Iwo Jima. Sixty-two thousand Japanese troops were stationed on Halmahera, the Moluccan island the Spanish and Portuguese knew as Gilolo, and on which they had fought their tiny battles. It was pounded into submission by General MacArthur. Nearby Morotai became the base for American Superfortress bombers taking off to destroy Japanese positions in the Philippines. A few totems of these contests survive in the Moluccas. Sunken Japanese warships provide havens for innumerable fish species and sport for divers. The rusting skeletons of anti-aircraft guns and armoured cars are being reclaimed by the jungle, alongside crumbling Portuguese and Dutch forts that stand witness to the great spice contests of earlier times.

32. The Portuguese fort on the northern coast of Ternate.

For all its size, the Pacific, an oceanic Amazonia, is not inexhaustible. Its empty spaces have become a source of extraction and a dumping ground for the world's dirty business. The USA carried out twenty-three nuclear tests on Bikini Atoll in the late 1940s and early 1950s. The coral reefs around Australia, veterans of centuries, are bleaching as temperatures rise. A convection current of plastic particles, known as the Great Pacific Garbage Patch, circulates in the north-east corner of the ocean, and at night the million-kilowatt lamps of squid fishing fleets, duping their prey with artificial moons, are visible from space.

Cerro Rico, the man-eating mountain of Potosí, remains – a monument to the tragedies of European conquest. Over the centuries 3 million enslaved Quechua Indians laboured in the oxygen-starved mines, and the extraction goes on today, in conditions little improved from the past: 16,000 miners hack away at the rock with simple hand tools, the darkness pierced only by their headlamps. The rewards are unequally distributed. By the age of 50, a man is broken; pulmonary diseases from the fine dust carry many off. The mountain itself is teetering on the brink of environmental catastrophe. Riddled with 60 miles of mineshafts, it has been hollowed out like a Swiss cheese. Engineers are trying to assess the possibility that the whole mountain might simply fold inwards and collapse. The city of Potosí, with the fine architecture of its colonial heyday, squats in its shadow.

On Cebu, each year on 27 April, the Filipino people re-enact the battle of Mactan, now named Lapulapu day, after the chieftain who resisted foreign rule. For them it is a foundation story, the start of national identity, yet the influences of the European incursion are complex. Simultaneously, Magellan is honoured for introducing Christianity to the Philippines and the special relic of his coming, *Santo Niño de Cebu*, the small figure of the infant Christ that the Spanish brought, then rediscovered, is deeply venerated. Magallanes is a common Filipino surname. The Portuguese still have a presence in Macau, though their numbers are in decline.

'The world's mine oyster, which I with sword will open,'[10] Shakespeare wrote in the closing years of the long sixteenth century.

AUTHOR'S NOTE

In the early stages of writing this book, during a brief ceasefire between COVID lockdowns, I was standing in the nave of Gloucester Cathedral, one of the great buildings of the medieval world. Its massive Romanesque columns still bear the ghostly scorings of chisels and their masons' marks. The east window, the size of a tennis court, was at the time of construction the largest in the world. It was completed in the early 1350s, not a moment too soon. The Black Death was already hitting England and would kill the master craftsmen who fashioned its brilliantly coloured panes of glass and halt such extraordinary projects. The plague, like COVID, was the fruit of global connections, carried out of the heart of Asia in Venetian and Genoese ships.

Looking up from the nave, the evidence for a connected world was literally right above me. Our planet was rotating slowly overhead – a globe based on NASA photographs taken from space. This outsized art installation was so big that it shrank the enormous building in which it was contained. For those of us from the northern hemisphere this was a realignment of understanding, giving us a perspective we seldom have. We were looking up from below, at the southern oceans, a visual reminder that our world is 70 per cent water. At its base the polar continent of Antarctica. Australia span into view, an ominous brown, untouched by forgiving rain, then the blue of the Pacific, banded by swirls of white cloud – a riptide vortex of terrific winds. Europe was all but invisible.

If the Black Death was a harbinger of global connections, the sixteenth century witnessed the acceleration of understanding of this one world. The explosion of exploration, cartography, printing and long-distance trade brought rich descriptions and the growing awareness of the wonders, opportunities and costs of globalisation. 'Although we call them the 'Old World' and the 'New World', that's because we only came across the latter recently, and not because there are two worlds; there is but one',[1] as Inca Garcilaso de la Vega remarked in 1609. In Gloucester Cathedral it was self-evident.

ACKNOWLEDGEMENTS

This book rests on the work of generations of writers about the 'Age of Discovery', as the Europeans have dubbed it. I am grateful to these many historians more knowledgeable than myself for their scholarship and their insights, from which I have learned, and for the collections of sixteenth-century archives and printed sources that have disseminated an astonishing wealth of eyewitness accounts of adventure, disaster and anthropology. I have just dipped a finger in this great ocean. Among the many books from which I have benefited I particularly valued Oskar Spate's *The Spanish Lake*, a seminal history of the early exploration of the Pacific, Felipe Fernández-Armesto's *Straits*, Martin J. Noone's lively account of the European arrival in the Philippines, *The Islands Saw It*, whose publisher I have been unable to trace, and the short inspirational work by Peter Gordon and Juan José Morales on the birth of globalisation, *The Silver Way*, from which I have borrowed the quotation by Inca Garcilaso de la Vega at the front of my book. The publications of the Hakluyt Society have been invaluable throughout. I have also gained from the comments of Yale's two expert readers, Zoltán Biedermann and an anonymous other.

In this book's creation my thanks are to Yale University Press for their enthusiasm and their attention to detail, to Julian Loose who commissioned it, to my agent Andrew Lownie, to Ron and Rita Morton for hospitality on trips to the Cambridge University Library, to the indispensable London Library, and, as ever, to Jan.

NOTES

Collisions

1. Wallace, vol. 1, 3.
2. Ibid., 4.

1 The Heaven of Francisco Serrão

1. Pires, vol. 1, lxxxviii and lxxix.
2. Ibid.
3. Ibid., lxxix.
4. Castanheda, 155–6.
5. Barros, 584.
6. Pires, vol. 2, p. 302.
7. Barros, 587.
8. Ibid., 586.
9. Villiers, 'Trade and society', 743.
10. Barbosa, vol. 2, 203.
11. Ibid., 199.
12. Pires, vol. 1, 215.
13. Lagoa, vol. 1, 155.
14. Pires, vol. 1, 208.
15. Ibid., 206.
16. Barbosa, vol. 2, 201–2.

2 Maps and Speculations

1. Fernández-Armesto, 72.
2. https://en.wikipedia.org/wiki/Johannes_Sch%C3%B6ner_globe (accessed 6 November 2023).
3. Guillemard, 71.
4. Morison, 319.
5. Ibid.
6. Ibid.

7. Fernández-Armesto, 43.
8. Bergreen, 33.
9. Ibid., 34.
10. Ibid., 46.
11. Ibid., 58.
12. Pigafetta, vol. 1, 36.
13. Guillemard, 80.
14. Ibid., 81.
15. Ibid., 82.
16. Ibid., 83.
17. Ibid.
18. Ibid., 82.
19. Ibid., 127.
20. Fernández-Armesto, 117.

3 The Molucca Fleet

1. *Magellan*, 354.
2. Pigafetta, vol. 1, 33.
3. Ibid., 35.
4. Ibid.
5. Bergreen, 90.
6. Pigafetta, vol. 1, 37.
7. Ibid., 45.
8. Ibid., 43.
9. Ibid.
10. Ibid., 47.
11. Ibid., 49.
12. Mitchell, *Elcano*, 179.
13. Transylvanus, in *Magellan*, 392.
14. Ibid., 392.
15. Ibid., 393.
16. Navarette, vol. 4, 190.
17. Ibid., 192.
18. Guillemard, 122.
19. Morison, 319.
20. Transylvanus, in *Magellan*, 394.
21. Ibid.
22. Albo, in *Magellan*, 338–9.
23. Pigafetta, vol. 1, 65.
24. Ibid.
25. Ibid., 67.
26. *Descripción de los reinos*, 193.
27. Bergreen, 187.
28. Navarette, vol. 4, 43.
29. Pigafetta, vol. 1, 73.
30. Ibid., 69–71.
31. Mafra, in *Magellan*, 193.

32. Barros, 641.
33. Ibid., 641–2.
34. Ibid., 643–5.
35. Pigafetta, vol. 1, 83.
36. Mafra, in *Magellan*, 197.
37. Ibid., 195.

4 To the Spice Islands

1. Fernández-Armesto, 217.
2. Transylvanus, in *Magellan*, 396.
3. Pigafetta, vol. 1, 85.
4. Ibid., 89.
5. Ibid., 83–5.
6. Ibid., 85.
7. *Descripción de los reinos*, 196.
8. Pigafetta, vol. 1, 85.
9. Ibid.
10. Ibid., 93.
11. Ibid.
12. Ibid., 95.
13. Ibid., 91.
14. Ibid., 99.
15. Ibid., 103.
16. Ibid.
17. Ibid., 109.
18. Ibid., 111.
19. Ibid., 113.
20. Ibid., 119.
21. Ibid.
22. Ibid., 123.
23. Ibid., 135.
24. Ibid.
25. Ibid., 137–41.
26. Ibid., 157.
27. Ibid.
28. Ibid., 163.
29. *Descripción de los reinos*, 201.
30. Ibid., 202.
31. Pigafetta, vol. 1, 171.
32. *Descripción de los reinos*, 201.
33. Pigafetta, vol. 1, 171.
34. Ibid., 173.
35. Ibid., 173.
36. Ibid., 175.
37. Ibid., 177.
38. Ibid.
39. Ibid., 179.

40. Ibid., 181.
41. Morison, 439.

5 Circumnavigators

1. Pigafetta, vol. 2, 65.
2. Ibid., 79.
3. Ibid., 69.
4. Ibid., 105–7.
5. Ibid., 67.
6. Ibid., 105.
7. Ibid., 111.
8. Barros, 587.
9. 'La Lettre d'Antonio de Brito', 13–14.
10. Pigafetta, vol. 2, 161.
11. Mitchell, *Elcano*, 89.
12. Ibid., 80.
13. Bergreen, 380.
14. Mitchell, *Elcano*, 89.
15. Pigafetta, vol. 2, 185–7.
16. Mitchell, *Elcano*, 89.
17. Ibid., 158.
18. Ibid., 85.
19. Ibid., 106.
20. Ibid.

6 Cannon Fire on the Pearl River

1. Crowley, *Conquerors*, 41.
2. Ferguson, 1–2.
3. Schuman, 144–5.
4. Ferguson, 1–2.
5. Pires, vol. 1, xxv.
6. Ibid., 116.
7. Ibid.
8. Ibid., 120–1.
9. Ibid., 122.
10. Ibid., 123.
11. Ferguson, 5–6.
12. Ibid., 7.
13. Pires, vol. 1, xxviii.
14. Ibid., xxxi.
15. Ibid., xxxii.
16. Barros, 213, trans. Clive Willis.
17. Ibid., 214.
18. Pires, vol. 1, xxxiii.
19. Ibid., xxxiv.
20. Ibid., xxxv.

21. Barros, 301 and 307–8.
22. Pires, vol. 1, xxxvii.
23. Willis, xix.
24. Chang, 36
25. Ferguson, 103.
26. Ibid., 104.
27. Ibid.
28. Ibid.
29. Ibid., 106.
30. Chang, 51.
31. Ibid., 52.
32. Ibid., 50.
33. Ferguson, 104.
34. Ibid., 107.
35. Ibid., 107.
36. Ibid.
37. Ibid., 107–8.
38. Ibid., 109.
39. Ibid., 112.
40. Ibid., 113.
41. Ibid., 117–18.
42. Ibid., 157–8.

7 The Spanish Reply

1. *Alguns documentos*, 462.
2. Navarette, vol. 4, 304.
3. Ibid.
4. Ibid.
5. Ibid., 341.
6. d'Anghiera, 273.
7. Uncilla, 317.
8. Markham, 31–3.
9. Uncilla, 318.
10. Ibid., 319.
11. Ibid., 320.
12. Ibid., 321.
13. Ibid.
14. Ibid., 321–2.
15. Ibid., 323.
16. Ibid.
17. Ibid.
18. Ibid., 324.
19. Ibid.
20. Ibid.
21. Ibid.
22. Markham, 44.
23. Ibid., 45.

24. Uncilla, 327.
25. Ibid.
26. Ibid.
27. Mitchell, *Elcano*, 138.
28. Markham, 48.
29. Uncilla, 331.
30. Ibid.
31. Ibid., 332.
32. Ibid.
33. Ibid.
34. Ibid.
35. Navarette, vol. 5, 42.
36. Uncilla, 333.
37. Ibid.
38. Ibid.
39. Ibid.
40. Uncilla, 333.
41. Ibid., 342.
42. Markham, 49.
43. Uncilla, 344.
44. Ibid., 343.
45. Mitchell, *Elcano*, 146.
46. Markham, 50.
47. Ibid.
48. Uncilla, 345.
49. Markham, 51.
50. Ibid.
51. Uncilla, 348.
52. Ibid., 352.
53. Ibid., 353.
54. Markham, 52.
55. Uncilla, 355.
56. Ibid., 356.
57. Mitchell, *Elcano*, 32.

8 Microwars

1. Uncilla, 356–7.
2. Ibid., 357.
3. Mitchell, *Urdaneta*, 25.
4. Ibid., 35.
5. Uncilla, 361.
6. Ibid., 363.
7. Ibid., 364.
8. Ibid., 363.
9. Wallace, vol. 2, 100.
10. Uncilla, 364–5.
11. Ibid.

12. Ibid., 368.
13. Ibid., 367.
14. Ibid., 368.
15. Ibid.
16. Ibid.
17. Ibid., 370.
18. Ibid., 371.
19. Ibid., 376.
20. Ibid., 374.
21. Fernández de Oviedo, 151.
22. Ibid.
23. Ibid., 104.
24. Ibid., 151.
25. Ibid., 376.
26. Ibid., 374.
27. Ibid., 380.
28. Ibid., 378.
29. Ibid., 381.

9 The Voyage of the *Florida*

1. Noone, 161.
2. Markham, 103.
3. Ibid.
4. Ibid., 104.
5. Ibid.
6. Ibid.
7. Navarette, vol. 5, 445.
8. Ibid., 453.
9. Markham, 113.
10. Ibid.
11. Ibid., 113–14.
12. Ibid., 114.
13. Ibid., 115.
14. Navarette, vol. 5, 477.
15. Markham, 116.
16. Ibid., 120–1.
17. Ibid., 121.
18. Ibid., 127.
19. Fernández de Oviedo, 152.
20. Ibid., 153.
21. Ibid., 157.
22. Ibid., 166.
23. Ibid.

10 'End the Suffering'

1. Kelsey, 63.
2. Ibid., 80.

3. Ibid.
4. Ibid., 85.
5. Ibid.
6. Ibid.

11 'The Infernal Labyrinth'

1. Galvão, 39.
2. Ibid., 71.
3. Coleridge, vol. 1, 372.
4. Diffie and Winius, 375.
5. Galvão, 75.
6. Ibid., 327.
7. Miller, 2.
8. Galvão, 285.
9. Ibid., 71.
10. Crowley, *Conquerors*, 365.
11. Diffie and Winius, 374.
12. Galvão, 73.
13. Barros, 385.
14. Galvão, 291.
15. Ibid., 86.
16. Ibid., 67.
17. Ibid., 43.
18. Ibid., 137–9.
19. Ibid., 87.
20. Ibid., 159.
21. Ibid., 161.
22. Ibid., 157.
23. Ibid., 159.
24. Ibid., 147.
25. Ibid.
26. Ibid., 6.
27. Crowley, *Conquerors*, 174.

12 The Haven of Death

1. Thomas, *Rivers of Gold*, 458.
2. Pires, vol. 1, xxxi.
3. Hakluyt, vol. 1, 217.
4. Skelton, 102.
5. Hakluyt, vol. 1, 228.
6. Ibid.
7. Ibid., 218.
8. Ibid., 230.
9. Ibid., 215.
10. Ibid., 216.
11. Williamson, 102.

12. Evans, 38–9.
13. Dalton, 180.
14. Ibid.
15. Pires, vol. 1, liv.
16. Ibid.
17. Dalton, 181.
18. Hakluyt, vol. 1, 241.
19. Mayers, 54.
20. Hakluyt, vol. 1, 237–8.
21. Mayers, 54.
22. Hakluyt, vol. 1, 239–40.
23. Ibid., 249.
24. Ibid., 250.
25. Ibid.
26. Ibid., 272.
27. Ibid., 273.
28. Ibid., 273.
29. Ibid., 274.
30. Ibid.
31. Ibid.
32. Ibid.
33. Ibid., 275.
34. Ibid., 276.
35. Ibid., 253.
36. Ibid., 279.
37. Ibid., 276.
38. Ibid., 278.
39. Ibid., 292.
40. Ibid., 290.
41. Ibid., 291.
42. Ibid.
43. Ibid., 279–80.
44. Ibid.
45. Ibid., 281.
46. Ibid.
47. Ibid.
48. Ibid., 282.
49. Ibid., 298.
50. Ibid., 285.
51. Gordon, 243.
52. Hakluyt, vol. 2, 265.

13 'Fear Our Greatness, Respect Our Virtue'

1. Chang, 71.
2. Pereira et al., xxiii.
3. Ibid., xxiii–iv.
4. Chang, 83.

5. Ibid.
6. Pereira et al., xxxii.
7. Braga, 'The first Sino-Portuguese treaty'.
8. Ibid.
9. Willis, xxiii.
10. Villiers, 'The origins of the first Portuguese communities'.
11. Lidin, 71.
12. Diffie and Winius, 395.
13. Pereira et al., 8.
14. Ibid., 121.
15. Ibid., 131.
16. Ibid., 120.
17. Ibid., 116.
18. Ibid., 131.
19. Ibid., 146.
20. Ibid., 110.
21. Ibid., 137.
22. Ibid., 138.
23. Ibid., 112.
24. Ibid., 128–9.

14 Cracking the Code

1. Noone, 264.
2. Ibid., 265.
3. Mitchell, *Urdaneta*, 115–16.
4. Noone, 267.
5. Ibid., 270.
6. Ibid., 273.
7. Ibid., 272.
8. Ibid., 276.
9. Ibid., 289.
10. Ibid., 287.
11. Mitchell, *Urdaneta*, 103–4.
12. Noone, 287.
13. Ibid., 284.
14. Ibid., 287–8.
15. Ibid., 297.
16. Ibid., 299.
17. Ibid., 300.
18. Ibid., 319.
19. Ibid.
20. Ibid., 322.
21. Ibid., 326.
22. Ibid.
23. Ibid., 334.
24. Ibid., 335.
25. Ibid., 336–7.

26. Ibid., 338.
27. Ibid., 384.
28. Ibid., 385–6.
29. Ibid., 400.
30. Ibid., 415.
31. Ibid., 388.
32. Ibid., 375.
33. Ibid., 393.
34. Ibid., 405.
35. Ibid., 416.
36. Spate, 104.

15 Galleons of Desire

1. Greenfield.
2. Spate, 191.
3. Careri, 478.
4. Ibid., 481.
5. Ibid., 487.
6. Ibid., 489.
7. Ibid., 490.
8. Ibid., 490.
9. Ibid., 492.
10. Ibid., 502.
11. Carletti, 71.
12. Ibid., 57.
13. Ibid., 491.

16 Going Global

1. Gage, 55.
2. Ibid., 56–9.
3. Crowley, 'The first global empire', 40.

Damage

1. Fuller, 217.
2. Giráldez, 30.
3. Ibid., 57.
4. Frankopan, 212.
5. Las Casas, in Wagner and Parish, 203–4.
6. Wallace, vol. 2, 243.
7. Giráldez, 40.
8. Crowley, *Conquerors*, 181–2.
9. Transylvanus, in *Magellan*, 395.
10. *The Merry Wives of Windsor*, Act II, Scene 2.

Author's Note

1. Gordon and Morales, 31.

BIBLIOGRAPHY

Abulafia, David. *The Boundless Sea*, Allen Lane: London, 2019.

Alguns documentos do archivio nacional da torre do tombo acerca das navagacoes e conquistas portuguguezes, Lisbon, 1892.

Atwell, William. 'Ming China and the emerging world economy c.1470–1650', in *The Cambridge History of China*, vol. 8, *The Ming Dynasty, Part 2: 1368–1644*, ed. Denis C. Twitchett and Fredick W. Mote, Cambridge University Press: Cambridge, 1998.

Barbosa, Duarte. *The Book of Duarte Barbosa*, 2 vols, Hakluyt Society: London, 1918.

Barlow, Roger. *A Brief Summe of Geographie*, Hakluyt Society: London, 2010.

Barros, João de. *Décadas da Ásia*, vol. 3, Part 1, Lisbon, 1777.

Bergreen, Laurence. *Over the Edge of the World*, HarperCollins: London, 2003.

Boxer, C.R. *Fidalgos in the Far East 1550–1770*, Martin Nijhoff: The Hague, 1948.

—— *The Great Ship from Amacon*, Centro do Estudos Históricos Ultramarinos: Lisbon, 1959.

Braga, J.M. 'The first Sino-Portuguese treaty made by Leonel de Souza in 1554', https://www.icm.gov.mo/rc/viewer/20001/747 (accessed 6 November 2023).

—— *The Western Pioneers and their Discovery of Macau*, Instituto Português de Hong Kong: Hong Kong, 1950.

Brook, Timothy. *Vermeer's Hat*, Profile Books: London, 2009.

Burnet, Ian, *Spice Islands*, Rosenberg: Kenthurst, NSW, 2013.

Careri, Gemelli. *A Voyage round the World*, London, 1704.

Carletti, Francesco. *My Voyage around the World*, Methuen: London, 1965.

Castanheda, Fernão Lopes de. *Historia do descobrimento e conquista da India pelos Portugueses*, Lisbon, 1833.

Catz, Rebecca D. *The Travels of Mendes Pinto*, University of Chicago Press: Chicago, 1989.

Chang, T'ien-Tse. *Sino-Portuguese Trade*, Brill: Leyden, 1934.

Clare, Horatio. *Orison for a Curlew*, Little Toller Books: Beaminster, 2015.

Coleridge, Henry. *The Life and Letters of St Francis Xavier*, 2 vols, Burns and Oates: London, 1872.

Crowley, Roger. *Conquerors: How Portugal Seized the Indian Ocean and Forged the First Global Empire*, Faber: London, 2015.

—— 'The first global empire', *History Today*, vol. 65, no. 10 (October 2015).

d'Anghiera, Pietro Martire. *The First Three English Books on America*, trans. Ricard Eden, Birmingham, 1885.

Dalton, Heather. *Merchants and Explorers: Roger Barlow, Sebastián Cabot, and Networks of Atlantic Exchange, 1500–1560*, Oxford University Press: Oxford, 2016.

De Sousa, Ivo Carneiro. *The First Portuguese Maps of China in Francisco Rodrigues' Book and Atlas (c.1512)*, ResearchGate, 2013, https://www.researchgate.net/publication/279192054_The_First_Portuguese_Maps_of_China_in_Francisco_Rodrigues'_Book_and_Atlas_c1512 (accessed 6 November 2023).

Descripción de los reinos, costas, puertos e islas que hay desde el Cabo de Buena Esperanza hasta los Leyquios por Fernando de Magallanes, Madrid, 1920.

Diffie, Bailey W. and Winius, George D. *Foundations of the Portuguese Empire, 1415–1580*, University of Minnesota Press: Minneapolis, MN, 1977.

Evans, James. *Merchant Adventurers*, Phoenix: London, 2013.

Ferguson, Donald, ed. and trans. *Letters from Portuguese Captives in Canton, Written in 1534 and 1536*, Byculla, 1902.

Fernández de Oviedo y Valdés, Gonzalo, *Spanish and Portuguese Conflict in the Spice Islands: The Loaysa Expedition to the Moluccas 1525–1535*, Hakluyt Society: London, 2021.

Fernández-Armesto, Felipe. *Straits: Beyond the Myth of Magellan*, Bloomsbury: London, 2022.

Flynn, Dennis O. and Arturo Giráldez. 'Born with a "silver spoon": The origin of world trade in 1571', *Journal of World History*, vol. 6, no. 2 (Fall 1995), pp. 201–21.

—— 'Cycles of silver', *Journal of World History*, vol. 13, no. 2 (2002), pp. 391–427.

Frankopan, Peter. *The Silk Roads: A New History of the World*, Bloomsbury: London, 2015.

Fuller, Errol. *The Great Auk*, privately published: Southborough, 1999.

Füssel, Stephan. *Gutenberg and the Impact of Printing*, Ashgate: Aldershot, 2005.

Gage, Thomas. *The English-American his Travail by Sea and Land*, London, 1686.

Galvão, António. *A Treatise on the Moluccas*, Jesuit Historical Institute: Rome, 1971.

Gaskell, Jeremy. *Who Killed the Great Auk?*, Oxford University Press: Oxford, 2000.

Ghosh, Amitav. *The Nutmeg's Curse*, London: John Murray, 2021.

Giráldez, Arturo. *The Age of Trade*, Rowman and Littlefield: Lanham, MD, 2015.

Gordon, Eleanora C. 'The fate of Sir Hugh Willoughby and his companions: A new conjecture', *Geographical Journal*, vol. 152, no. 2 (July 1986), pp. 243–7.

Gordon, Peter and Juan José Morales. *The Silver Way*, Penguin: Melbourne, 2017.

Greenfield, Patrick. 'Story of cities #6: How silver turned Potosí into "the first city of capitalism"', *Guardian*, https://www.theguardian.com/cities/2016/mar/21/story-of-cities-6-Potosí-bolivia-peru-inca-first-city-capitalism (accessed 6 November 2023).

Guillemard, F.H.H. *The Life of Ferdinand Magellan*, George Philip & Son: London, 1891.

Hakluyt, Richard. *The Principal Navigations, Voyages, Traffiques and Discoveries of the English Nations*, vols 1 and 2, J.M. Dent: London, undated.

Hamel, Iosif. *England and Russia: Comprising the Voyages of John Tradescant the Elder, Sir Hugh Willoughby, Richard Chancellor, Nelson, and Others, to the White Sea, etc.*, Richard Bentley: London, 1854.

Humayun Akhtar, Ali. *1368: China and the Making of the Modern World*, Stanford University Press: Stanford, CA, 2022.

Kelsey, Harry. *The First Circumnavigators*, Yale University Press: New Haven, CT and London, 2016.

Krondl, Michael. *The Taste of Conquest*, Ballantine Books: New York, 2008.

Lach, Donald F. *Asia in the Making of Europe*, vol. 1, *The Century of Discovery*, University of Chicago Press: London, 1965.

Lagoa, João António de Mascarenhas. *Fernão de Magalhāis: A sua vida e a sua viagem*, 2 vols, Seara Nova: Lisbon, 1938.

Lane, Kris. *Potosí: The Silver City that Changed the World*, University of California Press: Oakland, CA, 2019.

Langdon, Robert. *The Lost Caravel Re-explored*, Brolga Press: Melbourne, 1988.

'La Lettre d'Antonio de Brito', *La Géographie* (January–February 1928), pp. 1–16.

Lidin, Olaf G. *Tanegashima: The Arrival of Europe in Japan*, NIAS Press: Copenhagen, 2002.

Lyon, Eugene. 'Track of the Manila galleons', *National Geographic* (September 1990).

Magalhães-Godinho, Vitorino. *L'Économie de l'empire Portugais aux XVe et XVIe siècles*, SEVPEN: Paris, 1969.

Magellan (collection of sources), Dodo Press: Moscow, undated.

Markham, Clement. *Early Spanish Voyages to the Strait of Magellan*, Hakluyt Society: London, 1911.

Mathers, William M. 'Nuestra Señora de la Concepción', *National Geographic* (September 1990).

Mayers, Kit. *North-East Passage to Muscovy: Stephen Borough and the First Tudor Explorations*, Stroud: Sutton, 2005.

Miller, George, ed. *To the Spice Islands and Beyond*, Kuala Lumpur: Oxford University Press, 1996.

Mitchell, Mairin. *Elcano: The First Navigator*, Herder Publications: London, 1958.

—— *Friar Andrés de Urdaneta, OSA*, Macdonald and Evans: London, 1964.

Morison, S.E. *The European Discovery of America: The Southern Voyages*, New York: Oxford University Press, 1974.

Muller, Kal. *Spice Islands: The Moluccas*, Periplus Editions: Berkeley, CA, 1990.

Navarette, Martín Fernández de. *Colección de los viajes y descubrimentos que hicieron por mar los españoles desde fines del siglo XV*, vols 4 and 5, Imprenta Nacional: Madrid, 1837.

Noone, Martin J. *The Islands Saw It*, Helicon Press: Baltimore, MD, undated.

Pereira, Galeote et al. *South China in the Sixteenth Century: Being the Narratives of Galeote Pereira, Fr. Gaspar da Cruz, Fr. Martín de Rada (1550–1575)*, ed. and trans. C.R. Boxer, Hakluyt Society: London, 1953.

Pettegree, Andrew. *The Book in the Renaissance*, Yale University Press: New Haven, CT and London, 2010.

Pigafetta, Antonio. *Magellan's Voyage around the World*, 2 vols, ed. and trans. James Alexander Robertson, Arthur H. Clark Company: Cleveland, OH, 1906.

Pires, Tomé. *The Suma Oriental of Tomé Pires*, 2 vols, Hakluyt Society: London, 1944.

A Precursor to Globalisation: The Galleon Trade between Manila and Acapulco (1564– 1815), film of a Yale NUS College panel discussion, 89 mins, https://www. youtube.com/watch?v=52FFtKONaio (accessed 9 October 2023).

Russell-Wood, John. *A World on the Move*, Palgrave Macmillan: London, 1993.

Schuman, Michael. *Superpower Interrupted: The Chinese History of the World*, Public Affairs: New York, 2020.

Skelton, R.A. *Explorers' Maps: Chapters in the Cartographic Record of Geographical Discovery*, Routledge and K. Paul: London, 1960.

Spate, O.H.K. *The Spanish Lake*, Croom Helm: London, 1979.

Taylor, E.G.R. *Tudor Geography: 1485–1583*, Methuen: London, 1930.

Thomas, Hugh. *Rivers of Gold: The Rise of the Spanish Empire 1490–1522*, Allen Lane: London, 2004.

—— *World without End: The Global Empire of Philip II*, Allen Lane: London, 2014.

Thomaz, Luís F.R. 'Atlas Miller: Cartographic secrets and the Magellan expedition', https://www.moleiro.com/en/press/atlas-miller-cartographic-fake-news. py (accessed 6 November 2023).

Torodash, Martin. 'Magellan historiography', *Hispanic American Historical Review*, vol. 51, no. 2 (May 1971), pp. 313–35.

Uncilla y Arroitajáuregui, Fermín de. *Urdaneta y la conquista de Filipinas*, University of Michigan: Michigan, MI, 2007.

Villiers, John. 'The origins of the first Portuguese communities in Southeast Asia', https://www.icm.gov.mo/rc/viewer/20004/800 (accessed 6 November 2023).

—— 'Trade and society in the Banda islands in the sixteenth century', *Modern Asian Studies*, vol. 15, no. 4 (1981), pp. 723–50.

Wagner, H.R. and Parish, H.R. *The Life and Writings of Bartolomé de las Casas*, University of New Mexico Press: Albuquerque, NM, 1967.

Wallace, Alfred. *The Malay Archipelago*, 2 vols, Dodo Press: Moscow, undated.

Williamson, James Alexander. *The Cabot Voyages and Bristol Discovery under Henry VII*, Hakluyt Society: Cambridge, 1962.

Willis, Clive. *China and Macau*, Ashgate: Aldershot, 2002.

Winchester, Simon. *Pacific: The Ocean of the Future*, William Collins: London, 2015.

Wright, Iona Stuessy. 'The first American voyage across the Pacific, 1527–1528: The voyage of Álvaro de Saavedra Cerón', *Geographical Review*, vol. 29, no. 3 (July 1939), pp. 472–84.

Wyman, Patrick. *The Verge*, Twelve: New York, 2021.

ILLUSTRATION CREDITS

Plates

1. Miller Atlas, *c.* 1519. The Print Collector / Alamy.
2. Aerial view of the Banda islands, photograph by Fabio Lamanna. Shutterstock.
3. Alonso Sánchez Coello, *View of the City of Seville*, *c.* 1576–1600.
4. Portrait of Ferdinand Magellan, sixteenth-seventeenth century. Art Collection 3 / Alamy.
5. *Santo Niño de Cebu*, *c.* 1520.
6. Detail of a map by Abraham Ortelius, 1590.
7. Richard Chancellor presents his credentials to Tsar Ivan, from *The Illustrated Chronicle of Ivan the Terrible*, sixteenth century.
8. Replica galleon *Andalucia*, 2010.
9. Port of Acapulco, lithograph, 1628.
10. Panorama of Mexico City, *c.* 1700.
11. Panoramic view from the belfry of the Jesuit church, Potosí, Bolivia, photograph by Noradoa. Shutterstock.
12. Johannes Vermeer, *Woman Holding a Balance*, *c.* 1664. Widener Collection / National Gallery of Art.
13. Detail of famille rose plate with ceramics process design, Qing Dynasty. Lou-Foto / Alamy.
14. Dish with IHS monogram, armillary sphere and Portuguese royal arms, *c.* 1520–40. Helena Woolworth McCann Collection, Purchase, Winfield Foundation Gift, 1967 / Metropolitan Museum of Art.
15. Kano Sanraku, six-panel folding screen, early seventeenth century. Album / Alamy.
16. Cinnamon, nutmeg, cloves and bamboo, from *Les Indes Orientales et Occidentales et autres lieux*, 1708. Penta Springs Limited / Alamy.

ILLUSTRATION CREDITS

In the text

ILLUSTRATION CREDITS

INDEX

Locators for illustrations are entered in *italics*

INDEX